POTSTICKER CHRONICLES

America's Favorite Chinese Recipes

A FAMILY MEMOIR

Stuart Chang Berman

WILEY

John Wiley & Sons, Inc.

Published by John Wiley & Sons, Inc., Hoboken, New Jersey.

Published simultaneously in Canada.

For general information on our other products and services or for technical support, please contact our Customer Care Department within the United States at (800) 762-2974, outside the United States at (317) 572-3993 or fax (317) 572-4002.

Wiley also publishes its books in a variety of electronic formats. Some content that appears in print may not be available in electronic books. For more information about Wiley products, visit our web site at www.wiley.com.

LIBRARY OF CONGRESS CATALOGING-IN-PUBLICATION DATA:

Berman, Stuart Chang.

Potsticker chronicles : America's favorite Chinese recipes: a family memoir / Stuart Chang Berman.

p. cm.

ISBN: 0-471-25028-7 (Cloth)

1. Cookery, Chinese.

TX724.5.C5 B46 2003

641.5951 21 a-cc   2003002605

Chinese Ink paintings by Dora Lee
Book design by Richard Oriolo

10 9 8 7 6 5 4 3 2 1

With Deepest Love, to Mom,

Who Waits Patiently for Me

by the Front Gate

CONTENTS

POTSTICKER CHRONICLES

POTSTICKER CHRONICLES

INTRODUCTION

餃
子

THIS BOOK IS A CELEBRATION OF family. There is much more to cooking than chopping, slicing, kneading, mixing, marinating, sautéing, grilling, baking, and seasoning. The recipes of every chef and cook, from celebrity chefs to grandmothers, express something essential in the lives of their creators. Philosophically, there is a simple beauty in how we sup upon our daily bread, using an assortment of raw ingredients to create a finished product of food that feeds our bodies and souls. It is this celebration of life and family through food that I hope to bring to my readers. It is for this reason that I intersperse family stories throughout my book.

I remember teaching my children to cook at an early age. They would sit at a small table and on small stools that I made for them out of scrap wood, their little fingers cutting vegetables with smaller dull knives. My son would diligently cut the vegetables in exact shapes and put them aside in neat piles. My daughter would cut a few pieces, eat them, and cut a few more pieces. I would praise the children for their help, assemble the ingredients, cook them, and with their mother, we would all sit down together at our dinner table and consume our "daily bread."

My professional life with food began well before I had children. When I was in graduate school studying history at Rutgers University, I took a job teaching Chinese cooking in a local adult-education program. It was a great job. It paid much better than working in the student cafeteria, and I got to eat for free on the days I taught the course. My students, who were all ages and from all walks of life and ethnic backgrounds, were wonderful. I learned from them as well, keeping their handwritten recipes to this day for baklava, Russian tea cookies, semolina halvah, and cheese focaccia. Little did I know that this part-time job would launch me on a lifelong endeavor that has led to writing this book.

Thanks to an old classmate of mine who was a journalist, the *New York Times* did a feature article on me, including photos of me with food I cooked. Someone from the television program *To Tell the Truth*, with Gary Moore, read the article and I ended up on the show. By now I had a master's degree in political science as well as in Chinese history, but because at that time there were no academic jobs available, I abandoned my doctoral pursuits in both fields. Because my mother had just been diagnosed with Parkinson's disease, I joined her in Washington, D.C., to help her run her renowned restaurant The Court of the Mandarins.

It was there that I was transformed from home cook to professional chef, assuming the dubious distinction of being a "restaurant owner/chef." I quickly realized that many of the problems we had at The Court of the Mandarins originated in the kitchen. Jealousies and factionalism tore kitchen staffs apart. Whole kitchen crews would walk out. Additionally, chefs would leave to open their own restaurants. If I were to survive in this business, it was clear I had to learn the kitchen and one day control it and everything that came out of it. So I hired an older Chinese chef from Shanghai and paid him well on one condition—that he teach me all he knew. He consented, although he knew it was highly unusual for an owner to work in the kitchen unless he had been a chef previously. I figured he would teach me about 80 percent of what he knew.

For the next few years, I worked in the kitchen during the day and in the dining room at night. Specifically, I cooked on the wok stove during our busy lunches. In the afternoons, I deboned and filleted whole chickens, cut and prepped meats and vegetables, and made sauces, dumplings, and pancakes. I still bear the scars of working in that kitchen, mostly burns and cuts.

I will never forget the first time I was on the stove during lunch. It was 110 degrees in the kitchen and, exhausted, I leaned the front of my body against the stove. I quickly became prostrated by the heat and, almost fainting, was dragged by the chefs into the walk-in refrigerator, where they sat me down until I regained my normal body temperature. Never again did I lean against the stove. Another time, since I was the lowest-ranking chef, regardless of being the owner, it was my job to sauté the whole dried chili peppers, an experience not unlike being tear-gassed. I understood then why it was such an unpopular task.

Starting at The Court of the Mandarins, I worked in restaurant kitchens for fifteen years. The restaurant closed in 1982 because the building was being demolished and replaced with a modern high-rise office building. For three years I taught at a Washington culinary school, working and socializing with and learning from chefs from all over the world. These prominent chefs were in between jobs, many on their way to becoming well-known restaurant owners. The most famous was a former executive chef at the White House. I also did consultant work for Time-Life cookbooks. Photographs of food I prepared and my recipes appeared in the Good Cook series *Dried Beans & Grains,* and in the Healthy Home Cooking Series *Fresh Ways with Pasta.*

In 1986, I opened the Wok 'n' Roll Restaurant in downtown Washington, introducing a new concept of putting the wok stoves open to view. Customers would place their orders, then watch the raw ingredients being assembled and stir-fried three feet in front of them, the food flipped in a one-handed wok, which, when lifted from the stove, would send a three-foot-high flame into the air. Until they got used to it, my customers would jump backward. It was an idea that came to me while I watched sushi chefs at a sushi bar preparing my entree. After I renovated the restaurant and established the menu, I worked as the head chef on the wok stove for four months to work out all the "kitchen kinks" and trained a former chef from the old restaurant to take my place. My mother, who was still active despite her Parkinson's, assumed the function of general manager. Our clientele was very different from the old restaurant. They were from all walks of life—the parking lot attendants as well as the people who parked at their lots, such as lawyers, secretaries, judges, computer people, and government workers. My mother treated them all equally, with the same charm, courtesy, and respect that she bestowed on the more celebrity oriented clientele of The Court of the Mandarins. To this day, I still meet people she knew at the Wok 'n' Roll, who ask after her.

In 1987, I built and opened our third place, The Mandarins Restaurant, in Silver Spring, Maryland, adjacent to a Washington Metro station. This was a fancy, full-service restaurant. Although I included popular favorites such as General Tso's Chicken, I developed a menu based on fusion cuisine, which utilized Chinese techniques and ingredients with European nouvelle presentations. One of my star dishes, Sichuan Blackened Shrimp, the recipe for which is in this book, consisted of traditionally fluffy and tender shrimp lightly blackened in a very hot wok with freshly cracked black, white, and Sichuan peppercorns, presented on a jade green coulis, the sauce made from pureed and strained fresh green chile peppers and fresh coriander. The Mandarins Restaurant received an excellent review in the *Washington Post*. Most attempts at fusion in the United States and Europe merely use Asian ingredients and do not utilize Chinese cooking techniques. Accordingly, I promoted wine with my cuisine and sponsored a wine tasting led by wine expert Robert Parker, who did a marvelous job matching my nouvelle and traditional dishes with Alsatian and German wines.

But it was my mother who taught me everything I know about the restaurant business. My first few years of training were in the "front of the house"—the dining room—where I learned dining room management and continental French service. She tried desperately to teach me the "Two Ts" of dining room service, tact and tolerance, neither of which is my strong suit. On one particularly busy evening, a good customer—we call them "old" customers in Chinese—came in for dinner with an attractive blond woman. My mother greeted him, "Good evening, Mr. Jones. So nice to see you again." She smiled at the woman and said, "Madame." I said, "Hello, Mr. Jones." And, turning to the woman, I said, "I hope you have a pleasant evening, Mrs. Jones." Sheepishly, they went to their table. In a whisper without opening her mouth and fluttering her eyes, a signal of her disapproval, my mother said to me "That's not Mrs. Jones." Well, I flunked Tact 101.

I tried to redeem myself by asking my mother to define *tact*. She did so by relating a story told to her by her English professor in Peking. A woman on an overnight train was getting ready for bed in the privacy of her compartment when a young male porter inadvertently came into the compartment. She was stark naked. The porter said, "Excuse me, sir," and departed, closing the door behind him. My mother said, "Now, that's tact." I responded by saying that if I were that woman, I don't know what would have bothered me more—being barged in on while I was naked or being mistaken for a man. My mother said to me, "You really just don't get the point, do you?"

Customers were surprised to be greeted by a female Chinese restaurant owner who spoke impeccable English and who was well read and erudite in her conversation. Still, it was her extraordinary charm that impressed the customers most, literally coating the dining room in her sense of cultured well-being. I could never learn it in a thousand years.

The Court of the Mandarins was her stage, her "theater-in-the-round." During the Watergate years, she used to exalt in the incidents that took place at the "Court," such as then Attorney General John Mitchell's screaming obscenities across the dining room at the *New York Times* reporters. Celebrities abounded. My mother had many dinner parties to which she invited notables from the media, Congress, and the arts. The mix was often volatile, and conversation was never dull. When I reminisced about her "theater-in-the-round," she always responded, "Those were the days." My mother passed away recently and I miss her so very much. This book is dedicated to her memory. So, it is most appropriate that I begin this book with the following story.

RED SHOES AND GREEN SOCKS

Even though I was born in New York City, as a child, I did not speak English, only Mandarin Chinese. Entering the first grade proved to be problematic, as I was placed in a class with retarded children and with Puerto Rican kids who did not speak English. My mother, who had just received a master's degree in English literature from Fordham University, made a scene at my school and had me placed in a regular classroom. From then on, she spoke only English to me at home, with the exceptions of singing Chinese songs and reciting Chinese nursery rhymes. In a year's time I was speaking English like the kid next door, but there were some difficulties during that year.

One snowy, winter day, I returned from school to our apartment on West 86th Street in New York City. I had forgotten or lost my key and could not get into the building. My mother was not yet home from work. There was no way I could communicate my dilemma to anyone, so I waited for my mother outside.

Although it was already dark, it wasn't too bad. I found a mound of snow by the sidewalk, left by snow shovelers. I got on top of it, squished myself down, and leaned back. This reclining chair of mine became pleasantly warm after a few minutes. Looking up into the black sky, my eyes followed big flakes of snow floating down slowly in the light of a street lamp, glittery white diamonds that melted on my face. I recited out loud a Chinese nursery rhyme that my mother had told me frequently about red shoes and green socks. My mother's rosy face appeared above me, and I was instantly happy.

She led me inside to the warmth of our apartment, gave me a hot bath, and dressed me in my pajamas, while reciting again "Red Shoes and Green Socks." She explained to me that her mother in China used to do the same for her when she was cold and hungry as a child. She said it was important I eat something hot, nutritious, and a little sweet.

Carrying me to the kitchen, she put a pot of porridge, which she called "Buddha's Porridge," on the stove; she had made it the day before. Meatless, it consisted of barley, red kidney beans, and deep red-colored Peking dates. When it was hot, she put some in a bowl and swirled in brown sugar. As I ate it, she told me the story behind "Buddha's Porridge."

According to her, Buddha and his disciples in the middle of the winter had not eaten in many days. Buddha instructed them to fan out into the countryside and beg for whatever food people could afford to give them. They did so while their master waited for them by a fire. The people from whom they begged were poor but gave what they could—a little barley, some millet, a few beans, some dried dates. Returning, the disciples assured their master that they now had food. They began to cook their meager ingredients by boiling them in a large pot. But dried ingredients take time to cook, so when the food, a porridge, was finally ready to eat, Buddha had died of starvation. Although I never knew the historical accuracy of this story, I do remember eating that porridge with great gusto.

I never saw the red shoes and the green socks, but still I hold the vision of shiny red patent leather shoes and bright green socks that invoke the sweet smell and taste of Buddha's porridge consumed on a wintry day. These sensations bundle the memories of my mother's warmth and nurturing love, which I will keep close to me forever.

Equipment
and Ingredients

LET'S DO AN EQUIPMENT REVIEW FIRST. True, I can cook Chinese food in any kitchen without a scrap of Chinese cooking equipment. True, I have cooked in such a kitchen.

I had a good college friend at Rutgers, named Siegfried, who told me that he was an Italian count of Tyrolian origin, that his mother was a famous European playwright, that his father was an Egyptologist, that he lived in a cas-tle in northern Italy, and that his grandfather was the renowned American poet Ezra Pound. I thought he was a pathological liar with a British accent from Hoboken, New Jersey. But he was a nice guy, and we became friends.

As it turned out, the summer of my senior year, I planned to take a stu-dent-style trip to Europe. I told Siegfried about it, and he replied, "Stuart, do come visit me at my family's castle in Merano."

"Sure," I said, thinking to myself that this guy would not let it go. He gave me a postcard of a castle and wrote his name and address on the back.

That summer I rolled into Merano, Italy, and made a feeble attempt to find Siegfried. Merano is a breathtakingly beautiful village nestled in the Italian

Alps that fade into an endless background of the snowcapped Swiss Alps. Characteristic of the region, Merano had three castles, a main castle near the apex of the mountain and two guard castles below. I went into a butcher shop and in very poor Italian asked where Siegfried's address was. Of course, no one understood me. I pulled out the postcard; the owner looked at the writing on the back and pointed out his front window to one of the castles. I was flabbergasted.

Making my way to that castle, I ignored the sign that said in five languages, "Beware of Vicious Dog. Trained to Attack Trespassers." When I got to the castle, I heard a rapid four-legged descent down the castle steps. My back up against the wall, a German shepherd leaped at my face and licked off the cold sweat. A voice from behind said, "He's really quite friendly. Couldn't hurt a fly, let alone attack. Welcome, Stuart."

Siegfried gave me an escorted tour of the castle. As we entered, I knocked over what looked like a plaster foot by an open door. Siegfried said that it was an Etruscan foot and that the Etruscans, predecessors of the Romans, made plaster replicas of the feet of their dead. Siegfried picked up the foot and placed it by the door, apparently using it as a doorstop. He said, "Don't worry. There's a million of them around here."

We walked through a small museum displaying ancient Egyptian artifacts in glass cases. Moving into an adjoining room, Siegfried introduced me to his playwright mother, who had been typing furiously on an ancient typewriter. As I entered an atrium area, I was introduced to an entourage of his friends, sipping wine made from the grapes of his estate. The guests included the son of the British ambassador and the daughter of the German ambassador. True to his American roots, there were others, like myself, of more plebeian origins—including a cosmetician from Hamburg, perhaps Siegfried's girlfriend.

Siegfried was most hospitable. He took another room in the east wing of the castle and let me stay in his room in the west wing. Earlier, he told me I was free to roam anywhere in the castle except for the east wing, which was sequestered. A bit "Jane Eyrish," I thought. As I unpacked, I noticed poems pegged to the wall, written on tattered and dog-eared pieces of paper. One, headed "To My Grandson, Siegfried," was a one-stanza poem about a metaphorical autumn of an old man and the anticipated spring of a young man. It was signed "Your Grandfather, Ezra."

Early the next morning, I stood on a small balcony outside my room, watching the morning mist being gently swept away by the emerging Tyrolian sun. In an elevated garden in the east wing, I observed a gray-haired man with a gray beard, clad in a brown coarse-cloth monk's robe, puttering in the garden, tending tomato plants. It was, of course, the famous poet himself.

I felt so ashamed and guilty about doubting Siegfried. My stay at the castle was a once-in-a-lifetime experience. I wanted to do something to express my gratitude. "I'm going to cook a Chinese feast for Siegfried and his friends," I thought.

Early the next morning, I went to the local market and bought vegetables, marvelous meat from that butcher shop, and soy sauce from a specialty store. I needed fish. Siegfried informed me that, being inland, the availability of fish was limited, expensive, and not very fresh.

"Never fear," I said, pulling out an 18-inch aluminum tube from my baggage. Showing Siegfried my five-piece fishing rod that was neatly packed into the tube, I asked him where I could go fishing. He replied that on the property next to him was a mountain stream, but if I got caught fishing there, it was a 100,000 lire fine.

"What's that—about ten bucks?" I asked.

"Don't be ridiculous. It's about 100 bucks," he replied.

Deciding to take the risk, I pitch-forked up some worms from a manure pile and headed out. The stream, only a few feet wide, gushed down the steep decline of the mountain. I couldn't conceive of any fish existing in that water without being swept down the mountain, but ten fish later I knew better. Those brilliant-colored brown trout were as cold as the icy water of the stream. I wanted one more, a good one. I went further downstream.

The mountain was so steep that I had to shimmy down on my rear end. I came to a waterfall that dropped down eight feet into a small pool. Trout, especially in small streams, are spooky. Baiting up with the biggest manure worm I had, I placed it above the fall, watching it being swept over the fall into the pool. The line moved slowly in a circle. A tremendous thump stopped its rotation, and after a dogged battle, I landed a sixteen-inch brown trout. I envisioned it as a centerpiece surrounded by the small trout like rays of the sun.

Siegfried was astounded by my piscatorial success. After stoking an old cast-iron wood-burning stove, I started to cook. The stove had different-size holes on its top that were covered with lids, which I removed with a crowbar-like tool. Flames from the fire leaped out of the holes, and I wished I had my woks. I settled for the kitchen's cast-iron and copper skillets and pots. The crowning dish would be the last dish, the trout.

Heating an extremely light olive oil that was virtually tasteless, which I preferred, in a large cast-iron skillet until it smoked, I pan-fried the lightly floured trout to a golden brown. Then I put the trout through a steaming, sizzling wash of soy sauce, fresh ginger, garlic, and stock made from the bones of range-raised chickens on the castle grounds. Reducing the heat, I simmered the trout in the sauce. "Needs mushrooms," I thought, so I asked Siegfried for some. He brought out a velvet-lined brass box in which he kept moist, black mushrooms that looked like round chunks of dull coal. Slicing up a bunch quickly, I added them to the trout.

Siegfried said dryly, "Those are Italian truffles from this region. They are about $350 an ounce."

"Sorry, man. Hey, Siegfried, do you have any dry white wine like a sherry?" I asked, tasting the sauce with a spoon.

Siegfried left and returned with a crusty old bottle and carefully removed the cork. Grabbing the bottle, I added a liberal dousing of the sherry to the trout. Tilting the skillet, the vapors flamed in a blue arc. The guests, who decided to dine "country style" at a long rough-hewn wooden table in the kitchen, oohed and aahed, inhaling the aromas of the simmering trout.

Clutching the crusty bottle of sherry to his chest, Siegfried said, "This is the last bottle of sherry willed to me by my great-grandfather. It came from our own sherry casks in 1889."

"Sorry, man."

It was one of the greatest meals I ever cooked. And I did it without my equipment. If you are home, it is just so much easier to invest in some cooking equipment.

CHINESE COOKING EQUIPMENT

How about a *wok*? I prefer the iron woks available in most Asian groceries. Handmade woks, beaten circularly with a ball-peen hammer to form the convex shape, are particularly nice since they heat more quickly on home stoves. The factory-made woks are also good, but a little heavier. I use woks with one long handle, because I cook Mandarin style, flipping the food with one hand like flipping an omelet. The handle should be as close to level with the top of the wok as possible. If you prefer the two-hand method, in which the food is tossed with spoons in both hands like tossing a salad, buy a two-handled wok with the semi-circular handles on opposite sides of the wok. Whatever kind of wok you decide on, buy a metal ring that fits snugly around the burner of your stove, on which the wok is also snugly placed. Various sizes are usually sold where woks are sold.

All new woks should be scrubbed with steel wool in hot, soapy water and then rinsed thoroughly (the woks are usually packed in machine oil). Dry the pot completely on an open stove. Be sure to watch it and not forget about it. Otherwise, you might smell a strange odor and find your kitchen on fire. Let the wok cool. Add 2 teaspoons of vegetable oil and rub it in thoroughly with a paper towel. These woks are not stainless steel, although stainless steel woks are available, which in my opinion are not as good. Some maintenance is required. After each use, repeat the above oiling; otherwise the wok will rust. If you forget sometimes, it's no big deal; just scrub the wok well, dry it on the stove, and oil it.

There are many nonstick woks on the market, which require no seasoning. Most of these have some sort of Teflon coating. Most are quite expensive. I don't like them because when oil is heated in them, it beads up, like water on a newly waxed car, altering the stir-frying process. Anyway, a well-seasoned and well-maintained iron wok uses just as little oil.

In addition to the wok and ring, a cover for the wok is also recommended. It is used to bring sauce to a quicker boil and also in steaming and braising.

Many of my students ask me, "Can I use a French chef's knife?" You can use a Boy Scout knife if you feel comfortable with it. But I do recommend that you try to use a *Chinese cleaver*. Avoid the very heavy cleavers used for chopping through bone—most Western cleavers are of this type. Chinese cleavers sold in department stores and culinary shops are usually pretty expensive. Stainless steel cleavers sold in Asian markets are just as good and a whole lot cheaper. I have found them as low as $7.50. All cleavers should be sharpened on a 30- or 35-degree angle.

I would also advise purchasing a 10-inch or 12-inch *stainless steel strainer* with holes in it like a colander and with a handle. This is an essential tool for stir-frying, specifically for the poaching-in-oil technique. Other equipment I have, but that is not absolutely necessary, is a stainless steel *ladle* and, for those who use the two-handed stir-fry method, a *shovel* (which looks like a metal sand-box toy). A slotted or nonslotted spoon can be used just as easily. I also recommend buying two different sizes of long-handled *brass mesh strainers*. These have a bamboo handle. I have two, one that is 6 inches in diameter, the other that is 12 inches in diameter.

For braising, a wok with a cover can be used, but, untraditionally, I prefer to use a cast-iron skillet or Dutch oven with a tight-fitting lid. For steaming, a wok and cover can be used, or a large pot with a cover is acceptable. In both, a circular tripod rack is used to elevate the steaming dish. For steaming fish, I actually prefer to use a turkey roaster with a tight-fitting lid; its oval shape fits the shape of a whole fish well. The aluminum multitiered steamers are good but not necessary. Forget about the bamboo steamers. They look all right as a display piece, but they do not steam well, are bacteria breeders, and impart a strange camphor-like taste to the food.

INGREDIENTS

My recipes rely largely on fresh meats and vegetables readily available in most supermarkets. I eschew the use of canned vegetables and prefer to exclude them from my recipes unless the fresh versions are unavailable. Canned water chest-nuts, for example, are mushy, starchy, and tasteless. Chinese restaurants use them as filler. By contrast, fresh water chestnuts are juicy, sweet, and fruity.

For unusual ingredients like fresh water chestnuts, and for Chinese ingredients used in sauces and seasonings, I shop at an Asian market. Some supermarkets have some ingredients, but quality and variety are limited.

When I was a kid, the only stores selling Chinese ingredients were in Chinatown. A special trip was necessary to buy basic ingredients such as soy sauce and sesame oil, and maybe a few paltry canned goods. There were just much fewer Asians in the United States at that time. I was one of three Asians in my high school, and that was in the suburbs of Washington, D.C. My grandmother made do by preparing many things from the old country from scratch.

What I remember most is my grandmother's back porch. Extending from the kitchen, it was elevated. The railings were painted picket-fence white, and the floor, a battleship gray. In the shady part of the porch, there was a line of knee-high stone crocks with lids. In front of these were numerous quart canning jars filled with mostly cabbage and some string beans and radishes. This was a pickle similar to kimchi, and the ancestor of sauerkraut. When I went out on the back porch, my grandmother would routinely warn me about going into the stone crocks. Her warnings tickled my curiosity, so one day I couldn't resist. Kneeling on the porch, I opened the lid on one of the crocks. Floating in an inky salty liquid were black spheres the size of tennis balls. They were peeled turnips preserved in a soy sauce and salt solution, which when ready, were sliced and julienned, then mixed with a little soy sauce and sesame oil and sometimes pine nuts. Served with rice or noodles, this was a standard side dish. I reached in and grabbed one, rotating it in my hand. I felt like throwing it against the apple tree for fun, but before I could do it, I heard a scolding voice from the kitchen, "What are you searching? You have dirty, stinky hands. Do not put that back, or you will ruin the others."

Although I loved eating these things, I developed a shame for them because they were so strange to Americans. When I was in the first grade, I was absolutely taken with a little girl who I thought looked like Alice in Wonderland. Sitting on a stone wall, we played a nonsensical game with pebbles. She wore a blue dress with a blue bow that tied in the back, white socks, and black patent leather shoes. A black hair band pulled her long blond hair back. Since my hair was black, her light hair bore intense fascination for me. Even more fascinating were her arms. I was in awe of the golden fleece of hair on her arms, and I ran my fingers across it softly. She said to me, "You don't have any hair on your arms." We were just in first grade. It was all innocent enough. I hope so, anyway. I just wanted to be her friend. Reaching down into my pocket, I heard a crinkling sound and brought out a Chinese sweetmeat of which I was particularly fond. Twist wrapped in a blue printed paper that for some unknown reason had a picture of an airplane on it, it was labeled "preserved plum," and that is exactly what it was. She asked what it was, and I replied that it was "Chinese candy." I gave it to her, thinking we would be friends forever. She unwrapped it and, with a disgusted look, said, "Ew-w, it looks like poo-poo." I was devastated.

A few years later, a couple of neighborhood girls came to my grandmother's house. My grandmother gave us a snack of milk and stale Fig Newtons, which she bought and hoarded about once a year. We wandered out onto the back porch, and the inevitable question came up as to what was in the stone crocks. I lifted the lid on one of the crocks and let the girls look in.

"Ew-w. What are they?" they asked.

By this time in my life, I had had enough humiliation about the things my people ate. So, I replied, "Bulls' balls, salty bulls' balls."

"Ew-w-w!"

This trauma extended well into adulthood.

"Stu, what are these, anyway?" a young woman asked starring at the opaque white sphere she was balancing on a teaspoon.

She looked at me and back at the sphere and at me again, brushing a curve of hair away from the end of her mouth. There was a graceful, ballet-like movement to her eyes, which seemed choreographed with the movements of her body. She would shift her body in the chair, cross her legs, cast her eyes downward momentarily, and look back at me, holding me captive. She was now half smiling, her mouth slightly open, appreciating my attention, but conveying concern.

"So, what are these, anyway?" she asked again.

"Lichees," I replied.

"Lichees? What are lichees?"

This was my first date with her, and I wanted to woo her with my consummate knowledge of Chinese food. The meal was going so well. She agreed that spring rolls were so much more delicate and tasty than the traditional thick and clumsy egg rolls, and that General Tso Chicken made sweet-and-sour chicken a dish of the past. She was wild about Peking duck, which I wrapped in a pancake for her, using only my chopsticks. I could have explained that lichees were a fruit and followed this with the story of the emperor who sent a caravan from Peking to southern China for the sole purpose of bringing back lichees for a favorite concubine who craved them. Romantic, perhaps, but too hokey Oriental for me. Unpleasant childhood memories of Chinese food and American girls began to resurface, and I felt myself falling back into old habits.

"They're sweet. It's a dessert. Go on. Try it. You'll like it," I insisted.

She put the lichee in her mouth and bit down slowly, swallowing with a visibly and audibly conspicuous gulp.

"I want to see you eat one," she said. She put another lichee on her spoon. Placing her elbows on the table, she leaned toward me and extended herself across the table. She placed the lichee in my mouth and withdrew the spoon, smiling. I could taste the faint, waxy scent of her lipstick.

I chewed slowly, rolled my eyes, and said, "Mmmm, good. And, they give you so much energy." She was quite suspicious now.

"Really, what are lichees?"

Uncontrollably, I replied, "Monkey's balls. Candied monkey's balls."

"Ew-w-w!" she said, putting down the spoon. "How can you do that to a monkey?"

"With a knife or scissors, I guess."

Some time later we went to a party together, and I introduced her to a Chinese woman, a college classmate of mine. I left her side to get some drinks. She turned to my friend and asked, "Are lichees really candied monkey's balls?"

Frowning, my friend turned to her and asked, "Who told you that? Stu?"

Despite my being exposed as a liar, we continued seeing each other, although this did have a "boy who cried wolf" effect on the culinary aspects of our relationship. One night, we met a group of my friends who lived in New York City. They were a motley crew, but being equally urbane and well traveled, they all had broad tastes in food. We went to a favorite Chinese restaurant of mine, a walk-up in the center of Chinatown. All deferred to me to order. The selection was innocent enough, although not typical of what Americans would order. Long cruller-like fried bread, served with finely julienned fresh ginger. Shanghai steamed pork dumplings, served in a bamboo basket. Tung Ting Shrimp, floating in white sauce with clouds of meringue. "Snowfish," or delicately steamed steaks of grouper. Pork with pine nuts and fresh shiitake mushrooms. This was a Shanghai restaurant, so soup was served last. I ordered a favorite of mine, 10 Ingredient Soup.

"Hey, Stu," one of my friends said, "Only two ingredients of this 10 Ingredient Soup are recognizable. The other eight are unidentifiable. Good, though." He continued to slurp through it.

Sitting next to me on a banquette, she picked out a triangle of white spongy substance from her soup bowl with her chopsticks and held it quivering in front of her.

"What is this, anyway?" she asked.

All eyes and ears were on her, so I had to reply, "That's the stomach of a large fish that is blown up with an air pump to stretch it and deep-fried. It's then dried and cut up and reconstituted in soup, mostly."

Laughing, she slapped me lightly on my arm with the back of her hand. She said, "I know you. You're up to your old tricks again."

The reality here, however, was that I wasn't making up the story and was telling the truth. It dawned on me at this point of my life that we Chinese do eat some rather strange things. Psychoanalytically, there may be an odd correlation in my life between strange food and intimate love. But, I don't want to think about this too much.

Without hesitation, she placed the triangular piece of blown up, deep-fried, reconstituted-in-soup fish stomach in her mouth and ate it.

She said, "You know, your big stories really get to me. I know it's my imagination, but this thing does taste a little fishy."

I brushed the hair away from the corner of her mouth, my hand lingering briefly on her cheek. She held my hand, entwining her fingers with mine, and moved close to me on the banquette. Taken with the moment, I told myself I would tell her about it later.

Let's start with the most important seasoning in Chinese cuisine, soy sauce. After that, you'll find ingredients listed in alphabetical order.

SOY SAUCE My recipes call for two types of soy sauce: black or dark soy sauce, made with molasses, and regular soy sauce, which is thinner. For the former, I prefer the Koon Chun brand from Hong Kong or one labeled "Mushroom Soy Sauce." Do not buy the one labeled "Double Black Soy Sauce." It is too thick and sweet for normal use. For regular soy sauce, I prefer one labeled light soy sauce, usually from the People's Republic of China. If you cannot get to an Asian market, Kikkoman soy sauce, sold in most supermarkets, is an acceptable substitute, although I believe it does not cook well in the wok. Forget about the La Choy brand; it's nothing more than salty black water.

CHILI PASTE There are numerous tins and jars of chili paste in the market, but I make my own:

> Soybean oil
> $1/2$ pound Asian dried red chili peppers
> $1/4$ cup cocktail peanuts, ground to a paste in a blender or food processor
> $1/4$ cup grated carrot

Open the windows and turn the exhaust fan on high; otherwise, cooking this recipe is like being tear-gassed. Heat 3 tablespoons oil to the smoking point in a wok. Add the chili peppers and stir-fry until darker red but not black, keeping in mind that the chilies will continue to cook after you turn the fire off and remove them from the heat. Put the stir-fried chili peppers in a blender or food processor and puree. Add the peanut paste and grated carrot, and blend for 30 seconds to grind to a paste. No salt is necessary. Put it in a jar and pour in enough vegetable oil to cover the chili paste.

OPTIONAL: Add 1 or 2 teaspoons Sichuan peppercorns, which are fragrant and not spicy, when stir-frying the chilies. This is the authentic chili paste used in Sichuan, China. A tincture of Sichuan peppercorns was used for anesthesia during the war, and, therefore, it is an acquired taste. If you chew one, you will notice that it will numb your mouth.

If you don't want to go through all this trouble, just buy the commercially prepared chili paste, sometimes labeled "chili sauce." I like the straight chili paste without garlic or beans, especially the ones from China. Vietnamese and Thai chili pastes and sauces are too sweet and contain tomato sauce. My recipes generally specify to use 1 teaspoon of chili paste, which is usually qualified by "or to taste and tolerance." In other words, use as much as you are comfortable with, even if it's just a pinch.

HOISIN SAUCE This is erroneously called "plum sauce." I use the Koon Chun brand, which is darker, thicker, and more flavorful. Others, such as Panda brand, are acceptable, however.

OYSTER SAUCE The oyster sauce I use is the most expensive of oyster sauces, the Hip Sing Lung brand from Hong Kong, selling for around $3.50. Its taste is clearly superior. I go through it quickly, but still I suggest you refrigerate it, or any other brand of oyster sauce, because they have a tendency to mold.

RICE My family is from northern China, so I prefer to eat short-grain rice, which is a bit stickier. My favorite is short-grain rice from Japan, specifically the Kokuho Rose brand, extra fancy. I also prefer a good long-grain rice, like Carolina brand. Rice is served with almost all Chinese dishes, except a few that are eaten with thin pancakes, such as Moo Shu Pork or Peking Duck.

To cook short-grain rice, use a heavy pot with a lid and merely add rice and water. I use an unusual method of measurement: I touch the tip of my fore-finger to the top of the rice and fill enough cold water to the first joint of my finger, or approximately 1 inch. This method is good for making up to 4 cups of rice. Cover the rice pot and put it on the stove over high heat. Let it come to a full boil, stir, and reduce the water to just above the rice. Reduce the heat to a low simmer, cover, and cook for about 13 minutes. Turn the heat off and let the rice sit with the cover on until you are ready to serve. Fluff with a large spoon after cooking and before serving.

To cook long-grain rice, put the rice in a pot and fill almost to the top with cold water. Using your hands, stir the rice around in a circular motion, "washing" the grains, and pour off the milky liquid. Do this three times, then add water according to the above "first joint of the finger" method described above. (My grandmother used to soak the rice in cold water for a half hour before washing, which made it even better.) Bring the rice to a full boil over high heat in a covered pot, stir it, and reduce the heat immediately to simmer or low. Cook for 15 minutes. Fluff with a large spoon after cooking and before serving.

If you eat a lot of rice, you may want to buy an automatic rice cooker. Use the above method for measuring water and/or washing, cover, set the switch to "cook," and the rest is done automatically. This is simple and convenient, especially when you have other dishes to cook. Almost every Chinese family has one.

SESAME OIL Of the many brands of sesame oil sold in the Asian stores, I prefer those from Japan, which have a consistently superior taste. The Kadoya brand is particularly recommended. Do not use cold-pressed sesame oil from health-food stores; it does not have the same toasted flavor.

VEGETABLE OIL Almost all Chinese restaurants use soybean oil. Likewise, the generic vegetable oil at most major supermarkets is now soybean oil, which is healthful and cheap. Oils labeled as "vegetable oil" often have cottonseed oil in them, which, not being regulated by the USDA, contains chemicals and other impurities.

Many people ask me if olive oil is all right to use for Chinese food, since it is the certifiably "healthful" oil. Virgin olive oil, which it is light, is acceptable, but it is not as good as other oils for stir-frying because it has a low smoking point. Despite the hype, don't use olive oil, which is right for Western cuisine but not for Chinese. If you want to use a particularly healthful oil, mix 1 quart each safflower oil, soybean oil, and peanut oil. This mixture produces linoleic acid, reportedly a diet aid and anticarcinogen. Use it for stir-frying or salad dressing.

VINEGAR Like wine, vinegar needs to hold its integrity when cooked in a hot wok. Keep the fancy herbed vinegars for salad dressing. For Chinese food, use apple-cider vinegar. Occasionally, I use a mixture of apple-cider and balsamic vinegar, which is similar to vinegar from Chekiang Province.

WINE Buy the cheapest possible wine, labeled "Pale Dry" or "Cocktail Dry Sherry," sold in any liquor store. I would not use any wine labeled as cooking wine because salt has usually been added to it. Some Chinese restaurants ferment their own rice wine, but I don't believe that this adds anything remarkable to the sauces. I came to the conclusion that chefs who made their own rice wine were more interested in drinking it than using it.

Techniques and Basic Sauces 烹調技術

THE KEY TO WHY MEAT—BE IT chicken, beef, pork, or seafood—in Chinese stir-fried dishes is so flavorful, tender, and moist is in its unique preparation and method of cooking. Essentially, the meat is first coated in a mixture of egg, cornstarch, and water and then "poached" in oil. The process involves heating at least 2 cups of oil to 280°F, which is not very hot. If you do not have a deep-frying thermometer, place a piece of meat in the oil. It should not sizzle like fried chicken, nor should it just sit in the oil. There should be a little action to it, with bubbles rising from the morsels like champagne bubbles in a glass. Just remember the following sayings: "Bubbles slow, no"; "Deep fry, do not try"; and "Bubbles steady, it's ready." The meat is poached in the oil and then added with vegetables to a sauce and stir-fried.

Caution is needed when working with large amounts of oil. The rules for safety in deep-fat frying are really no different from other kinds of cooking. From the time the heat is turned on under the oil to the time it is turned off, you must watch it carefully. Avoid phone calls; do not respond to amorous advances, crying children, or meddling in-laws. In other words, do not be distracted. It is a good idea to keep pets and children out of the kitchen. When using this method of poaching in oil, I prefer to use a wok with a ring that fits over my burner underneath the wok, giving it stability. Many newer woks on the market are heavy and have flat bottoms; these are acceptably stable. Use slow, steady movements when practicing this technique. Stir the meat slowly, turning it gently with a slotted spoon. Do not stir the oil so vigorously that it flows up and over the side of the wok. Use a stainless steel strainer or brass mesh strainer to remove the meat. And try not to drip oil over the side of the wok.

But, you say, the battle cry in the kitchen today is "fat free." A low-fat diet has become the secret to weight reduction, health, and long life. So be it. Just bear in mind that the lower the fat or oil content in food, the greater the compromise in taste and texture. When you cook for yourself or your family every day, you might want to keep the fat and oil as low as possible. When you are cooking for friends, you might want to increase the amount of fat and oil for taste's sake. That is why I have given three options for cooking stir-fried dishes: low oil, even lower oil, and hardly any oil.

LOW OIL This technique is merely the thorough draining of oil from meat that has been literally poached in oil. Remove the meat from the oil with an 8- or 10-inch net-style or perforated stainless steel strainer with a long bamboo handle or use a colander. Drain thoroughly for at least 10 minutes. This technique effectively keeps residual oil low without compromising the taste at all.

LOWER OIL This is the same technique as the above, except 2 to 4 cups of hot boiling water are poured over the meat in the strainer, rinsing away most of the oil. There is a compromise in taste, although it is minimal.

HARDLY ANY OIL I developed this technique originally for gall bladder sufferers. It essentially uses an "English bath" to remove almost all the oil. Although this may not sound very appetizing, an English bath is simply a pot of furiously boiling water. After draining the meat thoroughly in a strainer or colander, dump it in the boiling water, stir, count to 10 or 15, remove the meat from the water, and flush it again with one more cup of fresh boiling water. Since this is the most radical method to remove oil, it compromises taste the most, but it does provide an option for people who want to eat stir-fried food but cannot tolerate the fat.

The following is the basic recipe for coating seafood, chicken, beef, and pork before stir-frying.

> 1 egg white
> 3 tablespoons cornstarch
> 3 tablespoons cold water
> 1 pound seafood, chicken, or meat, prepared and/or cut for coating

Mix the ingredients well in a bowl, preferably with your hands. The consistency should be milky and velvety.

Throughout this book, I will repeat the following methods of meat preparation, as necessary:

PORTIONS

MY RECIPES ARE GENERALLY BASED on 1 pound of meat per dish. My students always ask me, "How many will that feed?" I always respond, "It depends on how hungry you are." It also depends on how many dishes you are making. Generally speaking, served with rice, the recipes will feed two or three people with good appetites. Obviously, if you are cooking for four people, cook two dishes; for six people, cook three dishes; and so on. Yields given for each recipe assume a moderate-sized meal, not just one dish served alone.

The Meats

The type of seafood, chicken, or meat used in a recipe is important for the final product. The following details how and what seafood and meats should be picked and how to prepare them for coating and poaching in oil.

SHRIMP Almost all shrimp are frozen. The "fresh" shrimp on the bed of ice in seafood stores and supermarkets are not fresh, merely defrosted. Prudence is needed in buying shrimp. I have the most trouble in supermarkets, where shrimp sometimes are not very fresh and are sometimes inedible. So I make a pain in the neck of myself by asking to smell one of the shrimp. I get some funny looks. If the sample shrimp smells like ammonia, it is spoiled, so don't buy it.

Most Chinese restaurants use only white shrimp, which are actually gray when raw. Tiger shrimp, although a bit tough, are also all right. If these shrimp have any red or pink tinges around the edges, it means that they are in the process of spoiling. Frequently, inept staff at supermarkets forget to defrost the shrimp slowly the night before in the refrigerator; so they defrost them quickly under hot running water, which is illegal in most states and causes rapid spoilage.

I prefer to use large shrimp, specifically, 21-25s, which means there are 21 to 25 shrimp to a pound. The 26-30s are also fine. Peel and devein the shrimp before using, even though this is not a whole lot of fun. Already peeled and deveined shrimp are available, but they are not nearly as good as the shrimp that you prepare yourself.

In peeling shrimp, rip off the little legs first and peel back the shell from the head to the tail. When you get to the tail, grab the tip and pull gently; you may be able to get the small piece of meat in the tail, which makes the shrimp more attractive when cooked. To devein shrimp, use a cleaver or a knife to cut into the back—the curved opposite side of the legs—slicing deeply through the body of the shrimp without cutting it in half lengthwise, but leaving a small donutlike hole in the middle. In effect, this is butterflying the shrimp. Rinse the shrimp individually under cold running water to remove the vein.

Shrimp with their heads on are now available in many areas. I would not use these shrimp for most stir-fried dishes, but I provide a wonderful, simple recipe for these beauties in the chapter on shellfish. It is a tasty and attractive dish, if you don't mind looking a shrimp in the eye before eating it. Chinese people eat these shrimp by first ripping the heads off and sucking out the savory contents, much as people from Louisiana do with crayfish.

SCALLOPS Good Chinese restaurants prefer to use the best possible frozen scallops, which are Locket brand scallops from Canada. Most scallops have a visible small muscle, similar to the muscle that allows clams to open and shut, and this has to be excised with a small, sharp knife. Of course, the best scallops are fresh, but since they vary in size, to use them for Chinese food it is necessary to cut them into equal-size pieces so they will cook at the same speed.

CHICKEN Chicken is the easiest of all meats to buy and to cook. Simply buy boneless chicken breast from your local supermarket. This white chicken meat can be used for all Chinese stir-fried dishes, though restaurants prefer to use chicken thighs and legs for "dark" Chinese dishes such as Gung Bao Chicken and Chicken and Cashews. They fillet the meat from the thighs and legs by hand, something only a professional Chinese chef can do efficiently. Luckily, these days most markets sell boneless chicken thighs. This meat is generally cubed, although for General Tso's Chicken and Orange Chicken, broad slices are used. Remove the "tube steak," or thin fillet, from boneless breasts with a boning knife or your fingers.

Depending on the recipe, I specify two preparations for chicken—cubed and sliced. For cubed, first cut the breast lengthwise into $\frac{3}{4}$-inch strips; then cut across the strips to produce $\frac{3}{4}$-inch cubes. Cut across the tube steaks also to produce these size cubes. For slices, cut the boneless breast lengthwise in half. Thinly slice each piece on the diagonal to produce strips. Both cubes and slices are coated the same.

BEEF The only beef cut recommended for Chinese food is flank steak, preferably Choice rather than Select grade, both of which are available in most local supermarkets. It is one of the leanest cuts of beef, but any fat that is visible should be excised with a thin-bladed boning knife. When cut properly, which is easy to do since the grain all runs in the same direction, it is also one of the most tender cuts of beef. To cut it properly, after trimming, cut the steak lengthwise *with* the grain into two pieces. Using either a cleaver or a long, thin-bladed carving knife held, on a diagonal, slice the meat *against* the grain, producing strips of steak approximately $\frac{3}{4}$ to 1 inch wide.

PORK The preparation for pork is the same as for beef. The cut used in Chinese restaurants is pork butt from the shoulder, which is inexpensive and fatty. The best cut of pork is the loin. If loin chops are used, cut the center, nonfatty piece out and discard the rest. Or buy boneless pork loin, trim it with a boning knife, and cut it into medallions. Slice the medallions on an angle to produce strips about $\frac{1}{2}$ inch thick.

BASIC SAUCES

The sauces in this book are all authentic. When made with my recipes, they are as good as, if not better than, the sauces in a Chinese restaurant, complex and nuanced, because each sauce for each dish is freshly made at the time of cook, ing. The *chow gwo,* or stir-fry chef, deftly uses his ladle to take measured amounts of a variety of ingredients arranged in pans on a cart or table next to the wok stove. Chicken stock comes from a 50-gallon stockpot in which chicken bones have been simmering since morning. After these ingredients are combined in the wok, cooked meats and vegetables are added, and with a few tosses, in a less than a minute the dish is ready and is served. This is why in a good Chinese restaurant stir-fried dishes are produced so quickly.

You don't have to be a professional Chinese chef and have trained since you were eight years old to make a good Chinese sauce. You can make the sauce ahead of time, measuring out the ingredients carefully according to the amounts I specify. You can also make multiple portions of a sauce and store the remain, der in glass jars or plastic containers, which keep a remarkably long time in the refrigerator.

My recipes call for sauces to be maintained "hot." This means bringing the sauce just to a boil and maintaining it at a bare simmer on a back burner to keep it out of the way. This is not done in a Chinese restaurant because wok stoves are so powerful. On a home stove, however, this technique prevents the food from overcooking.

The following are recipes for the three most frequently used sauces in Chinese food. Be assured, they are authentic. These are trade secrets and many have never been revealed before.

Garlic Sauce

1/4 cup chicken broth

6 garlic cloves, crushed and minced

1 tablespoon finely minced fresh ginger

1/4 cup ketchup

3 tablespoons dark soy sauce

2 tablespoons dry sherry

1/4 cup cider vinegar

5 tablespoons sugar

1 teaspoon chili paste, or to taste and tolerance

Stir all the ingredients together in a small saucepan. Bring to a boil, stirring to dissolve the sugar. Set aside or refrigerate in a tightly covered container.

White Sauce

MAKES ABOUT 1 1/4 CUPS

1 cup chicken broth

2 tablespoons dry sherry

1/4 teaspoon salt

1 teaspoon freshly ground white pepper

4 garlic cloves, crushed and minced

1 tablespoon sesame oil

Combine all the ingredients in a small saucepan and bring to a boil. Set aside or refrigerate in a tightly covered container.

VARIATION SICHUAN SAUCE Prepare White Sauce as described above. Stir in 1 teaspoon chili paste, or the amount to your taste and tolerance.

Brown Sauce I

1 cup chicken broth

3 tablespoons black or mushroom soy sauce

1 tablespoon regular Chinese soy sauce or Kikkoman

2 tablespoons dry sherry

6 garlic cloves, crushed and minced

3 tablespoons finely minced fresh ginger

1 tablespoon sugar

1 tablespoon sesame oil

1 teaspoon freshly ground white pepper

Combine all the ingredients in a small saucepan. Bring to a boil, stirring to dissolve the sugar. Set aside or refrigerate in a tightly covered container.

Brown Sauce II

I developed this brown sauce for my restaurant Wok 'n' Roll, where I was restricted from having a stockpot because there was not enough space under the hood, rendering it a fire hazard and against fire code, and, thus, could not make chicken stock. Many of my customers called this "Wok 'n' Roll's Famous Sauce."

1 cup water or chicken broth

2 tablespoons black soy sauce

3 tablespoons oyster sauce

2 tablespoons dry sherry

2 tablespoons ketchup

3 tablespoons sugar

4 garlic cloves, crushed and minced

1 tablespoon finely minced fresh ginger

1 tablespoon sesame oil

1 teaspoon freshly ground white pepper

Combine all the ingredients in a small saucepan and bring to a boil. If using soon, reserve over low heat. Otherwise, let cool, then store in the refrigerator in a tightly covered container.

CORNSTARCH MIXTURE

This is simply a blend of cornstarch and water used to thicken sauces, particularly thinner sauces. Blend the two together ahead of time and then, before using, be sure to stir the cornstarch off the bottom, where it settles like silt in a river. I always keep a little extra cornstarch/water mixture on the side in case the sauce needs thickening. Every brand, every box of cornstarch, depending upon how long its been on the shelf, has varying thickening power. Likewise, I also keep a little broth on the side to thin the sauce if it becomes gummy and too thick.

3 tablespoons cold water	1 tablespoon cornstarch

The amount of cornstarch mixture you will need varies depending upon the amount of chicken broth called for in the recipe. A good general rule of thumb is, for every ½ cup of broth, use 1 tablespoon cornstarch dissolved in 3 tablespoons water to thicken it. For every cup of broth, use 4 tablespoons cornstarch dissolved in ½ cup cold water. Of course, other liquids in the recipe will also affect the consistency, and soups require less thickening. Each recipe will give you the amount you need.

SOUPS AND APPETIZERS

湯·菜·饍·茶·小·食

SOUP IN MANY PARTS OF CHINA—Shanghai, for example—is served at the end of a meal. I like it at the end because it provides a light finish. Wonton soup holds special memories for me. Not only did my Lao·Lao make the best wonton soup ever, but she also frequently used to enlist my help in making it.

"*Ni shr langoudou*," Lao·Lao said, as I frantically tried to chop lean pork by hand with a Chinese cleaver. This means in Chinese, I am a "lazy bones," not a flattering term. She gave me another cleaver, and I chopped the pork with two hands. Flailing furiously with both cleavers, I chopped the pork until Lao·Lao, my maternal grandmother, rubbing the meat between her fingers, would grunt her approval. Finished, she took the meat and mixed it with chopped shrimp and seasonings redolent with garlic and sesame oil. With her correcting me numer-ous times, I finally shaped the wontons into perfect "nun's caps"—to her satis-faction, anyway. My next slave task was to gently strain the chicken stock that had been simmering for four hours; the stock had started as chicken backs in water, and the strained broth had better be clear.

Another large pot held water boiling vigorously. Lao·Lao delicately folded the wontons into the water and gave me a wooden spoon. "Stir with the back of it," she said. I did, slowly. I was a teenager, wiling away about girls with waist-length hair in plaid skirts and rose-colored stockings. But I peered into the pot. The wontons were like butterflies, circling madly. I had a genetic condition that affected all adolescents in my family: Chinese traditional doctors had classified us, my family, as "hot." I leaned over the pot of whirling wontons. Blip, blip, blip, and blip—I had a nosebleed and turned that boiling pot of water from clear to pink.

Lao-Lao took the pot and threw the contents into the sink, muttering *"Tou-yen,"* which can only be translated as "pain in the ass." But she was smiling. She said, "Your great grandfather was like that." The pets of the house were waiting anxiously outside the kitchen door. One dog and two cats, they cocked their heads simultaneously, knowing they would get the "dead butterflies" in the sink.

WONTON SOUP

SERVES 4 TO 6

½ pound ground pork

½ pound shelled and deveined shrimp, coarsely minced

1 bunch of scallions, 2 reserved, remainder finely minced

5 garlic cloves, crushed and minced

1 tablespoon finely minced fresh ginger

1 tablespoon black or mushroom soy sauce

1 tablespoon regular soy sauce or Kikkoman

1 tablespoon dry sherry

2 tablespoons sesame oil

1 package (8 ounces) square wonton skins (about 50)

1 egg white

4 cups chicken broth

1   In a mixing bowl, combine the pork, shrimp, minced scallions, garlic, ginger, both soy sauces, sherry, and sesame oil. Mix well with a pair of chopsticks. Place in a colander and let drain.

2   Place a square wonton skin in front of you with one point closest to you, like

a baseball diamond with you behind home plate. Place 1 teaspoon of filling in the center of the wonton. Dipping your forefinger into the egg white, brush the egg white on all edges of the wonton skins—that is, from home base to first base to second base to third base and back to home base. Fold the home-base corner to meet the second-base corner and seal the edges from second base to first base and second base to third base. Pinching the first-base corner with your right hand and pinching the third-base corner with your left hand, fold both corners in to overlap in front of the pitcher mound, as if the wonton were folding its arms in front of its chest. Seal the first-base corner to the third-base corner with a dab of egg white. Repeat with remaining wonton skins and filling. Line up the wontons on a lightly floured tray, like toy soldiers.

3   Bring a large pot of water to a boil. Gently slide the wontons into the boiling water and stir with a slow circular motion with a wooden spoon, preventing them from sticking to the bottom. When they rise to the surface and the water is again at a boil, add 1 cup of cold water. When the water boils again, add another cup of cold water. When the water comes to a boil for a third time, remove the wontons with a mesh strainer or a slotted spoon and place in a bowl.

4   Bring the chicken broth to a boil in a large pot. When at a boil, place the wontons in the soup. Do not overcrowd. Stir them in a circular motion and cook for 1 minute. If there are extra wontons, reserve them for later.

5   Place a portion of wontons in a soup bowl. Pour soup over them to fill the bowl. Sprinkle a little bit of the minced scallions on top and serve.

HOT-AND-SOUR SOUP

SERVES 4 TO 6

If you cook this soup according to this recipe, I promise that it will be the best hot-and-sour soup you will ever have. For an exceptionally tasty soup, substitute 3 tablespoons rendered chicken fat for the vegetable oil. My preferred method for rendering chicken fat is to boil chicken skins and fat, place the liquid in the refrigerator and after the fat congeals, skim it off and put it in a mesh strainer to drain for 1 hour. Put the rendered fat in a jar and refrigerate. For a spicier Hot-and-Sour Soup, add 1 tablespoon minced fresh chilies along with the garlic and ginger.

1/4 cup tiger lilies (also called dried lily flowers)	1/2 cup dry sherry
1/4 cup tree ear mushrooms	1/4 cup cider vinegar
3 tablespoons vegetable oil	5 teaspoons sugar
1 tablespoon finely minced fresh ginger	3 tablespoons sesame oil
3 garlic cloves, minced and crushed	1 piece of tofu, 3 1/2 inches square and 1 1/2 inches thick
1/2 pound boneless pork, sliced into strips 3 inches long by 1/2 inch wide by 1/16 inch thick	2 tablespoons cornstarch mixed with 1/4 cup cold water
1 quart chicken broth	2 eggs, beaten
2 tablespoons black or mushroom soy sauce	2 scallions, sliced on the diagonal into 1/2-inch pieces
	Freshly ground white pepper

1   Remove the heads and tails from the tiger lilies by pinching them off with your forefinger and thumb. (The tail is narrower and tougher than the body of the tiger lily.) The trimmed tiger lily should be approximately 2 to 3 inches long. Pour boiling water over the lilies and soak for 15 minutes. Rinse thoroughly in a colander under cold water and reserve.

2   Soak the tree ear mushrooms in boiling water for 15 minutes. Rinse them in a colander under cold water. Place them back in the bowl and soak again in boiling water for another 15 minutes. Rinse again thoroughly in a colander under cold water. Repeat this procedure for a third time. Drain and set aside.

3   Heat the oil in a wok until smoking. Add the ginger and garlic. Immediately

add the pork. Stir-fry for 30 seconds, then add the tiger lilies and tree ears. Stir-fry for 30 seconds.

4   Add the chicken broth, soy sauce, sherry, vinegar, sugar, and sesame oil. Bring to a boil and add the tofu; stir.

5   Stir the cornstarch mixture until smooth. Add it to the soup gradually, stirring it in. If the soup is too thin, make more cornstarch mixture and add a little at a time until soup is to desired thickness. If the soup is too thick, add some broth to thin.

6   Add the eggs, which will thicken the soup a little more. Stir in a circular motion for 30 seconds, then add the scallions and white pepper to taste. Stir and serve.

CHICKEN AND CORN SOUP

SERVES 2 TO 4

½ pound skinless, boneless chicken breast

1 package (8 ounces) frozen corn kernels, or 1 can (12 ounces) canned corn, or 3 ears fresh corn, kernels cut off the cob

4 cups chicken broth

2 tablespoons dry sherry

1 teaspoon salt

1 tablespoon sesame oil

2 scallions, finely minced

2 tablespoons cornstarch mixed with ¼ cup cold water

1   Remove the thin membrane that covers the chicken breast as best as possible. Finely mince the chicken.

2   Place the corn in a colander and rinse thoroughly under cold water. Drain well.

3   Bring the chicken broth to a full boil in a large pot. Add the minced chicken and corn. Stir well and cook for 10 seconds.

4   Add the sherry, salt, sesame oil, and scallions. Stir once.

5   Pour the cornstarch mixture into the solution gradually, stirring constantly. If the soup needs more thickening, make more cornstarch mixture and add it a little at a time until soup is desired thickness. Remember the soup should not be as thick as a sauce. If too thick, add a little chicken broth to thin it. Serve at once.

CRAB AND ASPARAGUS SOUP

SERVES 8

This is such an easy soup to cook, yet it is elegant enough for special occasions or banquets.

2 quarts chicken broth

3 cups $\frac{1}{2}$-inch pieces fresh asparagus, preferably thin, sliced on the diagonal

1 ear of fresh white corn, kernels cut off, or $\frac{1}{2}$ cup frozen white corn kernels (see Note below)

$\frac{1}{2}$ cup dry sherry

1 tablespoon freshly ground white pepper

$\frac{1}{2}$ cup cornstarch mixed with 1 cup cold water

1 pound fresh crab meat, picked over to remove any cartilage or shells

3 scallions, sliced on the diagonal into $\frac{1}{2}$-inch pieces

1   Bring the chicken broth to a boil in a large pot. Add the asparagus and corn; stir. Add the sherry and white pepper; stir. Cook for 3 minutes, or until the asparagus is bright green in color.

2   Stir the cornstarch mixture into soup, adding it gradually, until lightly thickened. The soup should not be as thick as a sauce.

3   Once the soup is thickened, add the crab meat and scallions. Stir well, and serve immediately.

NOTE To effectively cut corn kernels off the ear, stand the cob up vertically with the stem end on the cutting board. Slice down the length of the cob with a knife.

Hunan Honey Fish Soup

SERVES 4 TO 6

Honey adds a nice, mildly sweet touch to this soup. To enhance its appearance, you can add 1 cup of seedless green grapes just before serving.

4 cups chicken broth

1/2 pound haddock or sea bass fillet, or any other white meat fish, thinly sliced

1/4 cup honey

1 tablespoon freshly ground white pepper

1 teaspoon salt

1/4 cup cornstarch mixed with 1/2 cup cold water

1/4 cup medium-dry or cream sherry, like Dry Sack or Harvey's Bristol Cream

1   Bring the chicken broth to a boil in a large saucepan. Add the fish fillet, honey, white pepper, and salt. Return to a boil, then reduce the heat to low.

2   Stir the cornstarch mixture until smooth. Add the mixture gradually to the soup, while stirring constantly.

3   Add the sherry, stir, and serve.

Egg Roll Soup

This is the real egg roll. The other one is a misnomer, really a "spring roll" in the direct translation. I prefer this soup thin, without any thickener. If you prefer, though, you can use a cornstarch solution (4 tablespoons cornstarch to ¹/₂ cup cold water) to thicken the soup before adding the egg roll slices.

4 cups chicken broth	I teaspoon cornstarch
¹/₄ pound shelled and deveined shrimp, finely minced	I tablespoon cold water
	I tablespoon vegetable oil
2 scallions, finely minced	2 eggs, beaten with I tablespoon water
I egg white	¹/₄ cup finely minced aged ham, such as Smithfield
I teaspoon finely minced fresh ginger	

1   Bring the chicken broth to a boil in a large saucepan. Reduce the heat and keep the broth at a simmer.

2   Combine the shrimp, scallions, egg white, ginger, and cornstarch in a bowl. Add the cold water. Mix into a paste.

3   Heat the oil in a medium nonstick skillet.

4   Pour the beaten eggs into the pan. Reduce the heat to medium. Gently cook a thin pancake; when one side is done, in about 2 minutes, carefully turn with a spatula. When the second side is done, place the egg pancake on a plate. Let it cool for 10 minutes.

5   Spread the shrimp paste evenly on the egg pancake. Roll the pancake as tightly as possible into a cigar shape without making the shrimp paste ooze out the sides. With a sharp knife or cleaver, cut the egg roll on the diagonal into 2-inch slices that are ½ inch thick. Reserve carefully on a plate.

6   Turn the heat to high under the chicken broth. When it comes to a boil, reduce the heat to low. Gently slide in the egg roll slices. Add the ham. Stir gently with a wooden spoon one time and cook for 5 minutes, or until the filling in the egg roll turns pink. Serve at once.

WHOLE CHICKEN AND HAM SOUP

SERVES 8

This is an excellent whole meal in a dish, a soup best consumed on a cold, wintry day with snow drifts piling up against the side of your house.

½ pound boneless chunk of aged ham, like Smithfield

I whole chicken, 4 to 5 pounds

4 scallions, cut into 3-inch sections and smashed with a cleaver

I piece of fresh ginger, 1 ½ inches by 1 inch, peeled and smashed with a cleaver

I tablespoon salt

I tablespoon freshly ground white pepper

I cup julienned shiitake mushrooms

1   Boil the ham in a pot with water to cover for 10 minutes. Remove the ham and discard the water. Rinse the ham in a colander under cold water.

2   Place the chicken in a large pot and pour in cold water to cover. Add the parboiled ham, bring to a boil, and lower the heat to a simmer.

3   Add the scallions, ginger, salt, and white pepper. Simmer for 1 hour, skimming off the fat occasionally, or until the chicken is fork-tender. It should not be too firm, and the meat should not be falling off the bones.

4   Turn off the heat. Add the shiitake mushrooms and serve in large bowls with pieces of chicken and ham and some shiitake mushrooms floating on top.

Oxtail Noodle Soup

SERVES 8

On cold winter days, my chefs at the Mandarin Restaurant would cook oxtails for hours over a low flame. The broth itself was an elixir.

1 pound Shanghai white noodles

1 pound oxtails

1 tablespoon freshly ground white pepper

2 teaspoons salt

$\frac{1}{2}$ pound bok choy, washed well and sliced on the diagonal into 2-inch pieces

1   Boil the noodles for 5 minutes, then rinse in cold water and drain in a colander.

2   Place the oxtails in a large pot. Cover with water by 3 inches. Bring to a boil, reduce the heat to a simmer, and cook for 2½ hours, or until the meat is fork-tender.

3   Add the white pepper, salt, noodles, and bok choy. Cook 4 or 5 minutes, or until the bok choy is bright green. Serve in large bowls.

Drunken Chicken

SERVES 6 TO 8

Cooking the bird this way produces unbelievably tender, silky meat. I've called for a whole chicken, but if only white meat is desired, boil and marinate bone-in chicken breast halves instead. The bone is important because it adds significant taste to the marinade as well as body to the gelatin. If boneless meat is desired, take the meat off the bone after it has marinated and is chilled. Cut into thick slices.

1 whole chicken, 3¼ to 4 pounds	1 tablespoon freshly ground white pepper
2 tablespoons kosher salt	3 cups dry sherry

1   Rinse the chicken under cold water and pat dry with paper towels. Pull out the neck, gizzard, and liver from the cavity of the chicken.

2   Place the chicken in a large pot and pour in enough water to cover by 1 inch. Take the chicken out and drain in a colander. Meanwhile, bring the water in the pot to a boil. Return the chicken to the pot and bring to a boil again. Reduce the heat and simmer for 30 minutes. Remove the chicken and let it cool for 30 minutes. Reserve 3 cups of the hot stock.

3   Place the chicken on a cutting board. With a sharp cleaver or chef's knife, remove the legs, thighs, and wings. Disjoint the legs from the thighs and the wings from the drummettes. Cut the back from the breast. Chop the back into 4 pieces.

4   Dissolve the salt in the reserved stock and pour into a large bowl. Add the white pepper and sherry. Place the chicken pieces in this stock, cover, and refrigerate, turning the pieces every 4 to 6 hours, for at least 24 hours, or up to 3 days.

5   Remove the chicken from the marinade, which should have jellied. Place the chicken breast on a cutting board and cut in half lengthwise. With a heavy cleaver, chop the breast crosswise into 1-inch-thick pieces, with the bone. The back is not particularly attractive, so instead of serving it to guests, you may want to eat it when no one is looking. Spoon some jellied marinade onto a serving plate. Arrange the chicken breast pieces on top in the center. Decorate the ends of the plate with the drumsticks and thighs. Serve cold.

Deep-Fried Marinated Fish

SERVES 6 TO 8

This was my mother's recipe. She used whiting, a common saltwater fish, which I suggest below. However, if you prefer another fish, the technique works very well with almost any variety, including the bluefish I discuss on page 43.

2-pound whole whiting, cleaned, scaled, and gilled

$^{1}/_{3}$ cup black or mushroom soy sauce

2 tablespoons dry sherry

6 garlic cloves, minced

1 tablespoon finely minced fresh ginger

1 tablespoon freshly ground black pepper

3 tablespoons plus 1 teaspoon sugar

$4^{1}/_{2}$ cups vegetable oil

Dipping Sauce

3 tablespoons black or mushroom soy sauce

2 tablespoons dry sherry

2 tablespoons sugar

2 tablespoons sesame oil

3 tablespoons brown sugar

1   Wash the whiting thoroughly, inside and out. Pat dry with paper towels. Cut the fish into 1½-inch pieces with a knife or cleaver. Put all the pieces, including the head if desired, in a large bowl.

2   Combine the soy sauce, sherry, garlic, ginger, pepper, sugar, and ¹/₂ cup of the oil in a bowl. Whisk well. Pour over the fish chunks. Turn the fish until well coated. Marinate in the refrigerator for 12 to 24 hours, turning the fish every 2 or 3 hours.

3   Heat the remaining 4 cups oil to 350°F. Drain the fish in a colander. Deep-fry the fish until fork-tender, about 5 minutes. Drain in a fryer basket first, then on absorbent paper. A large brown paper grocery bag works nicely.

4   Mix the ingredients for the dipping sauce in a small saucepan. Bring the sauce to a boil, stirring constantly. Remove from the heat and pour into individual dipping bowls.

5   Serve the fried fish either hot or cold, with the dipping sauce.

AN AVID FISHERMAN, I love catching bluefish, but I am not crazy about eating them because they are oily. So when I catch a lot of bluefish, particularly large ones, I fillet them, and cut out the V-shaped dark meat that lays in the center of the fillet. Next, I chunk the fillet and mix it with this marinade, letting it rest in the refrigerator for 24 hours, turning the fish frequently. I then deep-fry some of the chunks, serving some right away with the dipping sauce. I place the remaining deep-fried chunks in plastic bags, tie them securely, and freeze them. If guests or friends drop by and I want to serve an appetizer quickly, I just take some of these chunks out of the freezer, spread them on a tray, and reheat them in a 350°F oven. I serve them with the same dipping sauce.

PICKLED WHITE AND RED RADISHES

SERVES 6 TO 8

15 red radishes, washed

1 Chinese white radish (daikon), 8 to 10 inches long and 2 inches thick

1/2 cup balsamic vinegar

3 tablespoons sugar

1 teaspoon salt

1   Top and tail the red radishes with a paring knife. Peel the white radish and cut into 1-inch chunks. Put both radishes in a colander and rinse thoroughly. Drain well.

2   Combine the balsamic vinegar, sugar, and salt in a small saucepan. Bring to a boil. Boil for 5 minutes or until reduced by half. Remove from the heat and let cool.

3   Place the radishes in a serving bowl. Pour the cooled balsamic mixture over the radishes and mix well. Refrigerate for at least 1/2 hour. Serve chilled.

Hot-and-Sour Cucumbers

SERVES 6 TO 8

4 cucumbers, 8 inches long, or 2 hydroponic cucumbers, 14 inches long

1/4 cup black or mushroom soy sauce

1 tablespoon dry sherry

6 tablespoons sugar

2 tablespoons cider vinegar

1 teaspoon crushed hot red pepper, or 1 teaspoon finely minced fresh chilies (jalapeño, serrano, or Asian)

1 tablespoon cornstarch mixed with 3 tablespoons cold water, or more as needed

1   Peel the cucumbers and slice in half lengthwise. With a spoon, scoop out the seeds and discard. Cut the cucumbers lengthwise into 1/2-inch-thick spears. If very long, cut in half crosswise.

2   Combine the soy sauce, sherry, sugar, vinegar, and hot pepper in a saucepan and bring to a boil.

3   Add the cornstarch mixture gradually, stirring constantly until the sauce is thick. It should be a little bit gummy, because the cucumbers will release water, thinning the sauce. (If the sauce is not thick enough, make additional cornstarch mixture and add a couple of teaspoons at a time to get the proper consistency.) Let cool.

4   Put the cucumber spears in a bowl. Give the sauce a stir with a wooden spoon and pour over the cucumbers. Place the cucumbers on a platter and serve immediately.

SESAME VEGETABLES

SERVES 6 TO 8

1 cup broccoli florets

1 cup sliced celery, in diagonally cut
1-inch pieces (2 stalks)

2 thin carrots, sliced diagonally into
1-inch pieces

1 cup snow peas, tips and strings
removed

½ cup thinly sliced white mushrooms

¼ cup distilled white vinegar

1 tablespoon sugar

1 teaspoon salt

1 teaspoon freshly ground white pepper

1 tablespoon sesame oil

1   Combine the broccoli, celery, carrots, snow peas, and mushrooms in a colander and rinse under cold water.

2   In a medium pot of boiling water, blanch the vegetables until the broccoli and snow peas are bright green and the carrots are bright orange. Drain thoroughly in a colander, then rinse immediately with cold water. Set the colander over a bowl, place 2 cups of ice on top of the vegetables, and refrigerate for ½ hour.

3   Combine the vinegar, sugar, salt, white pepper, and sesame oil. Whisk well.

4   Placed the chilled vegetables in a mixing bowl. Add the vinaigrette and toss to mix well. Serve on small plates or in small bowls.

SHRIMP CROQUETTES

SERVES 6 TO 8

Most Chinese restaurants call these shrimp balls. My mother gave them a more appropriate culinary name, for which I was grateful since I was getting tired of my customers saying, "I didn't know shrimp had any."

1 pound shrimp, peeled, deveined, and minced	1 teaspoon salt
1 teaspoon grated fresh ginger	1 egg white
1 teaspoon dry sherry	1 tablespoon cornstarch
	4 cups vegetable oil

1   Combine the shrimp, ginger, sherry, salt, egg white, and cornstarch in a bowl and mix well with a pair of chopsticks. Refrigerate for 30 minutes.

2   With your hands, form the shrimp mash into balls about the size of a golf ball (see Note below).

3   Heat the oil to 350°F. Gently deep-fry the shrimp balls until golden brown, about 5 minutes. Drain in a fryer basket or colander, then drain briefly on absorbent paper and serve hot.

NOTE: For better-looking shrimp croquettes, use small store-bought croutons, about ¼ inch, or make your own by cutting ¼-inch cubes from firm-textured white bread. After forming the shrimp balls, press the croutons into the balls all the way around and deep-fry. This doesn't add significantly to the taste, but it does enhance the appearance.

Sichuan Fried Chicken Wings in Garlic Sauce

SERVES 6 TO 8

For all buffalo-wing lovers. This is better, as all my former happy hour customers will tell you.

1 cup cornstarch

2 pounds fresh chicken wings

3 cups oil

SAUCE

1/4 cup chicken broth

8 garlic cloves, crushed and minced

2 tablespoons finely minced fresh ginger

1/4 cup ketchup

3 tablespoons black or mushroom soy sauce

2 tablespoons dry sherry

1/4 cup cider vinegar

5 tablespoons sugar

1 teaspoon chili paste, or to taste and tolerance

1   Combine the cornstarch and 1 1/4 cups cold water to make a batter; mix well. It may be necessary to stir the cornstarch back into solution frequently because it settles like silt in a river on the bottom of the bowl.

2   Place the chicken wings in the batter and turn well to cover the wings.

3   Heat the oil to 350°F. Deep-fry the chicken wings for 5 minutes, or until yellowish white in color. Drain and put aside for 5 minutes. Reserve the hot oil in the pot.

4   In this same oil, fry the chicken wings again at 350°F for 2 minutes. Drain thoroughly in a fryer basket or colander. Place on absorbent paper.

5   To make the sauce, mix the broth, garlic, ginger, ketchup, soy sauce, sherry, vinegar, sugar, and chili paste in a small saucepan and bring to a boil.

6   Place the chicken wings in a large mixing bowl. Pour the sauce over the chicken wings and toss until they are well coated with the garlic sauce. Arrange on a platter and serve.

Tea Eggs

Tea eggs not only taste great but are stunning looking. When shelled, the cracked eggs look like Chinese porcelain, and the solid-colored eggs nicely contrast the brown exterior with the bright yellow interior of the yolk.

10 hard-cooked eggs in their shells

3 tablespoons loose black tea

2 tablespoons salt

1 tablespoon freshly ground black pepper

5 star anise

2 tablespoons black or mushroom soy sauce

1 cup boiling water

1 teaspoon freshly ground nutmeg

1   Shell 5 of the eggs. Lightly crack the shells of the remaining 5 with a spoon, being careful to keep the shells intact.

2   Combine the black tea, salt, black pepper, star anise, soy sauce, and boiling water in a small saucepan. Let this solution steep for 10 minutes.

3   Place all the eggs in the tea solution and simmer, turning the eggs frequently, for 30 minutes, or until the liquid is reduced by more than half.

4   Remove the eggs. As soon as they are cool enough to handle, remove the cracked shells from the 5 eggs. The already shelled eggs should be a dark brown, while the cracked-shell eggs will have a mottled porcelain appearance. Quarter each egg lengthwise with a sharp small knife.

5   Arrange the eggs in a flower pattern on a platter. I like alternating 1 porcelain egg slice with 1 brown egg slice. Serve cold.

MARINATED MUSHROOMS

SERVES 6 TO 8

I like to keep a bunch of these mushrooms in a jar in the refrigerator just for snacking. They never last long.

1 pound button mushrooms, preferably small

3 tablespoons vegetable oil

1/2 cup chicken broth

2 tablespoons black or mushroom soy sauce

1 tablespoon dry sherry

1 1/2 tablespoons sugar

1 tablespoon sesame oil

1   Rinse the mushrooms briefly in a colander. Drain, wipe dry, and reserve.

2   Heat the vegetable oil in a wok over high heat until smoking. Add the mushrooms and stir-fry for 3 to 5 minutes, or until lightly browned. Add the chicken broth, soy sauce, sherry, sugar, and sesame oil. Reduce the heat to low and braise for 25 minutes.

3   The mushrooms can be served hot or cold. I prefer them cold. When serving cold, place them in a bowl or a jar and pour the sauce over, then refrigerate for a minimum of 12 hours, or overnight.

SEAFOOD 海味

AS AN AVID FISHERMAN, OF ALL seafood, I love fish the most. There is nothing more wonderful than catching a fish, cooking it, and eating it on the same day. The rule is, the fresher the better. Most of the time, of course, it is necessary to go to the store to buy fish. Many supermarkets carry fresh fish, but sometimes attention and care given to fish is lacking. Caution, therefore, is needed when purchasing.

As far as whole fish are concerned, first look at the eyeballs. They should be clear, shiny, and convex. If they are dimpled or sagging, it means the fish is not fresh. Second, ask to see the gills. The brighter red they are, the fresher the fish. Gills that are darker red are acceptable, but if they are gray, don't buy the fish. In outdoor seafood markets, which do not display seafood behind glass, I like to take my thumb and press the stomach. If the flesh bounces back, it is fresh. If it remains indented, it is not so fresh. If weird stuff oozes out of one or more of the orifices, don't buy the fish. This does not make me greatly popular with the fish vendors.

I learned most of these techniques from my grandmother. Taking her shopping was an all-day affair. We would start out at the local supermarket, where she would scrutinize everything: meat, produce, canned or bottled goods. After traveling each aisle at least twice, we would check out. My maternal grandmother, my Lao-Lao, who was five feet tall and weighed 170 pounds, would invariably take the shopping cart and butt into the line. She got a lot of dirty looks, which she always ignored, but no one really messed with my grandmother. She would also watch the cash register like a hawk and frequently, after everything was rung up, would smile and say to the cashier, "You wrong three cents." Next, we would go to the Chinese store, where at least a half-hour was spent arguing with the owners about the prices of many items. She was always successful in bargaining the prices down.

The last place we would go was to the outdoor fish market by the wharf. I particularly dreaded the ordeal of this experience. Finding the type of fish she wanted, she would open the gills and then press her thumb into the stomach of every fish. Selecting a possible candidate for purchase, she would then grab the fish with both hands and rip the fish out of the ice, smelling it from the head to the tail. Usually, there was "Hey, lady" from behind the counter. Holding the fish up, she would shout, "Not fresh!" and throw the fish down, sending ice all over the place. She would then bargain the price of the fish down. As we would leave, she usually muttered in Chinese a term that cursed the part of the anatomy of the fishmonger's mother—the part from which he was born. She spoke adorably in English, but in Chinese she could be a bit off-color.

Exhausted after one of these shopping expeditions, I got lost driving back. Although she did not drive, my grandmother knew the city streets well. With her directing me, we headed home. At one point she told me to turn left. I did, not seeing a "No Left Turn" sign, and was pulled over by a policeman, who gave me a $50 ticket. My grandmother protested, and the officer informed us that the traffic court was just up the street and we could appeal the ticket. She insisted that we go. When we appeared before the judge, she explained that my making that left turn was all her fault. The judge accepted her story and reduced the fine by half to $25. Looking up at him and smiling, she said to him in her adorable English, "$10?"

SHANGHAI STEAMED WHOLE FISH

SERVES 3 TO 4

This dish requires tableside service. After placing the magnificent fish before your guests, use a small spatula and a knife to cut along the backbone of the fish, avoiding the rib bone and serve it in 2- by 3-inch boned pieces. When serving the meat around the rib bones, be careful not to serve those rib bones. It may be advantageous to remove the rib bones individually with a pair of good tongs. Once the upper side of the fish is served, take a pair of chopsticks or a pair of tongs and sever the backbone just behind the head. Using the chopsticks or tongs, pull the tail toward the head, removing it and leaving the bottom side of the fish mostly bone free. You may still have to remove some remaining rib bones with the tongs. Spoon sauce over each portion of fish.

1½- to 2-pound whole white-fleshed fish, preferably black sea bass

1 teaspoon salt, preferably kosher salt

1 tablespoon vegetable oil

3 tablespoons dark or black soy sauce

2 tablespoons dry sherry

1 tablespoon sesame oil

1 piece of fresh ginger, approximately 3 by 1 inch, peeled and cut into thin julienne strips

1 bunch of scallions, cut into 3- to 4-inch julienne strips

1 piece of Sichuan mustard greens, approximately 3 by 1 inch, cut into thin julienne strips

1 piece of Smithfield Ham, approximately 3 by 1 inch, cut into thin julienne strips

1 square of tofu, approximately 3 by 3 by 1 inch, cut into ¼-inch-thick rectangles

1 teaspoon freshly ground black pepper

1 teaspoon freshly ground white pepper

1   The whole fish should be gutted, gilled, and scaled. Cut both sides of the fish with a knife on an acute 20- to 25-degree angle 4 or 5 times, slicing toward the head of the fish. Cut to the bone, not through it. Wash the fish thoroughly under cold running water. Dry thoroughly with paper towels. Rub the kosher salt into the inside and outside of the fish. Rub the vegetable oil into the inside and outside of the fish with your fingers.

Braised Fish Fillet in Garlic Sauce

SERVES 4

This recipe is a particularly good low-fat dish if a nonstick skillet is used.

2 tablespoons vegetable oil

1 pound fish fillets, cut into 3- or 4-inch pieces

SAUCE

1/4 cup chicken broth

8 garlic cloves, crushed and minced

1 tablespoon finely minced fresh ginger

1/4 cup ketchup

3 tablespoons black or mushroom soy sauce

2 tablespoons dry sherry

1/4 cup cider vinegar

5 tablespoons sugar

1 teaspoon chili paste, or to taste or tolerance

4 scallions, sliced on the diagonal into 1/2-inch pieces

1 tablespoon cornstarch mixed with 3 tablespoons of cold water (optional)

1   Use a sturdy deep skillet, cast-iron if possible. Heat the vegetable oil in a nonstick skillet until it reaches smoking point. Pan-fry the fillets and adjust the heat, if necessary, to prevent the fish from sticking to the pan. If necessary, add a little more oil. With two spatulas, turn the fish fillets and pan-fry to a golden color on both sides.

2   Mix the sauce ingredients and add to the pan. It will sizzle and bubble up. Lift the fillets gently with a spatula so that the sauce can get underneath the fillets. Reduce the heat to low and reduce the sauce a bit in volume for approximately 5 minutes, spooning sauce over the fillets constantly. Add the scallions. When the fish flakes easily, it is done. Do not overcook it.

3   With a spatula, carefully transfer the fillets to a serving platter. If the sauce is thick enough, as it should be if the reduction is done properly, pour it over the fish. If not, thicken the sauce a bit with the cornstarch mixture. The sauce should not be gummy or soupy. Pour it over the fish and serve.

2   Place the fish on an oval plate that will not break during steaming
soy sauce and sherry over the fish, then pour the sesame oil over the surface o
Turn the fish a few times in the marinade. Let it marinate at room temperatu
hour while making other preparations.

3   Place julienne strips of ginger, scallions, mustard greens, and ham a
top of the fish. Be sure to stick the strips in the slashes across the width of the fi
slices of tofu across the entire surface of the fish, overlapping them like card
taire. Grind some black and white pepper over the surface of the fish. Using
baster or tablespoon, baste the entire fish and all the ingredients on top of the
quently with the marinade for ½ hour to an hour.

4   Prepare the steamer, using an oval turkey roaster with the lid, by pl
metal rack in the turkey roaster and filling water to just below the surface of th
Cover and bring to a full boil. Carefully, with gloves or mitts, place the entire
marinating fish into the steamer on top of the rack. Cover tightly and steam for 1
utes. Remove the platter carefully and place on a larger serving platter, since the
will overflow the rim of the steaming plate. Serve.

Whole Steamed Flounder with Vegetables and Three Mushrooms

SERVES 2 TO 3

1½-pound whole flounder, fluke, or sole with the head on, gutted, gilled, and scaled

1 teaspoon kosher salt

4 tablespoons vegetable oil

1 bunch of scallions, sliced lengthwise into 3- to 4-inch strips

1 piece of fresh ginger, 3 by 1 inch, cut into 3-inch julienne strips

SAUCE

1 cup chicken broth

2 tablespoons dry sherry

¼ teaspoon salt

¼ teaspoon freshly ground white pepper

4 garlic cloves, crushed and minced

1 tablespoon finely minced fresh ginger

2 teaspoons sesame oil

1 cup snow peas or snap peas, with tips and strings removed

1 cup 1-inch slices of celery, cut thinly on the diagonal

½ cup sliced white mushrooms

½ cup sliced shiitake mushrooms

½ cup enoki mushrooms, with 1 to 2 inches of tail removed

2 tablespoons cornstarch mixed with ¼ cup of cold water

1   Wash the flounder thoroughly under running water. Dry with paper towels. Sprinkle the fish with salt on the inside and outside, rubbing it in gently. Rub 2 tablespoons of vegetable oil on the inside and outside of the fish with your fingers. Place the flounder on a heat-resistant platter. With a sharp knife or cleaver, slice the top of the flounder 4 or 5 times across the surface of the fish down to the tail, slicing at a 20 to 25-degree angle toward the head. Stuff the slits with scallions and ginger.

2   Prepare a steamer with a rack, filling it with water to the surface of the rack. Cover and bring to a full boil. Place the platter with the fish in the steamer. Cover tightly. Steam for 13 to 15 minutes.

3   In a separate saucepan, combine the chicken broth, sherry, salt, white pepper, garlic, ginger, and sesame oil. Bring to a boil and maintain at a simmer.

4   Heat the remaining 2 tablespoons vegetable oil in a wok until smoking. Stir-fry the snow peas, celery, and white mushrooms until the snow peas are bright in color. Add the heated white sauce to the vegetables.

5   Restir the cornstarch water mixture and thicken the sauce by adding the mixture a little at a time. The sauce should not be soupy or gummy. Add the enoki and shiitake mushrooms, stir in, and take the vegetables off the heat.

6   By this time, the fish should be done. With a fork, the fish should flake off easily from the bone and still be moist. Remove the plate from the steamer with gloves or mitts and place the plate of steamed fish on a larger serving platter.

7   Pour the vegetables, mushrooms, and white sauce over the fish. Serve at once.

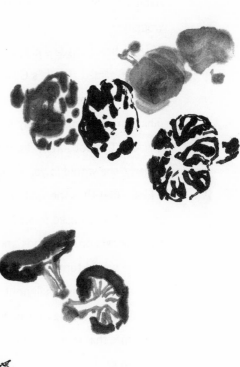

THE FOLLOWING RECIPE WAS HANDED DOWN to me by my other grandmother, my father's mother. I called her Neh-Neh, which is the name for "paternal grandmother" in the Shanghai dialect, Shanghai being the city of her birth. She came from a wealthy family, which always had cooks and, therefore, she did not learn to cook until she arrived in the United States. What an exemplary cook she became!

She was particularly fond of fish, especially whole fish, since whole fish with the head and tail on symbolize prosperity in the Chinese culture. I also like to think of them as representing the fullness of life. She also loved to catch those fish, two traits that I must have inherited from her. I spent one summer with her and other family members on a pristine lake in northern New Hampshire. Neh-Neh was intensely patient and, thus, made a great fisherwoman.

The family made daily journeys in a large inboard motorboat to a rocky cove we named "Uncle's Cove." My favorite time to fish with Neh-Neh was in the hours before sunset. Wearing a straw hat that she tied to her head with a pink scarf, she would deftly pull a hellgrammite, the ugly, threatening-looking larvae of the Dobson fly, from the bait box and impale it behind its neck. Quietly, she would lower her line to the bottom and then raise the bait about a foot. After that she waited patiently. Patience was not a strong suit of mine at age 13, but I used to sit and watch her in the amber glow of the receding day. The skin on her hands and her face was so smooth and soft. Finally, smiling, she would turn to me and say, "Stuart, I have dinner." A few minutes later, a four-pound smallmouth bass flopped onto the boat.

Always insisting on cleaning her own fish, with a small knife, she would make sure that every scale of the fish was removed. Marinating that fish in a solution of soy sauce, sherry, and sesame oil seasoned with ginger and scallions, she told me that she was making *suyu*. She always marinated the fish for a minimum of two hours, during which time she would baste it constantly. I fell asleep and awoke to her gentle nudge, looking up at her bespectacled face.

"The *suyu* is ready," she said. She gave me a bowl of rice and lifted a shimmering piece of fish with her chopsticks, placing it on my rice. It was delicious, and I ate heartily, which made her happy, as I was her "number-one grandson."

The meat and skin of the fish had all the flavors and nuances of the marinating, but the skin was still crisp, two seemingly contradictory characteristics of her *suyu* that I have never been able to duplicate. Neh-Neh then plucked the cheeks, which she considered the tenderest and tastiest part of the fish, with her chopsticks and placed them on my last spoonful of rice. Finishing, I touched her soft hand and said, "I love you, Neh-Neh."

Braised Whole Fish "Suyu"

SERVES 4

Sea bass is perfect for this recipe, but any whole white-meat fish will work; red snapper or grouper are fine. Of the freshwater varieties, bass, pike, and especially walleyes are great. Many Chinese people will use a few smaller fish, such as porgies or crappies or white perch. These tend to be a bit bony, however.

To serve this fish, use a knife that does not have to be sharp. I use a regular dining table knife and a small spatula. Cut along the top of the backbone from the head to the tail. Loosen the fish from the bone with the spatula. The bone should be below the meat. From the back of the ribs, section the fish into 2-inch portions by cutting it crosswide with a knife. With a spatula, lift off the sections from the backbone and serve on rice. Be sure to spoon some sauce over the meat. Next, lift out the backbone and as many rib bones as you can. You may want to pick out any remaining rib bones with a pair of tongs. With tongs, grab the tail and lift carefully, guiding the backbone with the dining room knife and lift the bone up and toward the head. This should remove all the major bones plus most of the rib bones. Cut the remaining meat into sections and serve.

1½-pound whole fish, such as black sea bass, gutted, gilled, and scaled

1 cup cornstarch

⅓ cup vegetable oil

3 (1-inch) chunks of peeled fresh ginger

6 garlic cloves, crushed and minced

½ bunch of scallions, cut into ½-inch lengths

¼ cup black or mushroom soy sauce

2 tablespoons dry sherry

2 tablespoons sugar

½ teaspoon freshly ground white pepper

2 tablespoons sesame oil

1   Rinse the fish thoroughly under cold running water. Pat it dry inside and out with paper towels. Grab some cornstarch with one hand and, holding the fish vertically over the sink with the other, lightly dust the fish with the cornstarch.

2   Using a frying pan or a skillet that will hold the whole fish, heat the vegetable oil until smoking. Place the fish in the pan and pan-fry on high or medium-high

heat until each side is golden brown in color, approximately 5 minutes on each side. Frequently lift the fish gently with a large spatula and add oil if necessary to prevent scorching or sticking.

3   Mash the ginger with the side of a cleaver or mallet and smash the sections of scallions.

4   Mix the soy sauce, sherry, sugar, garlic, white pepper, sesame oil, and ½ cup cold water. When the fish is pan-fried on both sides to a golden color, pour the premixed sauce over the fish. Add the crushed ginger and scallions. Lift the fish again with a long spatula so that the sauce can get underneath to prevent sticking. Cover tightly for 5 minutes. Turn the heat to simmer or low.

5   Gently and carefully using two spatulas, turn the fish in the sauce. Cover and cook for an additional 5 minutes.

6   Using a fork or a small knife, poke the meatiest part of the fish behind the head. The meat should flake off the bone easily. If not, cook uncovered for another 3 minutes and test it again. (If the sauce is reducing too quickly, add a little water or chicken broth.)

7   Place the fish with the two spatulas carefully and delicately on a serving platter and pour the sauce over the fish. Serve immediately.

Shanghai Steamed Chilean Sea Bass Fillet

SERVES 6

The first time I had Chilean sea bass was in a French restaurant. It was served in a simple beurre blanc sauce, and it was delicious. I vowed to develop a recipe for this remarkable fish. And so I have adapted it to my Shanghai fish recipe. Chilean sea bass fillets are usually as large as salmon fillets, sometimes thicker. I prefer to use a 2- to 3- pound fillet, but a 1-pound fillet is fine, too; just halve the ingredients in the recipe.

I also prefer to use a fillet that has the grayish black skin on one side, which serves the purpose of holding the fish together and sealing the flavors from underneath. This is not entirely necessary. And remember, the skin is inedible. Once the fish is cooked according to the following recipe, it literally melts in the mouth.

Tip: A single frozen green pea can be pressed into the center of each slice of tofu, making this dish more attractive.

3 pounds fresh Chilean sea bass fillet

¾ teaspoon salt, preferably kosher

1 piece fresh ginger, 3 by 1 inch, cut into thin julienne strips

1 bunch of scallions, cut into 3- or 4-inch strips

¼ ounce Sichuan mustard greens, cut into 2-inch strips

⅛ pound prosciutto ham, sliced paper-thin, cut into 3 by 1-inch rectangles

1 (3-inch) cake of fresh tofu, sliced ¼ inch thick and trimmed into 2 by 1-inch rectangles

3 tablespoons black or mushroom soy sauce

2 tablespoons dry sherry

1 tablespoon sesame oil

1 teaspoon freshly ground white pepper

1   Place the sea bass on a cutting board. With a large knife, preferably a Chinese cleaver, slice the fillet in the middle lengthwise *without* cutting all the way through the meat. If the skin is on the fillet, cut to the skin but not through it. Then, in an ice-cube-tray pattern, cut the fillet widthwise, again taking care not to cut all the way through. These width cuts should be made at a slight angle, not straight up and down. The whole fillet is now carved into approximately 2½ by 1½-inch cubes. Place

the fillet on a oval or round plate that will fit easily into the steamer. The plate should be sturdy enough so as to not break during the steaming process.

2   Place the julienned ingredients alternately into the vertical and horizontal cuts. Put the rectangles of ham over each cube, tucking any overlapping pieces into the vertical or horizontal cut near it. Place the remaining julienned ingredients over the surface of the fillet, crosswise. Place a cube of tofu on each cube of the fillet; trim the tofu to fit neatly.

3   Pour the soy sauce, sherry, and sesame oil over the fillet. Sprinkle the white pepper over the fish and baste the fillet frequently with a spoon or a turkey baster for 30 to 60 minutes.

4   Assemble the steamer in a pot with a tight-fitting lid, that is large enough to hold the plate of fish. Insert a metal rack into the pot and fill with water just under the surface of the rack. Cover and bring to a full boil. Place the plate with the fillet into the steamer, cover, and steam for 17 minutes. With mitts or gloves, remove the plate of steamed fillet and place on a larger serving plate. Use a small spatula and knife to scoop squares of fish onto individual serving plates. Spoon some sauce over the squares before serving.

FOR FRESHLY GROUND WHITE PEPPER, BUY whole white peppercorns in an Asian market. Put them either in a coffee grinder or a blender. Grind and reserve in a small jar for periodic use. The taste is fragrant and bears no resemblance to the gray powder that is sold in supermarkets.

CRISPY SQUIRREL FISH IN GARLIC SAUCE

SERVES 3 TO 4

While I was teaching how to cook squirrel fish, a student raised her hand and said she couldn't bring herself to eat a squirrel. I told her that the word referred to a flying squirrel, which the fish resembles after being filleted in a special way and deep-fried. The recipe looks complex, but much of the explanation involves how to remove the major bones from the fish while keeping the head and tail intact. Its final presentation is quite stunning and is, thus, suitable for special celebrations and banquets.

1 1/2- to 2-pound whole white fish, such as sea bass or red snapper

1/2 cup all-purpose flour

1/4 cup cornstarch

4 cups vegetable oil

SAUCE

1/4 cup chicken broth

8 garlic cloves, crushed and minced

1 tablespoon finely minced fresh ginger

1/4 cup ketchup

1/4 cup black or mushroom soy sauce

2 tablespoons dry sherry

1/4 cup cider vinegar

5 tablespoons sugar

1 teaspoon chili paste, or to taste and tolerance

1 tablespoon cornstarch mixed with 3 tablespoons cold water

1/2 bunch of scallions, sliced on the diagonal

1   The whole fish should be gutted, gilled, and scaled. For this dish, it is particularly important to tell the fishmonger to cut straight up the middle of the stomach to the gills. Sometimes fish cleaners will cut to the side just below the gills, which will ruin the appearance of the "squirrel" fish. Wash the fish thoroughly under cold running water. Pat dry with paper towels.

2   With a thin-bladed boning knife and a pair of needle-nose pliers, "squirrel the fish" by first cutting a slit on both sides of the back fins to the back bone. There are two sets of back fins. After the slits are made, with the pliers, grab the tail end of each fin and pull toward the head, thus removing the fin. Cut a slit on both sides of the anal fin, which is the fin just below the anus, and remove it with the pliers as well. Leave the two small fins on each side of the fish just below the gills on the stomach, which

after being fried will be part of the "wings." Make a neat incision on the top of the fish from the back of the head through the open slits where the fins have already been removed, all the way back to the tail. Carefully, with the tip of the boning knife, separate the meat from the spine on both sides, exposing the spine bone all the way to the tail. Using the tip of the knife, from the top, separate the rib meat from the ribs as far down to the belly of the fish as possible. From the anus to the tail, separate the bottom tail meat from both sides of the spine. With a kitchen shears or scissors (a small wire cutter is good), snip the spine just above the tail and just behind the head. Remove the skeleton, the spine, and rib bones carefully, using the needle nose pliers. Essentially, the fish, although whole, is filleted.

4   Place the "squirreled" fish on a cutting board with the top of the head facing up. Place the palm of your hand on top of the head above the eyes. Put your other hand on top of the first hand and flatten the head against the board, or you can smash the top of the head with the broadside of a cleaver, also flattening it. The fish should look kind of flat like a flounder. Sounds brutal, but the fish is already dead. (If you don't want the fish's eyes looking back at you when you smash its head flat, put a folded piece of paper towel on top of its head.)

4   Flour the fish lightly. Shake off any excess flour. Combine the cold water and cornstarch in a small bowl and mix well to make the batter. Dip the fish in the batter and coat thoroughly. In a wok, heat the oil to 350°F. Slide the fish into the deep-frying oil in its "flying position." Fry the fish to a golden color, approximately 5 minutes. Be sure that all parts, the head and the tail, of the fish are fried. Grip the tail of the fish with a pair of tongs, slide it up in the wok, and hold it in this position, so that the head can be fried. Then, grip the head and fry the tail in the same way. Remove the fish with a stainless steel or brass net strainer. Drain on absorbent paper towels or on a large paper bag.

5   Combine the chicken broth, garlic, ginger, ketchup, soy sauce, sherry, vinegar, sugar, and chili paste in a saucepan. Bring to a boil. Stir the cornstarch mixture back into solution and thicken the sauce by adding it a little at a time, so that the sauce is not soupy or gummy. Add the scallions to the sauce and stir in.

6   Place the deep-fried fish on a platter. Pour the sauce over it and serve.

Beijing Sweet-and-Sour Fish Slices

SERVES 3 TO 4

Traditionally, Beijing sweet-and-sour sauce is mild. To turn this into a hot-and-sour sauce, add 1 tablespoon of finely minced fresh chilies (serrano, jalapeño, or Asian) or 1 tablespoon of minced dried red chilies to the minced ginger when stir-frying in Step 3.

1 pound haddock fillets or any other thick white-meat fish fillet

1/2 cup all-purpose flour

1/4 cup cornstarch

2 cups plus 1 tablespoon vegetable oil

SAUCE

1/4 cup black or mushroom soy sauce

2 tablespoons dry sherry

2 tablespoons apple cider vinegar

5 tablespoons sugar

1 tablespoon finely minced fresh ginger

1 tablespoon cornstarch mixed with 3 tablespoons cold water

1   Slice the haddock fillets on a 45-degree diagonal into 1/2-inch-thick slices. Dredge the slices in the flour, lightly shaking off any excess. Mix the 1/4 cup cornstarch with 1 cup of cold water in a mixing bowl. This is the batter, and it should be thick but thin enough to stir.

2   Heat the deep-frying oil to 350°F. Stir the batter first, since it will settle. Put a few pieces of fish in the batter and coat well. With a pair of tongs, place the fish pieces one by one into the hot oil and fry until yellowish-white in color. Drain in the fryer basket and place on absorbent paper. Wait 5 minutes and re-fry in 350° oil briefly to a hard crispiness. Repeat with the remaining fish.

3   Mix the soy sauce, sherry, vinegar, and sugar together in a bowl and stir well. Set the sauce aside.

4   Heat the remaining 1 tablespoon vegetable oil in a wok to the smoking point. Stir-fry the minced ginger for 5 seconds. Add the sauce, stir, and bring to a boil. Stir the cornstarch mixture back into solution and add a little at a time to the sauce until thickened, which should not be soupy or gummy.

5   Turn off the heat. Add the deep-fried slices of fish. Toss gently 3 times, or until the crisp fish slices are well coated. Serve immediately.

IT IS MUCH SAFER AND EASIER to use an electric deep-fryer here, if you can. The indicator light goes off when the oil has reached the desired temperature. The only drawback to doing any deep-frying indoors is it can fill the house with the smell of oil, so I use mine on the back porch. There are special deep-fryers appropriate for small apartments, which filter out the vaporized oil.

CRISPY FISH FILLET WITH ROASTED SEASONED SALT

SERVES 4

Traditional "roasted salt" is kosher salt with crushed Sichuan peppercorns, but I prefer the mix below, which is my own and has more pizzazz. It is also great to use as a seasoning on any meat for barbecuing.

1 package dried bean curd skin (see Note)

2 egg whites, lightly beaten

1 pound haddock fillets or any other thick white-meat fish fillets

4 cups vegetable oil

ROASTED SEASONED SALT

4 tablespoons kosher salt

1 teaspoon crushed Sichuan peppercorns

1 teaspoon freshly ground black pepper

1 teaspoon freshly ground white pepper

1 tablespoon minced fresh chili (serrano, jalapeño, or Asian), with seeds

1   Soak the 1 or 2 sheets of bean curd skin in cold water for 1/2 hour, or until soft. Drain and pat dry with paper towels.

2   Beat the egg whites with a whisk until foamy. Trim the haddock fillets to be brick shaped. Dip and coat the fillets in egg white. Place the fillet in a bean curd sheet and roll, keeping the brick shape. Overlap the bean curd skin by 1 inch and seal with egg white. Trim the ends flush with a knife or scissors. Set aside.

3   Heat the oil for deep-frying to 350°F. Deep-fry the bean curd skin–wrapped fillets until crisp and bright yellow in color. Drain first in the fryer basket and then on absorbent paper towels or a brown paper bag.

4   Heat a cast-iron frying pan or some other heavy skillet over high heat until hot. Add the kosher salt, Sichuan peppercorns, black pepper, and white pepper to the pan. Stir quickly and constantly for 1 minute. Add the chili and stir for 1 more minute. Remove immediately from the pan and place the roasted salt in individual dipping bowls.

5   Place the fried fillet on a cutting board and cut into 1-inch slices on a slight diagonal. Serve at once.

NOTE Widely available in Asian markets, these are flat yellow sheets. They look a bit like wrinkled vinyl.

SICHUAN CUBED SWORDFISH

SERVES 4

I learned this recipe from a chef from Sichuan Province, who used it to cook large carp he caught in the Tidal Basin near the Jefferson Memorial. I figured if he could turn Potomac River carp into a delectable dish, then it had to be great for swordfish. And, so it is.

For more color and taste, ½ cup thawed frozen green peas can be added with the swordfish cubes to the sauce.

1 pound swordfish steak, skin removed	1 teaspoon chili paste, or to taste and tolerance
1 cup cornstarch	1 teaspoon crushed Sichuan peppercorns
4 cups plus 1 tablespoon vegetable oil	3 garlic cloves, crushed and minced
2 tablespoons black or mushroom soy sauce	1 tablespoon finely minced fresh ginger
1 tablespoon dry sherry	½ cup chicken broth
1 teaspoon sugar	2 tablespoons cornstarch mixed with ¼ cup cold water

1   Cut the swordfish into 1-inch cubes. Lightly coat in cornstarch, shaking off any excess. Heat the deep-frying oil to 350°F. Deep-fry the swordfish cubes until golden in color, approximately 5 minutes.

2   Combine the soy sauce, sherry, sugar, and chili paste. Set the sauce aside.

3   Heat the 1 tablespoon vegetable oil in a wok until smoking. Stir-fry the Sichuan peppercorns, garlic, and ginger for 5 seconds. Add the chili sauce. Stir-fry for 10 seconds. Add the chicken broth and bring the sauce to a boil. Stir the cornstarch mixture back into solution and add to the sauce a little at a time, thickening it to a consistency that is neither soupy nor gummy.

4   Add the deep-fried swordfish cubes and toss gently so that the cubes do not break up. Cook in the sauce for 1 minute. Serve.

SHELLFISH

The first seafood dish—in fact, one of the first Chinese dishes I ever cooked—was from a recipe provided by my mother. I was a junior at Rutgers living in an apartment and had to cook for myself. Tiring quickly of hamburgers and hot dogs, I wrote my mother to send me some Chinese recipes because I craved Chinese food. One of the two recipes she sent me was a stir-fried shrimp in the shell, which is the basis of the Salt Shrimp with Fresh Chilies recipe in this book. And so I began my life in cooking.

My mother has a special connection to food. She is widely credited with introducing Washington, D.C., to high-ticket, northern Chinese cuisine, with her restaurant, The Court of the Mandarins, where I first received my chef's training.

But my food memories of her rest primarily in my travels all over the world with her. I will never forget taking an overnight train with her from Mexico City to Oaxaca. Waking to the gentle swaying of the train and the clicking of the tracks, I saw my mother sitting up in her Pullman bed in front of the window, waving to people with a yellow kerchief as we passed by. Stopping at a dusty station amid cacti, I saw a little barefoot girl in rags who was selling tamales from a straw basket for two cents a piece. My mother gave her ten American dollars, a veritable fortune, for the whole basket. Whispering *"gracias,"* the little girl ran away quickly. To this day, those meatless tamales, wrapped in banana leaves, remain the best I have ever had. According to my mom, they were naturally sweet, made from the white interior of the corn cob, which is ground and made into a paste.

Mom and I also traveled in the Peoples Republic of China at a time when travel by Westerners in China was rare. We went to all the famous restaurants—the Peking duck restaurant, which served fifty types of duck, and the Mongolian firepot restaurant. But my warmest memories were of the simple foods, the stuff of my mother's childhood in Beijing—"street food," as she called it. Candied crabapples on a stick. A huge bowl of wonton soup, the extraordinary filling made from pork, dried shrimp, and scallions. Some strange things, too, like red bean Popsicles that made my mouth pucker and sparrows roasted on an open fire. Mom was Americanized in that she had to have an American breakfast every morning. That was the only time we parted. Every morning, she would go to the "Western" dining room in the hotel for her greasy eggs, and I would go to the Chinese dining room for rice porridge, preserved duck eggs, a variety of kimchi-like pickles, "drunken" chicken, and salted fish. The only breakfast item we agreed on was coffee. In those days, there was plenty of tea, but no coffee in China, so we hand-carried with us the biggest jar of Maxwell House instant coffee we could find.

We had to exit China through Hong Kong. Before we embarked on a plane back to the States, we stopped at a traditional dim sum parlor for lunch. Dim sum, or *dian syin* in Mandarin, translates as "little hearts," one of those translations that gives you no idea of what it is. Loosely and more accurately translated, it means "snacks." That is exactly what Chinese people in Asia go to a dim sum parlor for: a snack. They are very much like Europeans at a café. They read the paper. Students do homework. Friends chat leisurely, all casually between sips of tea. Once in a while, they order a small plate of dim sum from a female hawker pushing a metal cart, who shouts out the type of dim sum she is selling. In China, there were many types of dim sum not available in the United States. Fresh coconut pastries wrapped in small coconut leaves. Fresh straw mushrooms. Fresh baby bamboo shoots with pork. Seeing only one solution to this dilemma, Mom ordered something from every cart, filling our table with small plates. When we finished, she ordered more. Before long, we had fifteen carts circling our table, ignoring the rest of the restaurant, the hawkers—who receive a percentage of the total dim sum they sell—all screaming out their types of dim sum simultaneously. It was a raucous lunch. Stuffed, we got onto the plane and were easily able to shun the pallid airline food.

SHRIMP IN GARLIC SAUCE

SERVES 4

This is, by far and bar none, the most popular Chinese seafood dish I know. In fact, it is better than its restaurant counterpart because it uses real garlic, not dried garlic reconstituted in water.

I pound large shrimp (21–25 shrimp per pound), peeled

I egg white

$\frac{1}{4}$ cup cornstarch

2 cups plus I tablespoon vegetable oil

SAUCE

$\frac{1}{4}$ cup chicken broth

$\frac{1}{4}$ cup apple cider vinegar

$\frac{1}{4}$ cup ketchup

3 tablespoons black soy sauce

2 tablespoons dry sherry

8 garlic cloves, crushed and minced

2 tablespoons finely minced fresh ginger

5 tablespoons sugar

I teaspoon chili paste, or to taste and tolerance

$\frac{1}{2}$ cup sliced fresh water chestnuts (optional)

I tablespoon cornstarch mixed with 3 tablespoons cold water

$\frac{1}{2}$ cup sliced scallions, on the diagonal in $\frac{1}{2}$-inch pieces

1   Using a cleaver or knife, slice the shrimp from the back, leaving a small donut-like hole in the center, essentially butterflying the shrimp. Be careful *not* to cut all the way through the shrimp. Rinse away any veins from each shrimp under cold water. Drain well.

2   Place the shrimp in a bowl and add the egg white, cornstarch, and water. Mix well. The consistency should be silky and the color milky.

3   In a large wok, heat 2 cups of the oil to 280°F; or place 1 shrimp in the oil and, when bubbles rise from it like champagne bubbles in a glass, add the rest of the shrimp. Turn the shrimp gently in the poaching oil. When they are white and fluffy, remove them with a stainless steel strainer or brass mesh strainer. Place the cooked shrimp in a colander to drain.

4   In a small saucepan, mix the chicken broth, vinegar, ketchup, soy sauce,

sherry, garlic, ginger, sugar, and chili paste. Stir well. Bring the garlic sauce to a boil, lower the heat to a simmer.

5   In a clean wok, heat the remaining 1 tablespoon oil to smoking. Add the sliced water chestnuts and stir-fry for 30 seconds. Add the garlic sauce, stir, and bring to a boil. Stir cornstarch mixture and bring to a boil, stirring until thickened. Add the shrimp. Toss and stir 3 times until well coated. Add the sliced scallions, stir them in, and serve.

Shrimp and Scallops in Garlic Sauce

SERVES 4

1/2 pound shrimp (about 12), peeled

1/2 pound scallops

2 egg whites

6 tablespoons cornstarch

2 cups plus 1 tablespoon vegetable oil

SAUCE

1/4 cup chicken broth

1/4 cup apple cider vinegar

8 garlic cloves, smashed and minced

2 tablespoons finely minced fresh ginger

1/4 cup ketchup

1 tablespoon black soy sauce or mushroom soy sauce

5 tablespoons sugar

1 teaspoon chili paste, or to taste and tolerance

1/2 cup peeled and sliced fresh water chestnuts (1/8-inch thick)

1 tablespoon cornstarch mixed with 3 tablespoons cold water

1/4 cup sliced scallions, on the diagonal in diamond shapes

1   Devein the shrimp by butterflying—that is, slice the back of the shrimp deeply with a sharp knife to create a donutlike hole in the middle. Do not cut all the way through; keep it whole in a butterfly pattern. Rinse each shrimp under running cold water to clean out any vein. Combine these shrimp in a bowl with 1 egg white, 3 tablespoons cornstarch, and 3 tablespoons cold water. Mix well and reserve. Then combine the scallops in a separate bowl with the remaining 1 egg white, 3 tablespoons cornstarch, and 3 tablespoons water. Mix well and reserve. Both the shrimp and scallop mixes should be milky and silky.

2   Heat 2 cups of vegetable oil in a wok to 280°F; or place 1 shrimp in the oil and, when bubbles come up from it like champagne bubbles in a glass, add the rest of the shrimp. Turn gently and when the shrimp are white and fluffy, remove them and drain in a colander. Skim the oil with a strainer to remove any remnants as best as possible.

3   Repeat the same "poaching in oil" procedure of Step 2 with the scallops. After draining in a colander, combine the scallops and shrimp in one common colander.

4   Combine the broth, vinegar, garlic, ginger, ketchup, soy sauce, sugar, and chili paste in a small saucepan and bring the garlic sauce to a boil. Reduce the heat to very low.

5   Heat the remaining 1 tablespoon of oil in a clean wok until smoking. Stir-fry the water chestnuts for 30 seconds. Add the heated garlic sauce. Stir. Bring the sauce to a boil.

6   Stir the cornstarch mixture into solution, since the cornstarch settles to the bottom. Add to the sauce and bring to a boil, stirring until thickened. If the sauce is too thick, thin it with a little more chicken broth.

7   Add the shrimp and scallops. Stir-fry for 30 seconds. Add the scallions and toss once. Serve immediately.

FOR A SPICIER VERSION, MINCE 1 TABLESPOON jalapeño, serrano, or Asian chilies, including the seeds. Stir-fry the minced chilies with the water chestnuts or before adding the sauce if not using water chestnuts.

STIR-FRIED SHRIMP AND VEGETABLES

SERVES 4

For those who prefer light, subtly flavored seafood with an array of vegetables. When served with a more robust or spicy dish, it provides a pleasant balance to the meal.

1 pound shrimp (21–25 shrimp per pound), peeled

1 egg white

3 tablespoons cornstarch

2 cups plus 3 tablespoons vegetable oil

SAUCE

1 cup chicken broth

2 tablespoons dry sherry

$\frac{1}{4}$ teaspoon salt or to taste

$\frac{1}{4}$ teaspoon freshly ground white pepper

4 garlic cloves, crushed and minced

1 tablespoon sesame oil

1 cup broccoli florets, cut 3 inches long and 1 inch wide

$\frac{1}{2}$ cup thinly sliced carrots, on the diagonal in 1-inch pieces

1 cup snow peas (or 1 cup snap peas), strings and tips removed

1 cup quartered mushrooms

$\frac{1}{2}$ cup thinly sliced celery, cut on a slant in $1\frac{1}{2}$-inch-long pieces

2 tablespoons cornstarch mixed with $\frac{1}{4}$ cup cold water

1   Butterfly the shrimp by cutting deeply with a sharp knife along the back, creating a small hole in the middle but not cutting through the shrimp entirely. Rinse away any veins. Mix the shrimp in a bowl with the egg white, cornstarch, and 3 tablespoons cold water. Mix well. The shrimp mixture should be milky and silky.

2   Heat 2 cups of vegetable oil in a wok to 280°F; or add 1 shrimp and, when bubbles come up from it like champagne bubbles in a glass, add the rest of the shrimp. Turn gently and cook until the shrimp are white and fluffy. Drain in a colander.

3   In a small saucepan, combine the chicken broth, sherry, salt, white pepper, garlic, and sesame oil. Bring the sauce to a boil and then reduce the heat to very low.

4   Combine the vegetables in a colander and rinse in cold water. Drain well. Heat the 3 tablespoons vegetable oil in a wok to the smoking point. Stir-fry the vegetables for 2 to 4 minutes, or until the vegetables are garden bright in color.

5   Add the reserved sauce. Bring the sauce just to a boil. Restir the cornstarch mixture into solution. Add the cornstarch mixture a little at a time until the sauce is thickened, which should not be gummy or soupy. If too thick, thin out with a little broth. If too thin, add more cornstarch mixture.

6   Once the sauce is thickened, add the shrimp. Toss 3 times and serve.

VARIATION SHRIMP SICHUAN Add 1 teaspoon chili paste, or to taste and tolerance, to the white sauce.

SHRIMP HUNAN

SERVES 4

1 pound shrimp (21–25 shrimp per pound), peeled

1 egg white

3 tablespoons cornstarch

2 cups plus 3 tablespoons vegetable oil

3 cups broccoli florets, cut 3 inches long by 1 inch wide

2 cups quartered mushrooms

SAUCE

1 cup chicken broth

3 tablespoons black or mushroom soy sauce

1 tablespoon regular soy sauce or Kikkoman

2 tablespoons dry sherry

6 garlic cloves, crushed and minced

1 tablespoon finely minced fresh ginger

1 tablespoon sugar

1 tablespoon sesame oil

1 teaspoon freshly ground white pepper

2 tablespoons cornstarch mixed with 1/4 cup cold water

1   Devein the shrimp by butterflying—slicing the back of the shrimp with a sharp knife to expose a small hole in the middle. Be careful not to cut the shrimp in half. Rinse away any veins. Mix the shrimp with the egg white, cornstarch, and 3 tablespoons cold water. This mixture should be milky and silky.

2   Heat the 2 cups of oil in a wok to 280°F; or place a shrimp in the oil and, when bubbles come up from the shrimp like champagne bubbles in a glass, add the rest of the shrimp. Turn gently in the oil and cook the shrimp until they are white and fluffy, approximately 7 minutes. Drain in a colander and reserve.

3   Combine the broccoli and mushrooms in a colander. Rinse under cold running water and drain well.

4   Combine the chicken broth, soy sauces, sherry, garlic, ginger, sugar, sesame oil, and white pepper in a small saucepan. Bring the sauce to a boil. Reduce the heat to simmer or low.

5   Heat the 3 tablespoons of vegetable oil in a clean wok until smoking. Add the broccoli and mushrooms and stir-fry for 2 to 4 minutes or until the broccoli is bright garden green. Add the hot sauce to the wok. Stir-fry for 30 seconds. When the sauce is

just at a boil, add the cornstarch mixture a bit at a time until the sauce is thickened. The sauce should not be soupy or gummy. If too thin, add a little more cornstarch. If too thick, thin with a little more chicken broth.

6   Add the shrimp and stir-fry for 30 seconds, then serve.

SALT SHRIMP WITH FRESH CHILIES

SERVES 3 TO 4

This is my daughter's favorite dish. We meet regularly at a Chinese restaurant in Washington, D.C., which features it.

I pound shrimp in shell with heads on (headless shrimp in shell can also be used), unpeeled	2 garlic cloves, smashed and minced
I tablespoon cornstarch	I teaspoon finely minced chilies (serrano, jalapeño, or Asian)
I cup plus I tablespoon vegetable oil	I tablespoon finely minced fresh ginger
½ cup sliced scallions, cut on the diagonal into ½-inch pieces	I teaspoon dry sherry
	2 teaspoons coarse kosher salt

1   Rinse the shrimp under cold water in a colander. Drain well. Toss the shrimp with the cornstarch, lightly coating the shrimp.

2   Heat the 2 cups of oil for deep-frying to 350°F. Deep-fry the shrimp with the shell on quickly until the cornstarch is crisp, approximately 2 to 4 minutes. Drain on absorbent paper or a brown paper bag.

3   In a clean wok, heat the 1 tablespoon of oil until smoking. Stir-fry the garlic, chilies, and ginger for 10 seconds. Add the shrimp. Stir-fry for 15 seconds. Add the sherry and stir-fry 10 seconds, then turn off the heat.

4   Sprinkle the shrimp with the salt. Toss once and serve.

SICHUAN BLACKENED SHRIMP

SERVES 3

When I opened my second restaurant, in addition to traditional dishes, I offered new dishes of my own creation that combined Chinese ingredients and cooking techniques with European presentations. Sichuan Blackened Shrimp is one of my most popular "fusion" creations. Please note that the only Chinese ingredient I use is Sichuan peppercorns. The process, however, particularly the poaching in oil, is Chinese. This is a stunning dish that tastes fantastic.

1 pound shrimp (about 23), peeled

3 tablespoons cornstarch

1 egg white

2 cups plus 1 tablespoon vegetable oil

1 tablespoon coarsely ground black pepper

1 tablespoon coarsely ground white pepper

1 teaspoon coarsely ground Sichuan peppercorns

SAUCE

1 cup chicken broth

1/2 cup fresh cilantro, coarsely chopped

3 tablespoons minced jalapeño, serrano, or Asian chilies, including seeds

1/2 medium green bell pepper, seeded and coarsely chopped

1 teaspoon salt

1 tablespoon dry sherry

2 tablespoons cornstarch mixed with 4 tablespoons cold water

GARNISH

1/2 lime, thinly sliced widthwise

2 fresh shiitake mushrooms, thinly sliced

1   Use a sharp knife and cut the back of each shrimp deeply, leaving a donut-shaped hole in the middle—do not cut all the way through the shrimp. Wash the shrimp under cold running water to remove any veins. Combine the shrimp with the cornstarch, egg white, and 3 tablespoons cold water. Mix well in a bowl. The consistency should be milky and velvety.

2   Heat the 2 cups of oil to 280°F; or place a shrimp in the oil and, when the bubbles rise from it like champagne bubbles in a glass, add the rest of the shrimp. Gently stir and cook until the shrimp are white and fluffy. Drain in a colander.

3   On a plate, combine the black pepper, white pepper, and Sichuan pepper-corns. Mix well. Roll the shrimp in the peppers and coat well. If necessary, add equal portions of more pepper.

4   In a blender, combine the chicken broth, cilantro, chili peppers, bell pepper, salt, and sherry. Blend well for 30 seconds. Strain through a fine sieve set over a bowl, reserving the liquid and discarding the pulp. In a saucepan, bring the sauce to a boil. Stir the cornstarch mixture back into solution, then thicken the sauce with the corn-starch mixture, adding it bit at a time. The sauce should not be soupy or gummy.

5   In a wok, heat the remaining 1 tablespoon of vegetable oil to the smoking point. Stir-fry the pepper-coated shrimp for 2 to 3 minutes. They should be slightly blackened.

6   Using a ladle, sauceboat, measuring cup with a spout, or some other pour-ing vessel, pour the sauce onto an opaque or white serving plate. Place 7 or 8 shrimp on top of the sauce to one side of the plate.

7   Make one cut in each lime slice from the rind to the center. Twist each slice into a figure eight and place 2 or 3 slices side by side on the other side of the plate from the shrimp. In front of the lime slices, fan out 5 or 6 slices of shiitake mushrooms. Serve immediately.

SWEET-AND-SOUR SHRIMP

SERVES 4

This is the sweet-and-sour shrimp that everybody remembers from Chinese restaurants throughout the United States. I call the sauce "red lollipop sauce."

1 pound shrimp (21–25 or 26–30 count per pound)

1 1/2 cups cornstarch

2 cups all-purpose flour

2 eggs

4 cups plus 6 tablespoons vegetable oil

2 teaspoons baking powder

SAUCE

1 orange

1 lime or lemon, or 1/2 lime and 1/2 lemon

2 tablespoons finely minced fresh ginger

1 cup sugar

1/2 cup apple cider vinegar

2 tablespoons ketchup

1/2 teaspoon salt

1 tablespoon red food coloring (optional)

1 medium green bell pepper, seeded and cut into 1-inch diamond shapes

1 medium onion, cut into 1-inch cubes

1 cup 1-inch chunks of pineapple, preferably fresh (reserve any residual juice)

1 tablespoon cornstarch mixed with 3 tablespoons cold water

1   Devein the shrimp by butterflying them. Cut into the back of the shrimp without cutting all the way through, leaving a small donutlike hole in the center. Rinse away the veins. Roll the butterflied shrimp in 1 cup of the the cornstarch to coat well.

2   In a large bowl, mix the flour, 1/2 cup of cornstarch, eggs, 1/4 cup of the vegetable oil, and cold water with a sturdy whisk. Add the baking powder and mix in. Let the batter sit for approximately 10 minutes, or until small bubbles start rising to the surface.

3   Heat the 4 cups oil to 350°F. Place a handful of shrimp in the batter and stir to coat well. Deep-fry until yellowish white in color. Drain and deep-fry the shrimp a second time until golden yellow, about 15 seconds, but do not let get brown. Drain in the deep-fryer basket and then put the shrimp on absorbent paper. (Paper towels are fine, but I use paper bags from the supermarket.)

4   In a medium saucepan, place 2 cups of cold water and bring to a boil. Squeeze in the juice of the orange and lime or lemon, then add the ginger, sugar, vinegar, ketchup, salt, and food coloring. Bring to a boil and cook for 20 minutes, or until the liquid is reduced by almost half. Set the sweet-and-sour sauce aside, covered to keep warm.

5   Heat the remaining 2 tablespoons oil in a wok to the smoking point. Stir-fry the green pepper, onion, and pineapple for 5 minutes or until the green pepper is bright green. Add the sweet-and-sour sauce, plus any residual pineapple juice. Bring to a boil.

6   Stir the cornstarch mixture back into solution and add it a little bit at a time until the sauce is thickened, not soupy or gummy.

7   Add the deep-fried shrimp. Toss 5 times, or until well coated, and serve immediately.

Scallops and Snow Peas

SERVES 4

1 pound sea scallops

1 egg white

3 tablespoons cornstarch

2 cups plus 1 tablespoon vegetable oil

SAUCE

1 cup chicken broth

2 tablespoons dry sherry

1/4 teaspoon salt

1/4 teaspoon freshly ground white pepper

4 garlic cloves, crushed and minced

1 tablespoon sesame oil

1/2 pound snow peas or sugar snap peas, with tips and strings removed

1/2 pound sliced fresh water chestnuts (optional)

1 teaspoon finely minced fresh ginger

2 tablespoons cornstarch mixed with 1/4 cup cold water

1   Combine the scallops with the egg white, cornstarch, and 3 tablespoons cold water. Mix well in a bowl. The consistency should be milky and silky.

2   Heat the 2 cups of vegetable oil in a wok to 280°F; or place 1 scallop in the oil and, when bubbles rise from it like champagne bubbles in a glass, put the rest of the scallops in the oil. "Poach" them in the oil, turning them gently, until the scallops are fluffy, approximately 2 to 4 minutes. Drain in a colander and set aside.

3   Combine the chicken broth, sherry, salt, white pepper, garlic, and sesame oil in a small saucepan. Place the small saucepan on a back burner, bring the sauce to a boil, and then reduce the heat to a simmer.

4   Heat the remaining 1 tablespoon of vegetable oil in a wok to the smoking point. Stir-fry the snow peas or sugar snap peas and water chestnuts, if using, for 1 minute. Add the ginger and stir-fry for 15 seconds.

5   Add the heated sauce. Stir-fry for 30 seconds. Stir the cornstarch mixture back into solution, then add it a little at a time to thicken the sauce.

6   When the sauce is thickened, add the scallops, stir-fry for 1 minute, and serve.

TO REMOVE THE TIPS AND STRINGS from the snow peas or sugar snap peas, use your finger and thumb to snap the tip off, and pull downward to remove the strings. Do this at each end of the snow pea or sugar snap pea and remove on both sides.

I AGREE WITH JAMES BEARD THAT one of the best vegetables, seasonably available in the spring, is asparagus. The following recipe and its variation are delicate, but distinctive Chinese seafood recipes with asparagus. I particularly like crab with asparagus, both of which are the most delicate-tasting of their respective food groups.

SCALLOPS AND ASPARAGUS

SERVES 4 TO 6

1 pound scallops

1 egg white

3 tablespoons cornstarch

2 cups plus 3 tablespoons vegetable oil

SAUCE

1 cup chicken broth

2 tablespoons dry sherry

$1/4$ teaspoon salt

$1/4$ teaspoon freshly ground white pepper

4 garlic cloves, crushed and minced

1 tablespoon finely minced fresh ginger

1 teaspoon sesame oil

1 pound asparagus, sliced on the diagonal into 1-inch pieces

1 tablespoon cornstarch mixed with 3 tablespoons cold water

1   If the scallops still have the small muscle in the base, cut out this muscle with a small, sharp knife. Mix the scallops with the egg white, cornstarch, and 2 tablespoons water.

2   Heat the 2 cups of oil in a wok to 280°F, or place a scallop in the oil, and when the bubbles coming up from the scallop are like bubbles in champagne, add the rest of the scallops. Stir slowly and gently until the scallops are cooked, approximately 7 minutes. Take one out and cut it in half to check and see if it's cooked, but don't overcook the scallops. Drain in a colander.

3   In a saucepan, combine the broth, sherry, salt, white pepper, garlic, ginger, and sesame oil. Bring the sauce to a boil and reduce to simmer or low.

4   In a wok, heat the 3 tablespoons of oil until smoking. Stir-fry the asparagus

until bright green, approximately 10 minutes. Add the hot sauce and bring just to a boil.

5   Restir the cornstarch mixture into solution and add to the wok a little at a time until the sauce is thickened, not soupy or gummy. When thickened, add the scallops. Stir-fry for 2 minutes, then serve.

VARIATION CRAB AND ASPARAGUS For Crab and Asparagus, substitute 1 pound fresh crab meat for the scallops. Make sure to "pick" it first to remove any shell fragments. Add it at the very end, after thickening the white sauce; do not deep-fry first. Toss five times and serve.

The following recipe was handed down to me by my father, Morley Chang. Most restaurant versions of black bean sauce are made by sprinkling on a handful of salted black beans while stir-frying. The end result is tasteless, utilizing nothing of the bean, and is wholly unattractive, the whole black beans resembling rodent droppings. Morley released the powerful taste of the salted black bean by softening the bean in boiling hot water and then mashing it. The finished paste, redolent of the bean, garlic, ginger, soy sauce, sesame oil, and the tart touch of vinegar, rendered the simple black mussel into heavenly food.

But that was his culinary knack—to blend and refine taste and technique. Morley taught me to know whether a recipe was good or not by merely reading it, and, if it was not but had potential, to adjust it to perfection. Once, from his favorite seafood specialty shop in Greenwich Village, he was able to buy fresh razor clams, flown in from the State of Washington. He cooked them for me just past raw in butter over medium-low heat with garlic, shallots, sherry, and fresh chervil. His Shanghai seafood sensibilities never let him overuse any one seasoning so as to permit the peak enhancement of the seafood. The memory of those razor clams will never leave me. It was clear to me when he made the clams that his culinary talent was based on perception rather than invention.

MUSSELS IN BLACK BEAN SAUCE

SERVES 2 TO 3

Although its sister recipe for clams and black bean sauce is better known, I much prefer to use mussels. Use only black mussels, preferably with orange-colored meat. The big gray mussels often sold in seafood markets taste like clay. When cooked properly in black bean sauce, black mussels are tender, brimming with a taste of the sea, the true morsels of the sea that they are.

I pound mussels

2 tablespoons salted black beans

2 tablespoons black or mushroom soy sauce

I tablespoon dry sherry

I tablespoon cider vinegar

2 teaspoons sugar

6 garlic cloves, crushed and minced

I tablespoon finely minced fresh ginger

I tablespoon sesame oil

3 tablespoons vegetable oil

4 scallions, cut on the diagonal into $1/2$-inch pieces

1   Scrub the mussels under cold running water and de-beard them by pulling the beards out with a pair of pliers. Set into a bowl. Discard any mussels that are open and do not close after being tapped with a spoon or your finger.

2   Using a mortar and pestle, or using a bowl and some sort of masher, mash the salted black beans. Add 2 tablespoons of boiling water. Soak for 2 to 3 minutes or until the beans are soft. Mash again to a paste. Add the soy sauce, sherry, vinegar, sugar, garlic, ginger, and sesame oil. Mash and stir. Set the sauce aside.

3   Heat the vegetable oil in a wok or a large saucepan with a lid until smoking. Add the mussels and stir-fry gently without breaking the shells for 3 minutes. Cover tightly and steam for approximately 3 to 5 minutes, or until the mussels are opened. Discard any that do not open.

4   Add the black bean sauce, stir gently without breaking the shells, and cover for 10 to 15 minutes.

5   Add the scallions, toss, and serve.

VARIATION CLAMS IN BLACK BEAN SAUCE Substitute 1½ dozen small cherrystone or littleneck clams, scrubbed and rinsed under cold water. Clams open less easily than mussels, and sometimes have to be "helped" by prying them open. Nevertheless, discard any clams that do not open.

THE REAL LOBSTER CANTONESE

SERVES 2

½ pound ground pork

1½-pound lobster, preferably from Maine

1 pound fresh water chestnuts, peeled, washed, and coarsely chopped

SAUCE

2 tablespoons salted black beans

2 tablespoons black soy sauce

1 tablespoon dry sherry

1 tablespoon apple cider vinegar

1 teaspoon sugar

6 garlic cloves, crushed and minced

1 tablespoon finely minced fresh ginger

1 tablespoon sesame oil

3 tablespoons vegetable oil

1 cup chicken broth

2 tablespoons cornstarch mixed with ¼ cup cold water

1 egg, beaten

4 scallions, cut on the diagonal into ½-inch diamonds

1   In a medium skillet, sauté the pork over medium-high heat, breaking up any lumps, until the meat is brown with no trace of pink, about 5 minutes. Drain to remove fat.

2   Using a cleaver or a heavy knife, chop the lobster into 1½-inch pieces. Clean the cavity, then remove and discard the fingerlike lungs. This should be done while the lobster is alive. It sounds and looks cruel, but what do you think it's going through when you dump it into boiling water? Put the pieces in a bowl and reserve the juices and the coral, if it doesn't freak you out.

3   Using a mortar and pestle, or a bowl with some sort of masher, mash the black beans. Add 2 tablespoons of boiling hot water and mash again into a paste. Add the soy sauce, sherry, vinegar, sugar, garlic, ginger, and sesame oil. Mash into a paste and mix well. Set the black bean paste aside.

4   Heat the vegetable oil in a wok until smoking. Add the lobster and stir-fry until the shells are mostly red, about 3 minutes. Add the chopped water chestnuts and stir-fry 2 more minutes. Drain in a colander.

5   Add the black bean paste to the wok and stir-fry 1 minute. Add the chicken broth. Cover and bring the sauce to a boil. Stir the cornstarch mixture. Add it to the sauce a bit at a time until it is thickened, which should not be too thin or too gummy. From about 12 inches above the wok, pour the egg into the sauce in a thin stream, simultaneously stirring in a circular motion with your other hand. This will result in thin threads of egg instead of large clumps.

6   Add the lobster, cooked pork, and scallions. Toss gently 3 times, then serve.

SHANGHAI SAUTEED CRAB IN THE SHELL

SERVES 4

This recipe is generally used by Chinese families for leftover crabs from the previous day. For a spicier version, add 1 teaspoon, or to taste and tolerance, finely minced chili pepper (jalapeño, serrano, or Asian) to the smoking oil before adding the sauce, and stir-fry for 5 seconds.

1 dozen hard-shell crabs, boiled for 20 minutes

½ cup all-purpose flour

6 tablespoons vegetable oil

SAUCE

1 cup chicken broth

3 tablespoons dry sherry

6 garlic cloves, crushed and minced

1 tablespoon finely minced fresh ginger

2 tablespoons cornstarch mixed with ¼ cup cold water

1 egg, lightly beaten

3 scallions, sliced on the diagonal

1   Open each cooked crab by removing the "button" and prying the top shell from the body. Clean the crab by removing the fingerlike lungs, but save the yellow eggs (optional). Take a heavy knife or cleaver and cut each crab in half. Each half should have its own set of claw and legs. Dip each cut side of each half in the flour.

2   In a flat skillet large enough to fit the crab halves, heat 5 tablespoons of the vegetable oil to smoking. Place the crab halves floured side down, with the legs and claws up, in the hot oil. You may have to stack the crab halves against and next to each other to prevent them from falling over. Fry the floured halves until golden brown, about 3 to 5 minutes. Remove the crabs and drain on absorbent paper.

3   Mix the broth, sherry, garlic, and ginger in a small saucepan. Bring the sauce to a boil and reduce the heat to very low.

4   In a clean wok, heat the remaining 1 tablespoon of oil to the smoking point. Add the sauce and stir. Bring to a boil, then add the cornstarch mixture a little at a time to thicken the sauce; it should not be soupy or gummy. Add the beaten egg, which will thicken the sauce more, and stir vigorously 3 times in a circular motion.

5   Add the crab, crab eggs if using, and scallions. Stir-fry for 1 minute, then serve.

WHEN I WAS 13 YEARS OLD, I remember being at my grandparents' house, watching television. My Lao-Lao, my maternal grandmother, handed me a small folding table and an empty bowl, telling me I could eat in front of the T.V. I set up the table. She then served me a bowl of rice and a good-size bowl of snails cooked in black bean sauce. Opening a safety pin, she showed me how to eat snails. First, she flipped out the little lid that covered the snail's opening. Then she reached into the snail with the point of the safety pin and slowly extracted a curlicue of brownish black meat, discarding the shell in the empty bowl. She did this a few more times, placing the snail meat on the rice. Taking a spoonful of the sauce, she ladled it on top of the snails. I was in heaven. Eating snails in this way is quite labor-intensive, but they taste so great that they should be eaten slowly to appreciate them.

Decades later, my daughter sat next to me in a highchair in a small Chinese restaurant where I took my family regularly on Sundays. The snails arrived piping hot. Slivers of fresh green chili peppers peeked out between the shells. Their fresh peppery taste balanced and enhanced the dish. Methodically, I used a safety pin, removing the snail lid, extracting its meat, and placing the little curlicues on rice. My daughter watched me intently. As I spooned some sauce over the snail meat, a warm gush of memory flooded through me as I remembered my grandmother.

"It's odd," I thought, "How things get handed down from generation to generation in the strangest ways."

Using the chopsticks, I took a bit of snails, sauce, and rice and placed it in my daughter's mouth. I waited to savor her reaction. Her eyes widened and, as she chewed, she smiled. At 2 years old, she knew what was good.

"Mo," she said, as I reached for another.

An American couple sitting at the table next to us were aghast.

The woman asked, "How can your baby eat that?"

"With great relish and joy."

My daughter has always had a fine appreciation of good food, and she still does. In addition to snails, she has always loved fish, particularly steamed fish, and she is crazy about Maryland blue crabs. Today, she eats crabs with no seasoning or dipping sauce so she can fully enjoy their delicate, sweet flavor. We get together regularly at our favorite local restaurant for Salt Shrimp with Fresh Chilies (page 79) and sliced marinated pigs' ears.

I believe that her exquisite appreciation of food is integrally connected to her creative talents, specifically singing. Even as a child, she would sing songs she knew and songs she made up. Her voice was good then, but it has evolved into one of empowered resonance and tonal clarity that I liken to church bells ringing on a crisp, cold winter's day. When she sings, I can't help but swell with emotion, a wave that crests with her voice. I remember particularly at a friend's wedding when she went to the mike and sang Patsy Cline's "Crazy," silencing a loud and raucous crowd who turned their attention to her in awe.

Since then, training has brought her voice to new levels, as well as increased her appreciation and knowledge of music, especially jazz, ferrying her to a higher plateau of enlightenment. She has grown so much creatively and intellectually, with the speed and depth of her progress fueled by her own enthusiasm and curiosity. "Coming into her own," she has indeed blossomed. And I like to imagine that the bud of that blossom was her first taste of snails in black bean sauce with fresh chilies.

Snails in Black Bean Sauce with Fresh Chilies

SERVES 3 TO 4

1 pound snails, commonly available in Chinese seafood stores and often other fish markets, particularly in urban areas

2 tablespoons minced fresh chilies (jalapeño, serrano, or Asian)

2 tablespoons salted black beans

3 tablespoons boiling water

1 tablespoon dry sherry

1 tablespoon apple cider vinegar

1 tablespoon black soy sauce

2 teaspoons sugar

6 garlic cloves, crushed and minced

1 tablespoon finely minced fresh ginger

1 tablespoon sesame oil

3 tablespoons vegetable oil

1   Put the snails in a colander and wash thoroughly. Drain. Place the minced chilies on top of the snails as they drain.

2   Place the salted black beans in a mortar or in a sturdy bowl and use a pestle or some sort of masher to mash the beans. Add the boiling water. Let sit for 3 to 5 minutes, or until the beans are soft. Mash the black beans into a paste, then add sherry, vinegar, soy sauce, sugar, garlic, ginger, and sesame oil. Mash again.

3   Heat the vegetable oil in a wok until smoking. Stir-fry the snails and chili peppers for 5 minutes.

4   Add the black bean paste and stir-fry for 1 minute. Cover and steam over low heat for 15 minutes, then serve.

STEAMED CLAM SOUFFLE WITH SAUSAGE RICE

SERVES 4

My mother used to cook this next dish for me when I was a kid. It was one of my favorites. She would serve me a bowl of sausage rice first, the Chinese sausage having effused its sweet flavors into the rice. After permitting me to grab a piece of sausage with my chopsticks, she would put a large, rounded scoop of the custard-like egg on top of the rice and place two clams to the side of it. Then she would spoon some of the soufflé's rich broth over it all. Clams and pork bond and combine with egg so harmoniously that the trio of tastes should be savored slowly and deliberately.

4 eggs, beaten	4 littleneck or small cherrystone clams
$\frac{1}{2}$ cup chicken broth	I tablespoon sesame oil
$\frac{1}{4}$ teaspoon salt	Sausage Rice (recipe follows)
2 scallions, finely minced	

1   Combine the beaten eggs with the broth, salt, and scallions in a mixing bowl. Whisk until well mixed.

2   Put the clams in a heat-resistant bowl. Place a footed rack in a large pot that will hold this bowl and has a tight-fitting lid. Fill the pot with water to the surface of the rack and bring to a boil. When at a full boil, place the bowl of clams in the steamer. Cover tightly and steam for 10 to 15 minutes, or until the clams are open.

3   Add the egg mixture to the bowl of steamed clams. Put the bowl back into the steamer. Add water, if needed, and steam for 15 minutes. Remove the bowl from the steamer with mitts or gloves. The eggs should be like a soufflé.

4   In a small frying pan, heat the sesame oil to smoking. Pour it over the egg and clam soufflé, and serve over Chinese Sausage Rice (recipe follows).

CHINESE SAUSAGE RICE

SERVES 4

2 cups short-grained rice, preferably Japanese	3 Chinese pork sausages (5 inches long), sliced on the diagonal $1/8$ inch thick

1   Place the rice in a pot with a tight lid or in a rice maker. Add enough cold water until the water is 1 inch above the surface of the rice. Cover and bring to a full boil. (If using a rice cooker, just cover and press "cook.")

2   When the water is at a full boil, uncover. Stir once and boil the water until it is just above the surface of the rice. Scatter the sausage slices evenly over the rice. Cover and reduce the heat to low. A rice maker will automatically go to "low." Simmer for 13 to 15 minutes.

IF LONG-GRAIN RICE IS PREFERRED, put the rice in a saucepan that has a tight-fitting lid. Fill the pot with cold water. By hand, swirl and wash the rice. Pour off the excess water, which is milky. Do this two more times, or until the water is almost clear. Then, add water to 1 inch above the surface of the rice and proceed with the above steps.

CHICKEN

MY GOVERNOR'S CHICKEN, OR GUNG BAO Chicken, is not like the one served in most Chinese restaurants. It has vegetables. It is colorful. The sauce is different. But it is mine, and I consider it my "Johnny Appleseed" recipe, which I have proliferated all over the world, everywhere I have traveled.

It is also the one dish that symbolizes the origins of my marriage, the beginning of my adult life, the wellspring of a family yet to come. I was a junior at Rutgers when I met Eileen. Soon we moved into an efficiency apartment that cost $60 per month. The kitchen was the size of a closet, barely holding a small gas stove, a refrigerator, and a sink; yet much had evolved from that inadequate little kitchen. While most poor college students lived on franks and beans or Spaghetti-Os, I cooked a lot of Chinese and Western food, using inexpensive ingredients. I remember buying 52-cent packages of chicken gizzards. The meat would be filleted from their tough gristle shells, sliced, and stir-fried with a variety of vegetables, which later became the basis of another one of my dishes, T'ai Chi Chicken. Even white-meat chicken was cheap in those days, although it was a treat for us. And so, my Governor's Chicken was born.

There was a ritual to how Eileen and I would cook Governor's Chicken. I would coat the chicken. Eileen would peel the scallions and ginger. I would cut the peppers into diamond shapes while she would concoct the sauce. After she flaked the dried red chilies over the rest of the vegetables in a colander, she would rinse them under cold water and hand the colander to me. I would stir-fry the dish to completion. This balletic pas de deux remains luminescent in my memory, the glow in which I bask in the good memories of my marriage, which, although long term, did not last, although my Governor's Chicken has, presumably into eternity.

GOVERNOR'S CHICKEN

SERVES 4 TO 6

This type of dish is generally referred to by Chinese people as "dry cooked" because there is relatively little sauce. The sauce just lightly coats the ingredients.

1 pound skinless, boneless chicken breasts

1 egg white

4 tablespoons cornstarch

2 cups plus 3 tablespoons vegetable oil

2 medium green bell peppers, seeded and cut into 1-inch diamond-shape pieces

1 medium red bell pepper (optional), seeded and cut into 1-inch diamond-shape pieces

1 bunch of scallions, peeled and cut on the diagonal into ½-inch pieces

1 tablespoon finely minced fresh ginger

2 dried hot red chili peppers, or to taste and tolerance

1 cup cocktail peanuts

SAUCE

3 tablespoons soy sauce

2 tablespoons dry sherry

3 garlic cloves, crushed and minced

2 teaspoons sugar

¼ teaspoon salt

1   Cut the chicken into ¾-inch cubes. Combine the cubes with the egg white, 2 tablespoons of water, and 3 tablespoons of the cornstarch. Mix well. Heat the 2 cups oil in a wok to 280°F; or put one piece of chicken in the oil and, when the bubbles ris-

ing from it are like champagne bubbles, add the rest of the chicken. Stir the chicken slowly and cook until the pink is no longer visible. Drain in a colander.

2   Combine the bell peppers, scallions, and ginger in a colander. Rinse in cold water. With a pair of scissors, cut the hot peppers lengthwise and then cut again widthwise, flaking the bits on top of the vegetables in the colander.

3   Combine the soy sauce, sherry, garlic, sugar, salt, 2 tablespoons of cold water, and the remaining 1 tablespoon cornstarch. Mix well.

4   Heat the 3 tablespoons oil in a wok until smoking. Stir-fry the vegetables for 5 minutes, or until bright in color. Add the chicken cubes and stir-fry for 30 seconds. Add the cocktail peanuts and toss 3 times.

5   Restir the sauce and add it to the chicken and vegetables. Toss 5 times quickly and serve.

TO MAKE THIS RECIPE TASTE PERFECT, I occasionally fry my own peanuts, the taste of which is sensational. To do so, heat ¼ cup vegetable oil in a wok or a skillet (not a nonstick one) over high heat until the smoking point. Add 1 cup of raw peanuts and stir constantly. When the color changes from white to brownish white, drain immediately in a colander and let the peanuts sit for 15 minutes. They will continue to cook to a golden brown. (If the peanuts are taken off the heat when they are golden brown, they will turn to dark brown and taste burned.)

CHICKEN AND CASHEWS SHANTUNG STYLE, THE recipe that follows, always reminds me of an incident I will title as "Swordfight at The Court of the Mandarins." My mother has largely been attributed with introducing true Mandarin cuisine from northern China to Washington, D.C., at her restaurant, The Court of the Mandarins. She was the first, for example, to put Mandarin lamb dishes on the menu. She believed fervently that the American palate was capable of embracing authentic Chinese cuisine, but that it needed "training" to do so. The only problem was that she became somewhat authoritarian in the zeal of her mission "to train." As a liberal and civil libertarian, she emphatically denied this. "Rubbish," she would say. But when it came to what went on in her restaurant, she was the Dowager Empress.

My mother did not allow soy sauce to be placed on the tables of her dining room. One rainy evening, an elegantly dressed woman in her seventies arrived at The Court of the Mandarins and requested a table for one. She began by ordering a dry Bombay gin martini, straight up with an olive. When it arrived, she sipped it and lit up a thin, expensive cigar. After finishing her Crab and Asparagus Soup, she began on her lamb-filled potstickers and ordered another martini. Upon finishing her potstickers and her martini, she ordered a third martini and was well through it when her entree, Chicken and Cashews, arrived.

"I want some soy sauce," she said.

The gauntlet had just been thrown down. The waiter brought my mother to her table.

"Madame?" inquired my mother, who always addressed female customers as "Madame" because it was her style. She also instructed her dining room staff, who were all Chinese, to do so since they could not pronounce "ma'am," and, if they tried to use Ms. or Miss, it would come out as "Missy."

"I want some soy sauce," the lady said.

"Madame," my mother replied, "I understand your request for soy sauce. Most restaurants cook Chicken and Cashews with only hoisin sauce, rendering it excessively sweet. We, however, prepare this dish authentically and use a salty bean paste to give the dish the necessary salt balance. This is exactly the way it is done in Peking. So, Madame, there is no need for soy sauce."

"What kind of Chinese restaurant is this, anyway? All the other Chinese restaurants have soy sauce on their tables," the lady retorted.

My mother replied indignantly, and with just a trace of a British accent, "Madame, most certainly, we are not 'other Chinese restaurants.'"

The lady bolted up, grabbed her umbrella, and shook it at my mother, screaming, "Now give me my damn soy sauce or I'm really going to get angry!"

"I will not!" replied my mother defiantly.

Deftly, like a trained fencer, the lady lunged at my mother with her umbrella. Gracefully, my mother parried the blow, as she stepped to the side. The lady lunged again. My mother, shifting her weight, stepped to the other side as the point of the umbrella whizzed past her. In retrospect, it was like a scene from *Crouching Tiger, Hidden Dragon*. It took three waiters to restrain the woman, who screamed, "Give me some damn soy sauce!" as she was being led out of the restaurant.

The other patrons of the crowded restaurant were aghast, frozen, with their utensils dangling in mid air. A concerned customer asked my mother if she was all right, and she replied, "Quite all right, thank you."

Smoothing out her Chinese dress, my mother went to the next table filled with businessmen, and with her famous Deborah Kerr smile, inquired, "And, how is the Lamb Mandarin today, gentlemen?"

Chicken and Cashews Shantung Style

SERVES 4 TO 6

Authentic Peking (Beijing) cuisine uses bean sauce. I prefer the Koon Chun brand in a blue and yellow can, labeled "Bean Sauce," mixed with hoisin sauce. This reduces the sweetness and adds a little saltiness. Americanization of this recipe eliminated the bean sauce because many Americans preferred the sweetness of the hoisin sauce without the salt balance of the bean sauce.

Shantung province, just north of Beijing, is renowned for its cooking, as well as for Tsingtao beer (Shantung was once occupied by Germany, and, so, Tsingtao beer was originally German). The Shantung version of this dish, which I offer here, includes cucumbers, which I prefer, especially if using the optional bean sauce.

I pound skinless, boneless chicken breasts	$1/4$ cup hoisin sauce
I egg white	I tablespoon black or mushroom soy sauce
3 tablespoons cornstarch	2 tablespoons bean sauce (optional)
2 cups plus I tablespoon vegetable oil	I tablespoon dry sherry
2 cucumbers, peeled	$1/2$ teaspoon sesame oil
I cup cashews (preferably the deep-fried cocktail variety, not freeze-dried cashews)	

1   Cut the chicken into $3/4$-inch cubes. Mix the egg white, cornstarch, and 3 tablespoons water with the chicken cubes, coating well.

2   Heat 2 cups of the vegetable oil to 280°F; or place a cube of chicken in the oil and, when the bubbles from the chicken rise like bubbles in champagne, add the chicken. Turn the chicken gently in the poaching oil. Cook until the chicken cubes are white, approximately 7 minutes. Drain in a colander.

3   Cut the cucumbers lengthwise into $1/2$-inch slices. Cut again lengthwise into $1/2$-inch slices. Keeping the cucumber intact, slice across it, creating $1/2$-inch cubes.

4   Heat the remaining 1 tablespoon vegetable oil in a wok until smoking. Stir-fry the cucumber cubes for 15 seconds. Add the cashews, hoisin sauce, soy sauce, bean sauce, if using, and sherry. Toss 3 times. Add the chicken and stir-fry for 30 seconds.

5   Place the sesame oil in a Chinese ladle or kitchen spoon. Holding on to the wok firmly with one hand, with the other hand invert the ladle or spoon quickly and smack the stem of the spoon or ladle on the side of the wok, spraying the sesame oil across the chicken and cucumbers. Toss once and serve.

Chicken with Mixed Vegetables

SERVES 4 TO 6

Previously known as Moo Goo Gai Pan, this stir-fry is the "vanilla ice cream" of all Chinese dishes. If a restaurant does this dish well, it is likely other selections will be good. Likewise, if you can cook this dish successfully, it is likely you will quickly master many others.

Any combination of vegetables can be used in this chicken stir-fry. The ones listed here are most commonly used in a Chinese restaurant. During the summer season, when my garden is in full bloom, I use many of the vegetables it offers.

2 cups broccoli florets

1 cup quartered white mushrooms

1 cup snow peas or snap peas, strings and tips removed

2 thin carrots, peeled and sliced on the diagonal, or roll-cut or crinkle-cut (see box)

2 celery stalks, sliced on the diagonal

1 pound skinless, boneless chicken breasts

1 egg white

3 tablespoons cornstarch

2 cups plus 3 tablespoons vegetable oil

SAUCE

1 cup chicken broth

2 tablespoons dry sherry

$1/4$ teaspoon salt

1 teaspoon freshly ground white pepper

4 garlic cloves, crushed and minced

1 tablespoon sesame oil

2 tablespoons cornstarch mixed with $1/4$ cup cold water

1   Combine the vegetables in a colander and rinse thoroughly.

2   Slice each chicken breast half in half again lengthwise. Slice each piece crosswise diagonally into $1/8$-inch-thick slices. Combine the chicken slices with the egg white, cornstarch, and 3 tablespoons cold water. Mix well; the batter should be milky in color and velvety in consistency.

3   Heat 2 cups of the vegetable oil in a wok until 280°F; or until bubbles rise from a chicken piece placed in the oil like champagne bubbles in a champagne glass. Add the chicken and stir slowly in the poaching oil until the chicken is white in color, approximately 7 minutes. Remove the chicken and drain well in a colander.

4　Combine the broth, sherry, salt, white pepper, garlic, and sesame oil in a small saucepan. Bring to a boil on a back burner, reduce the heat to very low, and reserve.

5　Heat the remaining 3 tablespoons vegetable oil in a wok until smoking. Stir-fry the vegetables for 5 minutes, or until bright in color. Add the chicken and stir-fry for 30 seconds. Add the heated sauce. Stir the cornstarch mixture back into solution and add it to the sauce. Bring to a boil. Toss 5 times and serve.

VARIATION CHICKEN SICHUAN Add 1 teaspoon of chili paste, or to taste and tolerance, to the sauce when it is simmering.

TO ROLL-CUT CARROTS: Place a carrot on a cutting board horizontal to you. Putting your face over the carrot, look straight down at it. Place a cleaver or knife 1 inch from the tip of the carrot at a 35-degree angle when looking straight down at the carrot. Cut straight down at this angle. Roll the carrot one-quarter toward you on the board. Cut straight down again. Keep rolling and cutting until the carrot is finished.

TO CRINKLE-CUT CARROTS: Use a crinkle-cutting implement commonly used for crinkle-cutting french fries. Cut straight down on the carrot at a 45° angle, creating crimped $\frac{1}{8}$-inch-thick slices.

Moo Shu Chicken

SERVES 4 TO 6

The two essential ingredients of any *moo shu* dish are the tiger lilies and tree ears. The authentic *moo shu* dish has no cabbage in it at all, as Chinese restaurants added cabbage to this dish to reduce the expense of the other ingredients. It is also why this dish is erroneously served with "plum sauce," a misnomer for hoisin sauce. I much prefer to cook it the authentic way, without cabbage, but find that most Americans prefer to eat it with cabbage.

If you have trouble finding these ingredients in a Chinese market, you can try to ask somebody for them by saying they are used in *moo shu* dishes as well as hot and sour soup. But, good luck, since many people in Asian markets do not speak English.

All *moo shu* dishes are traditionally eaten with Mandarin pancakes, also used for Peking duck. These may be purchased in a Chinese market in the refrigerated or frozen section, or may be made by hand (see Mandarin Pancakes, page 208). I have even used warmed flour tortillas in a pinch.

1 pound skinless, boneless chicken breasts	S A U C E
1 egg white	1/4 cup chicken broth
3 tablespoons cornstarch	2 tablespoons black or mushroom soy sauce
2 cups plus 2 tablespoons vegetable oil	1 tablespoon regular soy sauce or Kikkoman
1 1/4 cups tiger lilies, frequently called lily flowers or buds	2 tablespoons dry sherry
1/2 cup dried tree ears (see Note)	2 garlic cloves, crushed and minced
1 small head green cabbage	1 tablespoon cornstarch mixed with 3 tablespoons cold water
1 tablespoon finely minced fresh ginger	1 bunch of scallions, cut on the diagonal into 1-inch diamond shapes
6 eggs	1/2 teaspoon sesame oil

1   Slice the breast halves in half lengthwise. Slice these strips crosswise straight down to produce 2-inch strips of chicken. Combine the sliced chicken in a mixing bowl with the egg white, cornstarch, and 2 tablespoons cold water. Mix well; the color should be milky and the consistency velvety.

2   Heat 2 cups of the vegetable oil in a wok to 280°F; or place a piece of chick

en in the oil and, when the bubbles from the chicken are like champagne bubbles, add the rest of the chicken slices. Cook the chicken in the poaching oil, turning slowly until white, approximately 7 minutes. Remove the chicken and drain in a colander.

3   Snip or pinch off the heads of the tiger lilies and the small tails, which are thinner and tougher than the main body of the lilies. Put them into a bowl and add hot boiling water to cover by 2 inches. Soak for 15 minutes. Dump the tiger lilies into a colander and rinse thoroughly with cold water. Return the tiger lilies to the bowl and again add hot water. Drain in a colander and rinse thoroughly with cold water.

4   Place the tree ears in a bowl and add boiling water to cover by 2 inches. Soak for 15 minutes. Place the tree ears in a colander and rinse thoroughly under cold running water. Place the tree ears in a bowl and add boiling water again. Repeat this procedure one more time, rinse them thoroughly with cold water, and drain well.

5   Quarter the cabbage head and remove the core. Thinly slice the cabbage as if making coleslaw so that the strands are approximately 3 inches long. In a large colander, combine the tiger lilies, tree ears, cabbage, and ginger. Rinse and toss well.

6   Beat the eggs well. Cook the eggs as if making scrambled eggs in a nonstick pan with a minimal amount of oil. Remove to a plate and set aside.

7   Combine the broth, soy sauces, sherry, and garlic, in a small saucepan. Heat the sauce to the boiling point and remove from the heat.

8   Heat the remaining 2 tablespoons vegetable oil in a wok to the smoking point. Add the tiger lilies, tree ears, cabbage, and ginger and stir-fry for 10 minutes. Add the chicken to the stir-fried ingredients and toss 3 times. Add the sauce to the wok and stir-fry for 30 seconds. Stir the cornstarch mixture back into solution. Add it to the sauce and bring to a boil, stirring until thickened. Add the scallions and toss 3 times.

9   Put the sesame oil in a Chinese ladle or a kitchen spoon. Inverting it, quickly hit the stem against the side of the wok spraying the sesame oil onto the ingredients of the wok. Hold the wok firmly with your other hand before doing this so you don't end up dumping the whole dish on the stove and floor, ending up with *moo shu* in the garbage.

NOTE This ingredient is also referred to as "dried vegetable" or "black fungus." Chinese translations of foodstuffs are neither accurate nor appetizing. I prefer to buy small tree ears rather than the large ones, which are chewier.

Chicken Hunan

SERVES 4

For a slightly hotter dish, chili paste can be added to the hot oil just before the broccoli and mushrooms are stir-fried. Heat and oil release the power of all chilies.

1 pound skinless, boneless chicken breasts, cut into $\frac{1}{8}$-inch-thick slices the size of a silver dollar

1 egg white

2 tablespoons cornstarch

2 cups plus 3 tablespoons vegetable oil

SAUCE

1 cup chicken broth

3 tablespoons black or mushroom soy sauce

1 tablespoon regular soy sauce or Kikkoman

2 tablespoons dry sherry

4 garlic cloves, crushed and minced

1 tablespoon finely minced fresh ginger

1 tablespoon sugar

1 teaspoon freshly ground white pepper

1 teaspoon chili paste, or to taste and tolerance

1 tablespoon sesame oil

1 pound broccoli, cut into florets 3 inches long and 1 inch wide

1 cup quartered white mushrooms

2 tablespoons cornstarch mixed with $\frac{1}{4}$ cup cold water

1   Place the sliced chicken in a mixing bowl. Add the egg white, cornstarch, and 3 tablespoons cold water. Mix well; the color should be milky and velvety in consistency.

2   Heat 2 cups of the vegetable oil in the wok until 280°F; or place a piece of chicken in the oil and, when bubbles come up from it like champagne bubbles, add the rest of the chicken. Stir slowly and cook until the chicken is white and no pink remains visible, approximately 7 minutes. Drain the chicken well in a colander.

3   Mix the broth, soy sauce, sherry, garlic, ginger, sugar, white pepper, chili paste, and sesame oil together in a small saucepan. Heat the sauce to the boiling point, at which time reduce the heat to low or simmer.

4   Place the broccoli and mushrooms together in a colander. Rinse under cold water and shake off any excess. In a wok, heat the remaining 3 tablespoons vegetable oil

to the smoking point. Stir-fry the broccoli and mushrooms until the broccoli is bright green in color, approximately 4 minutes. Add the chicken and stir-fry for 30 seconds, then add the sauce.

5   When the sauce is boiling in the wok, stir the cornstarch mixture back into solution. Add it to the wok and bring to a boil, stirring until the sauce is thickened. Serve at once.

Sweet-and-Sour Chicken

SERVES 4 TO 6

This "red lollipop" sweet-and-sour sauce is still a favorite. This recipe is originally from Trader Vic's. A deep-fryer with temperature control makes preparation a lot easier, and safer.

BATTER

2 cups all-purpose flour

1/2 cup cornstarch

2 eggs

1 1/4 cups plus 2 tablespoons vegetable oil

1 teaspoon baking powder

1 pound skinless, boneless chicken breast, cut into 3/4-inch cubes

2 cups plus 2 tablespoons vegetable oil

SAUCE

1 orange, cut in half

1/2 lime

1/2 lemon

2 tablespoons minced fresh ginger

1 cup sugar

3 tablespoons ketchup

1/2 teaspoon salt

1/2 teaspoon red food coloring (optional)

1 green bell pepper cut into 1-inch diamond shapes

1 large onion, cut into 3/4-inch cubes

1 1/2 cups 1-inch pineapple cubes, preferably fresh (juice reserved)

5 tablespoons cornstarch mixed with 1/2 cup cold water

1   To make the batter, combine the flour, cornstarch, eggs, 1 1/4 cups of the oil, plus 1 cup cold water in a medium bowl. Whisk until well blended and similar in appearance to pancake batter. Whisk in the baking powder. Let batter sit for 10 to 15 minutes.

2   In a large saucepan or deep-fryer, heat the oil to 350°F. Place the chicken pieces in the batter and mix well. Deep-fry the chicken in the hot oil until light yellow in color. Drain well, letting the chicken set for at least 5 minutes. Leave the oil over the heat. Fry the chicken pieces a second time briefly, until a light golden brown; drain.

3   Bring 2 cups of water to a boil in a wok or saucepan. Squeeze the orange and lime and lemon halves into the water, depositing the squeezed fruit into the water as well, rind and all. Add the ginger, sugar, ketchup, salt, and red food coloring, if

desired. Bring to a boil, stirring constantly until the sugar is dissolved. Continue to boil for about 15 minutes, stirring occasionally, until the sauce is reduced by almost half.

4   In a wok, heat 2 tablespoons of the vegetable oil until smoking. Stir-fry the green pepper, onion, and pineapple (reserving any residual juice) for 1 minute. Add the deep-fried chicken and toss 3 times.

5   Add the sweet-and-sour sauce and any reserved pineapple juice. When the sauce is beginning to bubble, stir the cornstarch mixture back into solution and add to the wok. Bring to a boil, stirring until the sauce is thickened. Toss twice and serve.

GENERAL TSO'S CHICKEN

S E R V E S   4

General Tso's Chicken and Chicken in Orange Sauce (given as a variation here) are unquestionably the most popular dishes in Chinese cuisine in the United States today. To make either one at home usually takes some practice, and it may take you one or two tries before you perfect the recipe. The size of the chicken slices is important. I find most people cut the chicken too small, and then it dries out in the cooking process. Also, crispness is a major factor. If the final product is soggy, it means either the chicken was not crisp enough and/or the final phase of stir-frying and caramelizing of sugar was not done quickly enough. The second frying is essential for crispiness and the temperature of the oil must be kept at 350°F. If the batter is sliding off during the final phase, this means the deep-frying was not done properly.

What is required most definitely, particularly in the final phase of stir-frying, is quickness and timing. It may be advantageous to cook this dish with the help of another person, because an extra pair of hands is very helpful.

1 pound skinless, boneless chicken breasts

1 cup cornstarch

BATTER

1 cup cornstarch

$\frac{1}{2}$ cup all-purpose flour

4 cups vegetable oil

SAUCE

1 cup chicken broth

3 tablespoons black or mushroom soy sauce

2 tablespoons dry sherry

1 tablespoon regular soy sauce or Kikkoman

4 garlic cloves, crushed and minced

1 tablespoon finely minced fresh ginger

1 tablespoon sugar

$\frac{1}{2}$ teaspoon white pepper

1 teaspoon chili paste, or to taste and tolerance

2 tablespoons cornstarch mixed with $\frac{1}{4}$ cup cold water

$\frac{3}{4}$ cup sugar

1 teaspoon sesame oil

1   Slice the chicken lengthwise into 4 pieces. Then cut crosswise on a 45-degree diagonal with a cleaver to create $\frac{1}{4}$-inch-thick slices about the size of a silver dollar.

Dust these pieces in the cornstarch, shake off the excess, and lay them out separately on a cookie tray.

2   To make the batter, mix together 1 cup cornstarch with flour and 1 cup cold water. The batter should be fairly thick, but not too thick to stir.

3   Heat the vegetable oil to 350°F. Add the chicken to the batter. Stir to coat well. Deep-fry the chicken pieces in the hot oil in batches without crowding until crusty and white, approximately 5 minutes; drain. Making sure that the oil remains at 350°F, fry the chicken pieces for a second time until golden yellow, approximately 1 minute. Drain and reserve on absorbent paper. (I like using brown paper bags from the super-market.)

4   In a wok, combine the broth, sherry, soy sauce, garlic, ginger, 1 tablespoon sugar, white pepper, and chili paste. Bring to a boil. Stir the cornstarch mixture back into solution and add it to the sauce, boiling until the liquid is thickened.

5   Add the deep-fried chicken pieces to the sauce and very quickly stir-fry, toss-ing 5 times, until the pieces are well coated with the sauce. Continuing to stir-fry con-stantly, add the ¾ cup sugar, pouring it from about 10 to 12 inches above the wok even-ly over the chicken pieces as you toss them. As soon as the sugar is caramelized, which will be indicated by a noticeable glaze, put the sesame oil in a kitchen spoon or Chinese ladle. Invert it quickly, hitting the handle against the side of the wok to spray the sesame oil over the chicken. Be sure to hold the wok firmly with the other hand or have a helper hold it when doing this. Toss once or twice and serve immediately.

VARIATION **CHICKEN IN ORANGE SAUCE** Instead of adding the sesame oil at the end, add 1 teaspoon of orange extract after the sugar has caramelized. Be sure to toss the ingredients well, spreading the extract.

CHICKEN AND CHESTNUTS

SERVES 4 TO 5

I love chestnuts, which, in fact, are indigenous to China. On cold days, my mother used to give me freshly roasted chestnuts to put into the pockets of my coat to keep my hands warm and to eat as I walked to school, as her mother did for her when she was a schoolgirl in Beijing.

2 cups raw chestnuts

1 pound skinless, boneless chicken breasts (about 2), cut into ¾-inch pieces

1 egg white

2 tablespoons cornstarch

2 cups plus 1 tablespoon vegetable oil

SAUCE

½ cup chicken broth

2 tablespoons black or mushroom soy sauce

1 tablespoon dry sherry

2 tablespoons light brown sugar

1 teaspoon sesame oil

½ teaspoon white pepper

1 tablespoon cornstarch mixed with 3 tablespoons cold water

1   Score a crisscross on the top of each chestnut. Place in a saucepan and cover well with cold water. Boil the chestnuts on high for 30 minutes. Add water if necessary. Drain the chestnuts, then rinse them in a colander under slow-running cold water for 10 minutes. When cooled, carefully remove the skins either by hand or with a small paring knife, attempting to keep each chestnut as whole as possible.

2   Combine the chicken with the egg white, cornstarch, and 3 tablespoons cold water. Mix well until milky in appearance and velvety in consistency.

3   Heat 2 cups of the vegetable oil in a wok to 280°F; or place a piece of chicken in the oil and, when the bubbles are like champagne bubbles, add the rest of the chicken. Stir slowly until the chicken is white, with no pink remaining visible, approximately 7 minutes. Drain well.

4   Combine the broth, soy sauce, sherry, brown sugar, sesame oil, and white pepper in a small saucepan. Stir well and bring to a boil. Remove the sauce from the heat.

5   Heat the remaining 1 tablespoon of vegetable oil in the wok until smoking. Add the sauce and stir well. Stir the cornstarch mixture back into solution and add it to the wok.

6   Add the chicken and chestnuts, and gently toss twice or until integrated into the dish, then serve.

CHICKEN AND WALNUTS

S E R V E S   4

The use of maple syrup in Chinese food is my own innovation. It is so much tastier in this recipe than the conventionally used hoisin sauce. Furthermore, soaking the walnuts in maple syrup counteracts the bitterness in the skin of the walnuts.

3 tablespoons black or mushroom soy sauce

2 tablespoons dry sherry

3 tablespoons plus 2 teaspoons cornstarch

2 cups plus 1 tablespoon vegetable oil

I pound skinless, boneless chicken breasts, cut into $\frac{3}{4}$-inch cubes

I egg white

$\frac{1}{4}$ cup real maple syrup

I cup walnuts

1   Mix the soy sauce, sherry, 2 teaspoons of the cornstarch, and 1 tablespoon cold water in a bowl. Mix the sauce well.

2   Combine the chicken cubes with the egg white, remaining 3 tablespoons cornstarch, and 3 tablespoons cold water. Stir well until the chicken is milky and silky in consistency.

3   Heat the 2 cups of the vegetable oil to 280°F; or place a piece of chicken in the oil and, when the bubbles from that piece of chicken rise like champagne bubbles, add the rest of the chicken. Stir slowly, and poach in the oil until all the chicken is white, with no pink remaining visible, approximately 7 minutes. Drain in a colander.

4   Combine the maple syrup and walnuts. Heat the remaining 1 tablespoon oil in a wok until smoking. Add the walnuts and maple syrup and stir once. Add the chicken and toss once.

5   Add the sauce, stir-fry for 15 seconds or until thickened, and serve.

CHICKEN AND ALMONDS

SERVES 4

1 pound skinless, boneless chicken
   breasts, cut into ¾-inch cubes

1 egg white

3 tablespoons cornstarch

2 cups plus 1 tablespoon vegetable oil

SAUCE

¼ cup chicken broth

1 tablespoon black or mushroom soy
   sauce

1½ teaspoons dry sherry

½ teaspoon freshly ground white
   pepper

1 cup whole almonds, skinless or with
   skin

¼ cup hoisin sauce

1   Combine the cubed chicken with the egg white, cornstarch, and 3 tablespoons cold water. Stir well until the chicken is milky and silky in consistency.

2   In a large wok, heat 2 cups of the vegetable oil to 280°F; or add a piece of chicken and, when the bubbles from that chicken rise like champagne bubbles, add the rest of the chicken. Stir the chicken gently and cook until the chicken is white with no pink remaining visible, approximately 7 minutes. Drain in a colander.

3   Combine the broth, soy sauce, sherry, and white pepper in a small saucepan. Heat the sauce to boiling, remove from the heat, and keep warm.

4   Place the remaining 1 tablespoon oil in the wok and heat until smoking. Stir-fry the almonds for 20 seconds. Add the drained chicken cubes and toss once. Add the sauce and stir-fry for 30 seconds.

5   Add the hoisin sauce and stir-fry well for 30 seconds, coating the chicken and almonds thoroughly in the sauce. Serve at once.

CHICKEN AND ASPARAGUS

SERVES 4

Cauliflower florets can be substituted for asparagus, also making a nice dish, though it will lack the color contrast.

1 pound skinless, boneless chicken breasts

1 egg white

3 tablespoons cornstarch

2 cups plus 2 tablespoons vegetable oil

SAUCE

1 cup chicken broth

2 tablespoons dry sherry

1/4 teaspoon salt

1/2 teaspoon white pepper

4 garlic cloves, crushed and minced

1 tablespoon sesame oil

1 pound thin asparagus, sliced on the diagonal into 1-inch pieces

2 tablespoons cornstarch mixed with 1/4 cup cold water

1   Slice the chicken breasts in half lengthwise, then cut crosswise on a 45, degree angle to create thin slices about 2 inches long and 1/2 inch wide. Combine the chicken in a bowl with the egg white, cornstarch, and 3 tablespoons cold water. Mix well. The color should be milky and the consistency velvety.

2   Heat 2 cups of the vegetable oil to 280°F; or place a piece of chicken in the oil and, when the bubbles rise from that piece of chicken like champagne bubbles, add the rest of the chicken and cook slowly until the meat is white and no pink remains vis, ible. Drain in a colander.

3   Combine the broth, sherry, salt, white pepper, garlic, and sesame oil in a small saucepan and bring to a boil. Turn the heat to low and keep warm.

4   Heat the remaining 2 tablespoons vegetable oil in a wok until smoking. Add the asparagus and stir-fry for 3 minutes, or until the asparagus is bright green. Add the drained chicken and stir-fry for 30 seconds.

5   Add the sauce, and when the sauce is boiling, stir the cornstarch mixture back into solution and add to the wok, boiling until the sauce is thickened. Serve at once.

T'AI CHI CHICKEN

SERVES 4 TO 6

This recipe has evolved from my poor student days when chicken gizzards were a mainstay ingredient. I have since eliminated them from my diet, but occasionally, I will add them to this recipe out of nostalgia. If you want to try them, use a small thin-bladed knife to carve out the meat from the gristle and tendon shells of a half pound of gizzards. The meat should be free of all tendons and gristle and oval shaped. Make crisscross cuts across the meat. Sauté for 5 minutes in 2 tablespoons of oil. The gizzard meat should look like tiny pine cones.

I pound skinless, boneless chicken breasts, cut into ¾-inch cubes

I egg white

3 tablespoons cornstarch

2 cups plus 2 tablespoons vegetable oil

I green bell pepper, cut into 1-inch diamond-shape pieces

I red bell pepper, cut into 1-inch diamond-shape pieces

½ cup bamboo shoots, sliced thinly into 1-inch pieces

I cup portobello mushrooms, cut into ½-inch cubes

½ cup quartered white mushrooms

½ cup fresh water chestnuts, peeled and sliced

4 scallions, sliced on the diagonal into diamond shapes ½ inch long

I tablespoon minced fresh ginger

SAUCE

3 tablespoons black or mushroom soy sauce

2 tablespoons dry sherry

4 garlic cloves, crushed and minced

I teaspoon sugar

½ teaspoon freshly ground white pepper

½ teaspoon Liquid Smoke

I tablespoon cornstarch

I cup smoked almonds

1   Combine the cubed chicken with the egg white, cornstarch, and 3 tablespoons cold water. Mix well until the appearance is milky and the consistency velvety.

2   Heat 2 cups of the vegetable oil in a wok to 280°F; or put a piece of chicken in the oil and, when bubbles start rising from it like champagne bubbles, add the rest of the chicken. Slowly turning the chicken in the poaching oil, cook until the meat is white with no pink visible, approximately 7 minutes.

3   Combine the green and red bell peppers, the bamboo shoots, portobello mushrooms, white mushrooms, and water chestnuts in a colander. Sprinkle the minced ginger on top.

4   Mix all the sauce ingredients and stir well.

5   Heat the remaining 2 tablespoons oil in the wok to the smoking point. Stir-fry the vegetables until bright in color, approximately 3 minutes, then add the chicken and stir-fry for 30 seconds. Add the almonds and scallions and toss 3 times. Add the sauce. Stir-fry for 15 seconds, or until the sauce thickens, and serve.

Velvet Chicken

SERVES 2

In Chinese cooking, *velvet* indicates that a dish that has finely pureed ingredients. The person who eats this dish is supposed to taste the full flavor of chicken without any sense of eating chicken. A nice addition is finely minced chives—or, better yet, yellow chives, which are available in Asian markets. Add ½ cup of either chives after adding the chicken to the sauce.

1 pound skinless, boneless chicken breasts

1 egg white

3 tablespoons cornstarch

2 cups plus 2 teaspoons vegetable oil

SAUCE

1 cup chicken broth

2 tablespoons dry sherry

¼ teaspoon salt

½ teaspoon freshly ground white pepper

4 garlic cloves, crushed and minced

1 tablespoon sesame oil

2 tablespoons cornstarch mixed with ¼ cup cold water

1   With a small, sharp knife, attempt to remove the thin membrane that encases the chicken breast as well as any fat or gristle. Thinly slice the chicken breast lengthwise and then thinly slice it crosswise, producing a mince. With a cleaver or a French knife, continue to mince the chicken as fine as possible. Use a food processor to finely mince, adding a little cold water at a time to facilitate pureeing the chicken.

2   Heat 2 cups of the vegetable oil in a wok to 280°F; or place a little bit of the chicken in the oil and, when the bubbles rise from it like champagne bubbles, add the rest of the finely minced or pureed chicken and poach in the oil. Be sure to separate the chicken as much as possible with a spatula or a kitchen spoon. Drain the minced chicken in a colander, and with the chopping motion of a spatula or a kitchen spoon, separate the chicken as best as possible and try to remove any clumps.

3   Combine the chicken broth, sherry, salt, white pepper, garlic, and sesame oil in a small saucepan and bring to a boil. Reduce the heat to simmer or low.

4   Heat the remaining 2 teaspoons vegetable oil in a wok to the smoking point, making sure to spread the small amount of oil around the base of the wok. Add the sauce and stir. Stir the cornstarch mixture back into solution and add it to the wok. Boil, stirring until lightly thickened. I prefer the sauce for this dish to be a little bit thinner than normal. Add the minced chicken, fold gently to coat with the sauce, and serve.

SHANTUNG FRIED CHICKEN

SERVES 2 TO 4

When I was a teenager, my mother met a Chinese chef at a neighborhood Chinese-American restaurant. Although he cooked the normal fare of Egg Foo Yung and Chop Suey, he was a chef trained in Shantung Province, which is renowned for its Mandarin cuisine. My sister was friends with his children, and, one night, we all had dinner at his apartment. It was a thrill to sample real Shantung food from a master chef. One of the dishes he cooked for me was the following recipe, which he made with baby chicken. He placed a whole bird in front of me, and it was so delicious that I ate the whole thing.

Perhaps this memory colors my opinion, but I believe this dish is most impressive when served with a whole Cornish hen or baby chicken (poussin) rather than with chicken pieces. Serve with Bok Choy in Oyster Sauce (page 229), which provides the perfect balance for this dish.

1 piece of fresh ginger, 3 by 1 inch	2 tablespoons sesame oil
4 garlic cloves, crushed and minced	1 tablespoon sugar
2 scallions, cut into 4-inch lengths and crushed with a cleaver or knife	2 baby chickens (poussins) or small Cornish hens, or 1 1/2 pounds cut up chicken
4 tablespoons black or mushroom soy sauce	4 cups vegetable oil, for deep-frying
2 tablespoons dry sherry	

1   Smash the ginger with a cleaver or large kitchen knife and put it into a large bowl. Add the garlic. Smash the scallion sections also with a cleaver or a knife and place in the bowl. Add the soy sauce, sherry, sesame oil, and sugar; mix well. Add the chicken or Cornish hen and marinate overnight in the refrigerator or for a full day, turning occasionally.

2   In a large saucepan or deep-fryer, heat the oil to 350°F. Drain the chicken well in a colander. Because of residual marinating liquid, there will be some splatter when you fry it, so stand back. Deep-fry the chicken in the hot oil until the skin turns light brown and the meat is no longer pink, 8 to 10 minutes. Remove and drain well. Pat dry with paper towels.

3   Serve whole or chop the chicken into sections and serve on lettuce leaves.

STEAMED WHOLE CHICKEN

SERVE 4

1 whole chicken, 4 to 5 pounds

1 tablespoon kosher salt

1 teaspoon freshly ground white pepper

1 teaspoon freshly ground black pepper

1 bunch of scallions, trimmed and cut into 3-inch lengths

1 tablespoon minced fresh ginger

1 tablespoon minced fresh hot chili pepper (jalapeño, serrano, or Asian)

SAUCE

1 cup chicken broth

2 tablespoons dry sherry

1/4 teaspoon salt

4 garlic cloves, crushed and minced

1 tablespoon sesame oil

2 tablespoons cornstarch mixed with 1/4 cup cold water

1   Rub the chicken with the salt, white pepper, and black pepper. Put a handful of scallions in the cavity of the chicken, then place the chicken in a large bowl.

2   Set up a steamer, preferably a large pot with a tight-fitting lid and a footed metal rack inside. Fill the pot with water to just below the surface of the rack, cover, and bring the water to a full boil. Uncover and place the bowl of chicken in the steamer. Cover tightly and steam for 1 hour. Be sure to add water if necessary, checking the water level after 20 minutes of steaming.

3   Remove the bowl carefully and remove the chicken carefully with tongs and an implement like a kitchen spoon stuck into the cavity of the chicken. Place on a serving platter.

4   Pour out the residual liquid that's in the bowl and bring to a boil in a saucepan. Add the remaining scallions, the ginger, and the hot pepper. Stir in the cornstarch mixture and boil until the sauce thickens. Remove from the heat.

5   With a cleaver or a large French knife, disjoint the chicken, cutting it into neat pieces and arranging them on the platter. Pour the sauce over the chicken.

Red-Cooked Chicken

SERVES 4 TO 6

"Red cooking" refers to the reddish color of the chicken when cooked in the following way. The soy sauce actually turns the meat reddish brown. A traditional braising technique, red cooking renders meat fork-tender and imbues it with the flavors of the braising sauce.

8 chicken legs	6 garlic cloves, crushed and minced
2 tablespoons vegetable oil	3 tablespoons sesame oil
1 cup chicken broth	3 tablespoons light brown sugar
1/3 cup black or mushroom soy sauce	1 teaspoon freshly ground black pepper
1/4 cup dry sherry	6 small hard-boiled eggs, peeled (optional)
2 tablespoons finely minced fresh ginger	

1 Separate the chicken legs into drumsticks and thighs. Pat dry.

2 Heat the vegetable oil in a heavy, large pan, such as a Dutch oven, with a tight-fitting lid. When the oil is at the smoking point, add the chicken. Pan-fry, turning once for 10 minutes, until nicely browned. Drain in a colander. Reserve 1 tablespoon of the oil and juices in the Dutch oven.

3 Reheat the oil in the pan and add the broth, soy sauce, sherry, ginger, garlic, sesame oil, brown sugar, pepper, and cold water. Stir well. Bring the sauce to a boil. Add the chicken and hard-boiled eggs, cover, and simmer for 30 minutes. Remove the lid and stir.

4 Continue to cook for 15 minutes longer. Remove 1 piece of chicken and probe with a fork. If the meat is still firm and tight, the chicken needs to cook a little longer. If the chicken breaks apart and falls off the bone, it has been overcooked. The desired consistency is somewhere between both of the above. Serve at once.

Meat

單菜肉類

Only Barbarians Eat Raw Meat

CHINESE NEW YEAR'S DINNER IN MY family was traditionally a Mongolian firepot feast. Preparation for it was exhaustive and required the participation of the whole family. The end result was a long, slowly unfolding banquet of meats, vegetables, tofu, and noodles, which each person cooked in hot, bubbling broth, in brass and copper firepots set right on the table. Each morsel was then dipped into bowls of sauce that everyone concocted from at least a dozen ingredients to suit his or her individual tastes. The highlight of the dinner was at the end, when the rich broth of the firepots was consumed, with the delicate flavors of all the foods that had been cooked in them. Firepot remains a family affair and, as such, is the best way to begin the first day of the Chinese New Year.

For our meal, two freshly scrubbed and polished firepots would be set on both ends of the dining room table. The brass pot was squatter than the copper one. Seeing them gleaming in the morning light of my grandmother's dining room, I always believed that one was the patriarch and the other, the matriarch—symbols of the family.

I remember one Chinese New Year's Day in particular. Everyone was busy preparing and assembling the raw ingredients for the firepot. White celery cabbage (Napa cabbage) was cut into squares, soft fresh tofu into cubes. Two days previously, other tofu had been sliced, arranged on a cookie sheet, and frozen. It was now being defrosted and drained, rendering the tofu into perforated, spongelike rectangles that would soak up the flavors of the firepot broth when cooked. Transparent rice noodles called "spring rain" were boiled and drained, and arranged in a concentric swirl on a large plate.

My aunts assembled the sauce ingredients into small, porcelain bowls. Crushed garlic was put into a little ice water. There was peanut sauce, the same kind used in *dan-dan* noodles, and a type of pickled tofu, called "red in snow." Small, potent chili peppers from my aunt's garden were chopped and marinated in Chekiang vinegar, similar to balsamic. Soy sauce. Sesame oil. Red chili paste. Most important, someone—usually my uncle—was the fire starter. In China, the embers of burning wood are used to stoke the firepots. But here, charcoal briquettes are used. This was a difficult and tedious task that required clever timing because the briquettes would have to be started outdoors and, when ready, brought indoors and placed carefully in the distinctive tall funnels of the firepots.

My mother's family is from northern China, so according to tradition, only three meats were strictly allowed: lamb, beef, and calf's liver. The calf's liver was thinly sliced. Not too much was prepared, since it is not popular with everyone, including me. In fact, those cooking it were confined to one firepot since it made the flavor of the final broth stronger. My cousin, who is as adept with a knife as I am, was carving and thinly slicing a leg of lamb.

I was slicing the beef. Only good-quality beef—specifically flank steak, choice grade or better—was used. This is also the type of beef used for Chinese stir-fried dishes, such as Beef and Asparagus, Hunan Beef, and Pepper Steak. To accomplish this task, I used a long, slender knife, like a German carving knife normally reserved for large roasts or turkey, which gave me a quick, neat slice. I arranged the meat, overlapping each piece slightly, on large, decorative platters so that the plates were covered in a sheet of red meat, symbolic of prosperity in the New Year.

By this time, the smells of the meal-to-be were swirling in the kitchen, like ghosts of temptation intoxicating me with hunger. I popped a slice of raw beef into my mouth when no one was looking, hoping to placate these ghosts and quell their screams. Um, good, I thought. I do love steak tartare, though it's not on the favorite food list of most Chinese. Then I sneaked a bowl of sauce—just some soy sauce, sesame oil, garlic, and green chili vinegar. I flipped another slice of raw beef into the sauce, let it sit for a minute, and ate it with great gusto. Um, fantastic, I thought, my eyes rolling. But my grandmother, my Lao-Lao, saw me.

Chopping her fist with her index finger extended into the air—her sign language for a scolding—she yelled, "Only barbarians eat raw meat!"

My grandfather, my Lao-Yeh, normally refined and nondemonstrative, laughed hysterically, as did the rest of the family in the kitchen. Chagrined, I continued to cut meat. Well, I thought, my Lao-Yeh's side of the family were "barbarians," specifically, Manchus, the rulers of the last dynasty, the Ch'ing Dynasty.

It is said in my family that there is an old family tree that proves my grandfather to be a descendant of Kubla Khan, a Mongolian, the other major northern barbarian people. It is also said that Kubla Khan had more than 300 hundred concubines, which probably made, at the least, one-third of China his descendants. As I chewed on the raw beef, I fantasized myself living day and night on my horse, traveling the northern steppes of China to conquer the Western hordes, sleeping on my horse, and, when hungry, opening a small vein in its neck to drink its blood for nourishment. Using a horsehair, I would tie the vein, reserving it for the next meal. My grandmother's voice shook me from my fantasy.

"But, I understand," she said smiling, "Your grandfather's family were all barbarians."

The raucous laughter of my family continued, but my grandfather was not laughing. Turning to my grandmother with one of his rarely displayed stern looks, he popped a slice of raw meat into his mouth.

HUNAN BEEF

SERVES 4 TO 6

1 pound flank steak, trimmed of fat and gristle

1 egg white

3 tablespoons cornstarch

2 cups plus 3 tablespoons vegetable oil

SAUCE

1 cup chicken broth

3 tablespoons black or mushroom soy sauce

1 tablespoon regular soy sauce or Kikkoman

2 tablespoons dry sherry

6 garlic cloves, crushed and minced

2 tablespoons finely minced fresh ginger

1 tablespoon sugar

1 tablespoon sesame oil

1 teaspoon chili paste, or to taste and tolerance

1 teaspoon freshly ground white pepper

3 cups broccoli florets

1 cup quartered mushrooms

2 tablespoons cornstarch mixed with ¼ cup cold water

1   Cut the trimmed flank steak in half lengthwise. Slice the halves on the diagonal across the grain with a cleaver or carving knife. The pieces should be approximately 3 inches long, 1 inch wide, and no thicker than ⅛ inch. Combine the sliced beef with the egg white, cornstarch, and 3 tablespoons cold water. Mix well. The redness of the beef should be somewhat milky and the consistency silky.

2   Heat 2 cups of the vegetable oil in the wok until 280°F; or place a piece of the beef in the oil and, when bubbles come up from it like champagne bubbles in a glass, add the rest of the beef. Stir occasionally while poaching the beef in oil, being sure to break up any clumps that may develop. Cook the meat until it's mostly tan in color (I prefer that a little bit of red remain to ensure that the meat is not overcooked) approximately 5 minutes. Remember that the meat will be cooked a second time. Drain the beef in a colander.

3   Combine the broth, the two types of soy sauce, sherry, garlic, ginger, sugar, sesame oil, chili paste, and white pepper. Put the sauce in a small saucepan and bring to a boil on a back burner. Turn the heat as low as possible.

4   Combine the broccoli and mushrooms in a colander and rinse under cold running water.

5   Heat the remaining 3 tablespoons vegetable oil in a wok until smoking. Add the broccoli and mushrooms and stir-fry for 3 to 5 minutes, or until the broccoli is bright green in color. Add the cooked beef and stir-fry for 1 minute.

6   Stir in the sauce. When the sauce just reaches a boil, stir the cornstarch mixture and add it a little at a time to the wok. Bring to a boil, stirring until thickened. The brown sauce should not be soupy or gummy. Toss 3 times and serve.

VARIATION For *Beef and Broccoli,* eliminate the mushrooms and chili paste.

Beef Sichuan

SERVES 4

1 pound flank steak, trimmed of fat and gristle

1 egg white

3 tablespoons cornstarch

2 cups plus 2 tablespoons vegetable oil

SAUCE

1/2 cup chicken broth

2 tablespoons black or mushroom soy sauce

1 tablespoon regular soy sauce or Kikkoman

1 tablespoon dry sherry

3 garlic cloves, crushed and minced

1 teaspoon finely minced fresh ginger

1 teaspoon sugar

1 1/2 teaspoons sesame oil

1/2 teaspoon freshly ground white pepper

1 teaspoon chili paste, or to taste and tolerance

3 carrots, sliced thinly into 2-inch julienned pieces

4 celery stalks, sliced thinly lengthwise into 2-inch-long julienne strips

4 scallions, sliced on the diagonal into 1/2-inch pieces

1 tablespoon cornstarch mixed with 3 tablespoons cold water

1   Slice the steak in half lengthwise. Cut the beef halves diagonally at a 45-degree angle against the grain into slices that are 3 inches long, 1 inch wide, and no more than 1/8 inch thick. Combine the sliced beef with the egg white, cornstarch, and 2 tablespoons cold water. Mix well. The beef should be milky in color and the consistency silky.

2   Heat 2 cups of the vegetable oil in the wok until 280°F; or place a piece of the beef in the oil and, when bubbles come up from it like champagne bubbles, add the rest of the beef. Stir the beef slowly in the oil and cook until the beef is tan in color with a small amount of pink remaining, approximately 5 minutes. Drain in a colander.

3   Combine the broth, both soy sauces, sherry, garlic, ginger, sugar, sesame oil, and white pepper in a small saucepan. Bring the sauce to a boil, then reduce the heat to low or simmer.

4   In a wok, heat the 2 tablespoons vegetable oil until almost smoking. Add the carrots and celery and stir-fry until the carrots are bright in color, approximately 3 minutes. Add the beef and stir-fry for 1 minute.

5   Add the sauce and bring to a boil. Stir the cornstarch mixture back into solution and add to the wok. Bring to a boil, stirring until the sauce is thickened. Toss 3 times and serve.

Pepper Steak

SERVES 6

1 pound flank steak, trimmed of fat and gristle

1 egg white

3 tablespoons cornstarch

2 cups plus 3 tablespoons vegetable oil

SAUCE

1 cup chicken broth

3 tablespoons black or mushroom soy sauce

2 tablespoons regular sauce or Kikkoman

2 tablespoons dry sherry

6 garlic cloves, crushed and minced

2 tablespoons finely minced fresh ginger

1 tablespoon sugar

1 tablespoon sesame oil

1 teaspoon freshly ground white pepper

3 medium green bell peppers, seeded, cored, and cut into 1-inch diamond-shape pieces

1 large white onion, cut into 1-inch cubes

2 tablespoons cornstarch mixed with $1/4$ cup cold water

1   Slice the trimmed flank steak in half lengthwise. Slice the beef halves diagonally at a 45-degree angle across the grain into pieces 3 inches long and 1 inch wide, and no thicker than $1/8$ inch. Combine the sliced beef with the egg white, cornstarch, and 2 tablespoons cold water. The redness of the beef should be milky in color and the consistency silky.

2   Heat 2 cups of the vegetable oil in the wok until 280°F; or place a piece of beef in the oil and, when the bubbles come up from it like champagne bubbles, add the rest of the beef. Stir slowly in the poaching oil. Cook until the beef is tan with just a little bit of pink, approximately 5 minutes. Drain it in a colander.

3   Combine the chicken broth, two types of soy sauce, sherry, garlic, ginger, sugar, sesame oil, and white pepper in a small saucepan. Bring the sauce to a boil and reduce the heat to low or simmer.

4   Heat the remaining 3 tablespoons vegetable oil in a wok to smoking. Add the green peppers and onion. Stir-fry for 3 minutes, or until the peppers are bright in color. Add the beef and stir-fry for 1 minute.

5   Add the sauce and bring to a boil. Stir the cornstarch mixture back into solution and add it to the wok. Bring to a boil, stirring until thickened. Toss 3 times and serve.

ORANGE BEEF

SERVES 4

Because of the thicker slices required for this dish, it is necessary to use a good quality flank steak, preferably Choice or better. Otherwise, the beef pieces can be a bit chewy. In my restaurant, we used only Prime Kenosha flank steak for this dish.

As with General Tso's Chicken, or Chicken in Orange Sauce (page 114), this dish must be done quickly, particularly in the final phase. Furthermore, it is essential that the beef pieces be crisp, which is ensured by a second frying.

1 pound flank steak, trimmed of fat and gristle

1 cup cornstarch

BATTER

1 cup cornstarch

½ cup all-purpose flour

4 cups vegetable oil, for deep-frying

SAUCE

1 cup chicken broth

3 tablespoons black or mushroom soy sauce

3 tablespoons regular soy sauce or Kikkoman

2 tablespoons dry sherry

4 garlic cloves, crushed and minced

1 tablespoon finely minced fresh ginger

¾ cup plus 1 tablespoon sugar

½ teaspoon freshly ground white pepper

1 teaspoon chili paste, or to taste and tolerance

1 tablespoon cornstarch mixed with 3 tablespoons cold water

1 teaspoon orange extract

1   Slice the steak in half lengthwise. Slice the halves on a 45-degree diagonal into 3-inch-long, 1-inch-wide, ¼-inch-thick pieces. Dredge these beef slices thoroughly in the cornstarch, shake off the excess, and set aside.

2   Mix the batter by combining the cornstarch, flour, and 1 cup cold water. Mix well with a whisk. Add the dredged beef pieces to the batter. In a large saucepan or deep-fryer, heat the oil to 350°F. Add the steak pieces in batches without crowding and fry until crisp and white, approximately 5 minutes. Drain in a colander. Fry the pieces a second time in 350°F oil until golden white in color, about 1 minute. Drain and

place on absorbent paper towels (I prefer to use a shopping bag from the supermarket).

3   In a wok, combine the chicken broth, both soy sauces, sherry, garlic, ginger, 1 tablespoon sugar, white pepper, and chili paste. Bring the sauce to a boil. Stir the cornstarch mixture into solution and add it to the wok. Bring to a boil, stirring until the sauce is thickened.

4   Add the pieces of fried beef to the thickened sauce. Stir-fry as quickly as possible until the beef pieces are coated in sauce. While still stir-frying, add the remaining ¾ cup sugar from approximately 10 to 12 inches above the wok, tossing quickly at the same time. (It may be helpful to have the assistance of someone to pour the sugar while you stir-fry.) As soon as the sauce is glazed, add the orange extract. Toss 3 times and serve immediately.

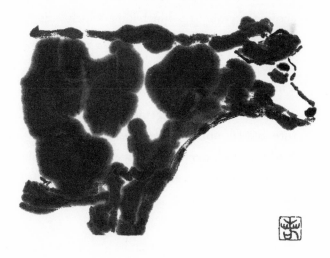

BEEF AND ONIONS

SERVES 4 TO 6

This was one of the first Chinese recipes I ever cooked. My family was on vacation in Ireland, and I was away at college. I quickly tired of eating hamburgers and hot dogs and wrote my mother frantically for her to send me some Chinese food recipes. Beef and Onions was one of two that she initially sent me.

It's a bit unorthodox, but frequently I make this dish and put it on a hard roll or a piece of baguette. Better yet, I'll add a slice or two of cheese and melt it briefly under the broiler for "Chinese Cheesesteak."

In recent years, I have minced up some jalapeño, serrano, or Asian chilies and put them in the marinade to give this dish a bit of a kick.

1 pound flank steak, trimmed of tough membrane and fat	2 tablespoons dry sherry
1 1/2 cups thinly sliced onions	2 teaspoons cornstarch
3 tablespoons black or mushroom soy sauce	3 tablespoons vegetable oil
	1 teaspoon freshly ground black pepper

1   Slice the steak in half lengthwise. Slice the halves at a 45-degree diagonal across the grain into 3-inch-long, 1-inch-wide, 1/8-inch-thick pieces.

2   Combine the beef in a mixing bowl with the sliced onions. Mix well. Add the soy sauce, sherry, and cornstarch. Mix well. Let the beef and onion mixture sit for a minimum of 30 minutes in the refrigerator.

3   Heat the vegetable oil in a wok until smoking. Add the beef and onion mixture. Stir-fry until the beef turns brown, being sure to break any clumps that develop. Add the black pepper. The beef and onions should have a little sauce that comes from the juices of the beef and onion as well as from the marinating ingredients. Serve at once.

BEEF AND ASPARAGUS
SERVES 4 TO 6

1 pound flank steak, trimmed of fat and gristle

1 egg white

3 tablespoons cornstarch

1 pound thin asparagus, sliced on the diagonal into 1-inch pieces

2 cups plus 3 tablespoons vegetable oil

SAUCE

1 cup chicken broth

3 tablespoons black or mushroom soy sauce

1 tablespoon regular soy sauce or Kikkoman

2 tablespoons dry sherry

4 garlic cloves, crushed and minced

1 tablespoon finely minced fresh ginger

1 tablespoon sugar

1/2 teaspoon freshly ground white pepper

2 tablespoons cornstarch mixed with 1/4 cup cold water

1   Slice the flank steak lengthwise in half. Slice each half against the grain on a 45-degree angle into 3-inch-long, 1-inch-wide, 1/8-inch-thick pieces. Combine the beef slices with the egg white, cornstarch, and 3 tablespoons cold water. Mix well.

2   Rinse the asparagus in a colander; drain.

3   Heat 2 cups of the vegetable oil in a wok to 280°F; or put a slice of beef in the oil and, when the bubbles rise from it like champagne bubbles in a glass, add the rest of the meat. Turn slowly in the poaching oil until the beef is cooked and tan in color with just a little bit of pink left, approximately 5 minutes. Drain in a colander.

4   Combine the chicken broth, both soy sauces, sherry, garlic, ginger, sugar, and white pepper in a saucepan and bring the sauce to a boil. Reduce the heat to low or simmer.

5   In a wok, heat the remaining 3 tablespoons oil to the smoking point. Add the asparagus and stir-fry until bright green. Add the beef and stir-fry for 1 minute.

6   Add the sauce and bring to a boil. Stir the cornstarch mixture back into solution and add it to the wok. Bring to a boil, stirring until thickened. Toss 3 times and serve.

Beef and Sugar Snap Peas in Oyster Sauce

SERVES 4 TO 6

1 pound flank steak, trimmed of fat

1 egg white

2 tablespoons cornstarch

2 cups plus 2 tablespoons vegetable oil

1 pound sugar snap peas, with strings and tips removed

1/3 cup oyster sauce, preferably Hip Sing Lung brand

1 tablespoon dry sherry

1   Slice the flank steak in half lengthwise. Slice the halves against the grain on a 45-degree angle into 3-inch-long, 1-inch-wide, 1/8-inch-thick pieces. Combine the beef slices with the egg white, cornstarch, and 3 tablespoons cold water. Mix well.

2   Heat 2 cups of the vegetable oil in a wok to 280°F; or put a slice of beef in the oil and, when the bubbles rise from it like champagne bubbles in a glass, add the rest of the meat. Turn slowly in the poaching oil until the beef is cooked and tan in color with just a little bit of pink left, approximately 5 minutes. Drain in a colander.

3   Put the snap peas in a colander, rinse, and drain.

4   Heat the 2 remaining tablespoons oil to smoking in a wok. Add the snap peas and stir-fry until bright in color, approximately 1 minute. Add the beef and stir-fry for 1 minute.

5   Add the sherry and toss 3 times. Turn off the heat and add the oyster sauce. Toss 5 times and serve.

Beef and Green Beans

1 pound flank steak, trimmed of fat and gristle

1 egg white

3 tablespoons cornstarch

2 cups plus 2 tablespoons vegetable oil

SAUCE

¼ cup chicken broth

2 tablespoons black or mushroom soy sauce

2 tablespoons dry sherry

1 tablespoon bean sauce, preferably Koon Chun brand

1 tablespoon sugar

4 garlic cloves, crushed and minced

1 tablespoon finely minced fresh ginger

1 pound green beans, ends removed and sliced on the diagonal into 2-inch pieces

1 tablespoon cornstarch mixed with 3 tablespoons cold water

1   Slice the flank steak in half lengthwise. Slicing across the grain at a 45-degree diagonal, cut the beef into 3-inch-long, 1-inch-wide, ⅛-inch-thick pieces. Combine the slices with the egg white, cornstarch, and 2 tablespoons cold water in a bowl. Mix well.

2   In a large wok, heat 2 cups of the vegetable oil to 280°F; or place a piece of beef in the oil and, when the bubbles rise from it like bubbles in champagne, add the rest of the meat. Turning the beef slowly in the poaching oil, cook until the beef is tan or grayish brown, approximately 5 minutes. Drain in a colander.

3   Combine the chicken broth, soy sauce, sherry, bean sauce, sugar, garlic, and ginger in a small saucepan. Heat the sauce to boiling; reserve over very low heat.

4   In a wok, heat the remaining 2 tablespoons oil until smoking. Add the green beans and stir-fry for approximately 10 minutes or until they are bright green.

5   Add the sauce, bring to a boil, then add the beef and stir-fry for 1 minute. Stir the cornstarch mixture into solution and add it to the wok. Bring to a boil, stirring until thickened. Toss 3 times and serve.

Stir-Fried Steak with Mixed Vegetables

SERVES 6

1 pound flank steak, trimmed of fat and
membrane

1 egg

3 tablespoons cornstarch

2 cups plus 3 tablespoons vegetable oil

1 cup broccoli florets, in 3-inch-long and
1-inch-wide pieces

1/2 green bell pepper, seeded and cut into
1-inch diamonds

1 celery stalk, thinly sliced on the diagonal into 2-inch slices

1 thin carrot, peeled, cut into 1 1/2-inch-
long pieces, then sliced paper-thin

1/2 cup snow peas, strings and tips
removed

1/2 cup quartered mushrooms

1/2 cup fresh water chestnuts, peeled,
washed, and cut into 1/8-inch slices

SAUCE

1 cup chicken broth

3 tablespoons black or mushroom soy
sauce

1 tablespoon regular soy sauce or
Kikkoman

2 tablespoons dry sherry

6 garlic cloves, crushed and minced

2 tablespoons finely minced fresh ginger

1 tablespoon sugar

1/2 teaspoon white pepper

2 tablespoons cornstarch mixed with 1/4
cup water

1   Slice the flank steak in half lengthwise. Slice the halves against the grain on
a 45-degree diagonal into 3-inch-long, 1-inch-wide, 1/8-inch-thick pieces. Combine the
slices with the egg white, cornstarch, and 3 tablespoons cold water. Mix well.

2   Heat 2 cups of the vegetable oil in the wok to 280°F; or put a piece of beef
in the oil and, when the bubbles rise from it like bubbles in champagne in a glass, add
the rest of the beef. Slowly turn the beef in the poaching oil and cook until the beef is
tan in color with some tinges of pink. Drain in a colander.

3   Combine the broccoli, green pepper, celery, carrot, snow peas, and mushrooms in a colander. Rinse in cold water; drain.

4   Combine the chicken broth, soy sauces, sherry, garlic, ginger, sugar, and
white pepper in a small saucepan and bring the sauce to a boil. Reduce the heat to low
or simmer.

5   In a wok, heat the remaining 3 tablespoons oil until smoking. Add the broc-coli, bell pepper, celery, carrot, snow peas, mushrooms, and water chestnuts. Stir-fry for 5 to 10 minutes, or until the broccoli and snow peas are bright green. Add the beef and stir-fry for 1 minute.

6   Add the sauce and bring to a boil. Stir the cornstarch mixture back into solution and add to the wok. Bring to a boil, stirring until thickened. Serve at once.

Moo Shu Beef

SERVES 4 TO 6

Moo shu dishes are traditionally eaten with Mandarin pancakes, which are also used for Peking duck. They may be purchased in a Chinese market in the refrigerated or frozen section or may be made by hand (see page 208). In a pinch, you can also substitute steamed flour tortillas.

1 pound flank steak, trimmed of fat and gristle

1 egg white

3 tablespoons cornstarch

2 cups plus 2 tablespoons vegetable oil

1¼ cups tiger lilies (also called lily flowers)

½ cup dried tree ears (see Note)

1 small head of green cabbage

1 tablespoon finely minced fresh ginger

6 eggs, beaten lightly

SAUCE

1 tablespoon black or mushroom soy sauce

2 tablespoons regular soy sauce or Kikkoman

2 tablespoons dry sherry

2 garlic cloves, crushed and minced

¼ cup chicken broth

1 tablespoon cornstarch mixed with 3 tablespoons cold water

1 bunch of scallions, cut on the diagonal into ½-inch pieces

½ teaspoon sesame oil

6 Mandarin Pancakes (page 208)

Hoisin sauce (optional)

1   Slice the flank steak lengthwise in half. Slice the halves across the grain at a 45-degree diagonal into 3-inch-long, 1-inch-wide, ⅛-inch-thick pieces. Combine the beef slices with the egg white, cornstarch, and 3 tablespoons cold water. Mix well. The redness of the beef should be milky and the consistency silky.

2   Heat 2 cups of the vegetable oil in a wok to 280°F; or put a piece of beef in the oil and, when the bubbles rise from it like bubbles in champagne, add the rest of the meat. Turning the meat slowly in the poaching oil, cook the meat until it is tan with some tinge of red, approximately 5 minutes. Drain in a colander.

3   Snip or pinch off the heads of the tiger lily buds and the small, thin tail, which is thinner and tougher than the rest of the body of the lily. Place the lilies in a

bowl and add hot boiling water to 2 inches above the buds. Soak for 15 minutes. Dump the buds into a colander, drain, and rinse thoroughly with cold water. Return the buds to the bowl and add hot water to cover again. Drain in a colander again and rinse thoroughly again with cold water. Soak the tree ears in hot water in the same way, drain, and rinse 3 times. Combined the drained tiger lilies and tree ears in a colander and mix well.

4   Quarter the cabbage and discard the core. Thinly slice as if making cole slaw and cut the strands so they are approximately 3 inches long. Combine the cabbage with the tiger lilies and tree ears. Rinse again in cold water. Add the minced ginger.

5   Cook the beaten eggs as if making scrambled eggs in a nonstick pan with a minimum amount of oil.

6   Combine both soy sauces, the sherry, garlic, and chicken broth in a small saucepan. Heat the sauce to boiling, remove from the heat, and set aside.

7   Heat the remaining 2 tablespoons vegetable oil in the wok until smoking. Stir-fry the cabbage, ginger, tiger lilies, and tree ears for 10 minutes. Add the beef and toss 3 times.

8   Add the sauce and bring to a boil. Stir the cornstarch mixture back into solution and add it to the wok. Bring to a boil, stirring until thickened. Add the scallions and toss 3 times.

9   Place the sesame oil in a Chinese ladle or a kitchen spoon. Holding the wok firmly, invert the ladle or spoon and quickly hit its stem against the side of the wok to spray the oil over the ingredients. Spoon 2 tablespoons of the Moo Shu Beef on the left side of a pancake. If desired, smear a small amount of hoisin sauce next to the mixture. Fold up the bottom flap, then gradually roll the left side of the pancake into the shape of a cigar or cone shape. Repeat for remaining pancakes. Serve immediately.

NOTE Tree ears are often labeled as "dried vegetable" or "black fungus." I recommend that smaller tree ears be used rather than the larger variety, which are much chewier.

Beef Fillet in Black Pepper–Cognac Sauce

SERVES 4 TO 6

This dish is reputedly the creation of a famous chef in Hong Kong, who originally called it XO Peppered Beef Fillet. Apparently, Remy Martin XO was originally used. Personally, I believe a decent cognac, like a Courvosier VS, is sufficient. Some Chinese in competition with Western glitz and glamour like to be flashy. This reminds me of a Chinese restaurant owner I knew who wore a big diamond pinky ring. An American customer admired it, and the owner took the ring off and gave it to the customer. As it turned out, the ring was a zircon, but it's the thought that counts. Anyway, it is likely that this recipe is that Hong Kong chef's attempt to be flashy in a hot culinary community that is becoming increasingly international. The result, however, is an excellent dish.

1 pound fillet mignon, cut into 1-inch-thick medallions	SAUCE
	¼ cup chicken broth
1 egg white	2 tablespoons mushroom soy sauce
2 tablespoons cornstarch	2 tablespoons dry sherry
¼ cup freshly ground black pepper	2 teaspoons sugar
4 tablespoons unsalted butter	¼ cup cognac
	1 tablespoon cornstarch mixed with 3 tablespoons cold water

1   Mix the beef medallions with the egg white, cornstarch, and 3 tablespoons cold water.

2   Heat the oil in a wok to 280°F; or put one of the medallions in the oil, and when bubbles rise from the medallion like bubbles in champagne, add the rest of the meat. Gently turn in the poaching oil until the medallions are beige brown in color, approximately 3 minutes; drain.

3   Place the black pepper on a plate and press each medallion in it to coat both sides. Melt 3 tablespoons of the butter in a large skillet over high heat. (I use an old French copper skillet.) Pan-fry the medallions on each side, gently turning them once,

1 minute per side, until rare, or until cooked to desired doneness. I believe emphatically that, because it is so lean, fillet should be rare. Transfer the medallions to a serving platter or individual plates.

4   Add the remaining tablespoon butter to the skillet and cook until it turns light brown. Immediately add the chicken broth, soy sauce, sherry, and sugar. Bring to a boil. Add the cognac. Carefully ignite the cognac with a long fireplace match. Flambé for 10 seconds, stirring the sauce constantly. If the flame does not go out, cover with any sort of cover, which will extinguish the flame.

5   Restir the cornstarch mixture into solution. Add it to the skillet and bring to a boil, stirring until the sauce is thickened. Pour the sauce over the medallions and serve at once.

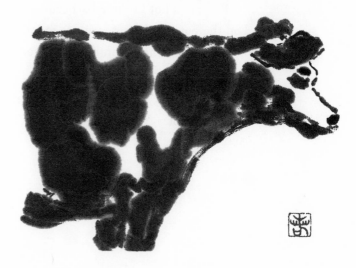

BARBECUED SHORT RIBS

SERVES 6

I absolutely adore beef short ribs, which, when marinated and grilled, become smoky, juicy morsels of meat that melt in your mouth.

3 pounds beef short ribs	1/4 cup crushed and minced fresh ginger
1/2 cup honey	2 tablespoons sugar
1/4 cup black or mushroom soy sauce	1 tablespoon chili paste (optional)
2 tablespoons dry sherry	3 tablespoons minced jalapeño, serrano, or Asian fresh green chilies (optional)
2 tablespoons sesame oil	
6 garlic cloves, crushed and minced	1 tablespoon freshly ground black pepper

1   Place the beef ribs in a baking pan that is at least 1 1/2 inches deep.

2   Combine the honey, soy sauce, sherry, sesame oil, garlic, ginger, sugar, chili paste, and fresh chilies. Mix with a whisk until well blended. Pour the marinade over the short ribs. Rotate and turn the ribs in the marinade to make sure they are well coated. Cover and refrigerate overnight or for a minimum of 8 hours, turning the ribs every 2 or 3 hours.

3   Prepare a hot fire in a barbacue grill with a lid. Grill the ribs, turning until browned on the outside, taking care not to let the ribs catch on fire from dripping fat. If they do flame, close the lid until the fire goes out.

4   After the ribs are seared all over, elevate the grill rack, or raise them to a higher rack, if possible. Close the lid, and open the top and side vents halfway. Cook for 20 minutes. Serve hot.

GROUND BEEF WITH PEAS AND ONIONS

SERVES 4

When I was a kid, my mother used to cook this dish for my birthday parties because, although it was Chinese food, most of the kids and their parents liked it. I remember one friend in particular, Duane, who refused to eat Chinese food, but he loved this dish because it reminded him of hamburgers. He's probably a food critic somewhere in the world today.

1 pound ground beef

2 tablespoons vegetable oil

1 cup frozen green peas

1 medium onion, chopped

2 tablespoons black or mushroom soy sauce

1 tablespoon dry sherry

2 garlic cloves, crushed and minced

1   In a large nonstick skillet or seasoned wok, cook the ground beef over medium-high heat, stirring to break it up, until browned, 5 to 10 minutes. Drain well in a sieve.

2   Heat the oil in a wok until smoking. Add the frozen peas and the onion and stir-fry for 3 to 5 minutes, or until the peas are bright green.

3   Add the cooked ground beef and stir-fry for 3 minutes. Add the soy sauce, sherry, and garlic. Stir well and serve.

MOO SHU PORK

SERVES 4 TO 6

The American version of this dish uses cabbage as a filler. The authentic version, which does not use cabbage, is infinitely better. Furthermore, Chinese restaurants serve *moo shu* dishes with hoisin sauce to boost the taste. With my recipe, none is needed.

Moo Shu Pork is traditionally eaten with Mandarin pancakes. To serve them pre-wrapped, place the Moo Shu Pork in a pancake, roll over one time, fold the end, and roll over again on the opposite side into a cone shape. I prefer to place the pancakes and the Moo Shu Pork on the table separately and let guests roll their own. It's so much more tactile and friendly this way.

I pound pork loin, trimmed of fat

I egg white

3 tablespoons cornstarch

$2^{1}/_{4}$ cups plus 3 tablespoons vegetable oil

$1^{1}/_{4}$ cups dried tiger lilies (also called lily flowers)

$^{1}/_{2}$ cup dried tree ears (see Note)

I tablespoon finely minced fresh ginger

2 cups thinly sliced cabbage (optional)

I bunch of scallions, cut on the diagonal into $^{1}/_{2}$-inch pieces

SAUCE

$^{1}/_{2}$ cup chicken broth

2 tablespoons regular soy sauce or Kikkoman

I tablespoon black or mushroom soy sauce

2 tablespoons dry sherry

2 garlic cloves, crushed and minced

I teaspoon sesame oil

6 eggs, beaten

I tablespoon cornstarch mixed with 3 tablespoons cold water

8 Mandarin Pancakes (page 208)

1   Slice the pork loin into $1^{1}/_{2}$-inch-long by $^{1}/_{2}$-inch-wide by $^{1}/_{8}$-inch-thick pieces. Combine the pork slices with the egg white, cornstarch, and 3 tablespoons water. Mix well.

2   Heat 2 cups of the vegetable oil in the wok to 280°F; or place a piece of pork in the oil and, when the bubbles rise from it like champagne bubbles in a glass,

add the rest of the pork. Turn gently and cook the pork until completely tan with no pink visible, approximately 7 minutes. Drain in a colander.

3   Trim the tiger lilies by snipping off the heads of the lilies as well as the tails, which are thinner and tougher than the rest of the bud. What should remain is a piece of tiger lily approximately 2 to 3 inches. Soak the lilies in boiling water, which should cover the lilies by at least 2 inches, for 15 minutes. Drain the lilies in a colander and rinse thoroughly in cold water.

4   Pour boiling water over the tree ears in a bowl and cover the tree ears with at least 2 inches of boiling water. Let soak for 15 minutes. Drain in a colander and rinse thoroughly in cold water. The tree ears should be greatly expanded. Repeat this process two more times.

5   Combine the tree ears with the lily flowers in a colander, and add the ginger. Stir in the cabbage.

6   Combine chicken broth, both soy sauces, sherry, garlic, and sesame oil. Set the sauce aside.

7   Heat ¼ cup vegetable oil in a wok until smoking. Slowly pour in the eggs from 12 inches above the wok in a thin stream, stirring vigorously with a long-handled wooden spoon in a circular motion. After all the egg is added, stir vigorously for 5 seconds, then immediately remove the scrambled eggs with a mesh strainer.

8   Heat the remaining 3 tablespoons vegetable oil in a wok until smoking. Add the vegetables in the colander and stir-fry for 10 minutes. Add the sauce, cover the wok with a lid, and bring the sauce to a boil. Add the pork and the scrambled eggs. Add the cornstarch mixture and bring to a boil, stirring until thickened. Toss 5 times and serve with Mandarin pancakes.

NOTE Tree ears are frequently referred to as "black fungus" or "dried vegetable." I prefer to use the small ones since the larger ones are much chewier and more suitable for soup.

PORK AND MUSHROOMS

SERVES 4

Although this was not on the menu at my restaurant, Wok 'n' Roll, I used to make this for myself for lunch. One day, a customer asked me what I was eating, and I let him have my lunch. He was wild about it. The next day, I put it on the menu.

1 pound boneless pork loin, trimmed and sliced into 1 1/2-inch-long by 1/2-inch-wide by 1/8-inch-thick pieces

1 egg white

3 tablespoons cornstarch

2 cups plus 2 tablespoons vegetable oil

2 cups quartered mushrooms

1 medium onion, cut into 1/2-inch cubes

SAUCE

1 cup chicken broth

3 tablespoons black or mushroom soy sauce

1 tablespoon regular soy sauce or Kikkoman

2 tablespoons dry sherry

2 garlic cloves, crushed and minced

3 tablespoons finely minced fresh ginger

1 tablespoon sugar

1 tablespoon sesame oil

1/2 teaspoon white pepper

2 tablespoons cornstarch mixed with 1/4 cup cold water

1   Combine the pork with the egg white, cornstarch, and 3 tablespoons cold water. Mix well. Heat 2 cups of the vegetable oil in a wok to 280°F; or put a piece of the pork in the oil and, when bubbles come up from the pork like champagne bubbles in a glass, add the rest of the pork. Turn slowly in the poaching oil. Cook until the pork is tan and no pink remains visible, approximately 5 minutes.

2   Combine the mushrooms and onion in a colander. Rinse briefly under cold running water.

3   Combine the chicken broth, soy sauce, sherry, garlic, ginger, sugar, sesame oil, and white pepper. Place the sauce in a small saucepan and heat to boiling. Reduce the heat to very low.

4   Heat the remaining 2 tablespoons vegetable oil in the wok until smoking. Add the mushrooms and onion and stir-fry for 5 minutes. Add the pork and sauce. Stir the cornstarch mixture back into solution. Add it a to the wok and bring to a boil, stirring until the sauce is thickened. Serve at once.

Pork in Garlic Sauce

SERVES 3 TO 4

For a spicier version of this dish, add minced jalapeño, serrano, or Asian hot pepper to the fried pork and scallions. Then stir-fry with the pork and scallions.

1 pound boneless pork loin, trimmed and cut into 2½-inch-long by ½-inch-wide by ⅛-inch-thick pieces

1 egg white

3 tablespoons cornstarch

2 cups plus 2 tablespoons vegetable oil

1 bunch of scallions, cut on the diagonal into ½-inch pieces

SAUCE

¼ cup chicken broth

8 garlic cloves, crushed and minced

1 tablespoon finely minced fresh ginger

¼ cup ketchup

3 tablespoons black or mushroom soy sauce

2 tablespoons dry sherry

¼ cup apple cider vinegar

⅓ cup sugar

1 teaspoon chili paste, or to taste and tolerance

1 tablespoon cornstarch mixed with 3 tablespoons cold water

1   Combine the pork with the egg white, cornstarch, and 3 tablespoons cold water. Mix well. Heat 2 cups of the vegetable oil in the wok to 280°F; or place a piece of pork in the oil and, when the bubbles rise from the pork like bubbles in champagne in a glass, add the rest of the pork. Turn slowly in the poaching oil and cook until the pork turns tan, with no visible signs of pink, approximately 5 minutes. Drain in a colander. Add the scallions to the pork and set aside.

2   Combine the chicken broth, garlic, ginger, ketchup, soy sauce, sherry, vinegar, sugar, and chili paste. Mix well in a small saucepan and bring to a boil. Reduce the heat to very low.

3   Heat the remaining 2 tablespoons oil in a wok until smoking. Add the reserved pork and scallions and stir-fry for 30 seconds. Add the garlic sauce.

4   Stir the cornstarch mixture back into solution. Add it to the wok and bring to a boil, stirring until the sauce is thickened. Serve at once.

AUTHENTIC PEKING SWEET-AND-SOUR PORK

This is the real McCoy and so much better than the "red lollipop" sauce version. Although sweet, it is not too cloying, and is delicate in flavor.

1 pound boneless pork loin, trimmed and cut into ¾-inch cubes

1 cup cornstarch

BATTER

2 cups all-purpose flour

½ cup cornstarch

2 eggs

1 cup vegetable oil

2 teaspoons baking powder

4 cups plus 3 tablespoons vegetable oil

SAUCE

½ cup chicken broth

2 tablespoons black or mushroom soy sauce

2 tablespoons regular or light soy sauce or Kikkoman

2 tablespoons dry sherry

6 tablespoons sugar

3 tablespoons apple cider vinegar

2 tablespoons ketchup

1 large onion, cut into cubes

2 green bell peppers, cut into 1-inch diamond-shape pieces

1 cup cubed pineapple, fresh or unsweetened canned

2 tablespoons cornstarch mixed with ¼ cup cold water

1   Dredge the pork cubes in the cornstarch. Shake off any excess.

2   Combine the flour, cornstarch, eggs, 1 cup vegetable oil, and 1 cup cold water. Blend well with a whisk; the batter should be the consistency of pancake batter. Add the baking powder and mix well. Let stand for 15 minutes, or until bubbles percolate from the batter.

3   Heat the 4 cups oil to 350°F. Place the dredged pork cubes in the batter and coat well. Fry the battered pork cubes until yellowish white, about 10 minutes. Drain in the fryer basket. Wait 5 minutes, then refry the pork cubes a second time until golden brown, about 1 minute; drain.

4   Combine the chicken broth, soy sauces, sherry, sugar, vinegar, and ketchup

in a small saucepan. Bring to a boil, then remove the sweet-and-sour sauce from the heat and set aside.

5   Combine the onion, green peppers, and pineapple in a colander. Reserve any residual pineapple juice.

6   Heat the remaining 3 tablespoons vegetable oil in a wok until smoking. Add the peppers, onion, and pineapple and stir-fry for 5 minutes, or until the peppers are bright green. Add the sweet-and-sour sauce along with any pineapple juice. Stir the cornstarch mixture back into solution and add it to the wok. Bring to a boil, stirring until the sauce is thickened. Serve at once.

Sweet-and-Sour Pork, Chinese-American Style

SERVES 4 TO 6

Many of my students say they prefer the Peking style of sweet-and-sour pork, but maintain that their children prefer the old-fashioned sticky-sweet "red lollipop sauce" found in Chinese-American restaurants. So here it is—for all you "kids" out there.

1 pound boneless pork loin, cut into ¾-inch cubes

1 cup cornstarch

BATTER

2 cups flour

½ cup cornstarch

2 eggs

1¼ cups vegetable oil

2 teaspoons baking powder

4 cups plus 3 tablespoons vegetable oil

SAUCE

1 orange

1 lime or lemon, or ½ lime and ½ lemon

1 tablespoon finely minced fresh ginger

1 cup sugar

3 tablespoons ketchup

½ teaspoon salt

½ teaspoon red food coloring (optional)

3 tablespoons vegetable oil for stir-frying

2 green bell peppers, cut into 1-inch diamond shapes

1 large white onion, cut into 1-inch cubes

1 cup cubed pineapple, fresh or unsweetened canned

5 tablespoons cornstarch mixed with ¼ cup cold water

1   Dredge the pork in the cornstarch. Shake off the excess.

2   Combine the flour, cornstarch, eggs, and 1¼ cups oil in a mixing bowl. Add 1 cup cold water. Blend well with a whisk until the batter is the consistency of pancake batter. Add the baking powder and mix well. Let stand for 15 minutes, or until bubbles percolate in the batter.

3   Place the dredged pork cubes in the batter and stir to coat well. In a large saucepan or deep fryer, heat the oil to 350°F; add the pork cubes and fry until yellowish white, about 5 minutes. Drain in a fryer basket or colander. Wait 5 minutes, then fry the pork cubes for a second time until golden brown, about 1 minute.

4   To make the sauce, bring 2 cups of water to a boil in a nonreactive medium saucepan. Add the juice of the orange and lemon and/or lime to the water. Stir in the ginger, sugar, ketchup, salt, and red food coloring, if using. Stir over high heat until the sugar is dissolved. Boil for 15 minutes, or until the sauce is reduced by almost half. Keep warm.

5   Heat the remaining 3 tablespoons vegetable oil in the wok until smoking. Add the green peppers, onion, and pineapple and stir-fry for 5 minutes, or until the bell pepper is bright green.

6   Add the sauce and any residual pineapple juice. When the sauce comes to a boil, stir the cornstarch mixture back into solution and add it to the wok. Bring to a boil, stirring until the sauce thickens.

7   Add the pork, toss 5 times to coat well, and serve.

PINE FOREST PORK

SERVES 3 TO 4

I learned this recipe when I was in China—specifically, when I was in Kwangchou (Canton). It is a delightful dish that uses fresh shiitake mushrooms and pine nuts. Shiitake mushrooms are very delicate in taste. They should be added to a dish after the heat is turned off. The most common mistake with fresh shiitakes is to overcook them. By slicing them thin and adding them at the very end, the heat of the dish will cook the shiitake mushrooms sufficiently.

1 pound boneless pork loin, trimmed and cut into $2^{1}/_{2}$-inch-long by $^{1}/_{2}$-inch-wide by $^{1}/_{8}$-inch-thick slices

1 egg white

3 tablespoons cornstarch

2 cups plus 2 tablespoons vegetable oil

1 cup sliced carrots, in 2-inch match-sticks

3 scallions, cut on the diagonal into $^{1}/_{2}$-inch pieces

3 tablespoons regular soy sauce or Kikkoman

2 tablespoons dry sherry

2 teaspoons cornstarch mixed with 2 tablespoons cold water

$^{1}/_{2}$ cup pine nuts

1 cup thinly sliced shiitake mushrooms

1   Combine the pork with the egg white, cornstarch, and 3 tablespoons cold water. Mix well. Heat the 2 cups of the vegetable oil in a wok to 280°F; or put a piece of pork in the oil and, when bubbles rise from it like bubbles in champagne in a glass, add the rest of the pork. Turn slowly in the poaching oil. Cook until the pork turns tan and no pink is visible, approximately 5 minutes. Drain in a colander.

2   Heat the remaining 2 tablespoons oil in a wok until smoking. Stir-fry the carrots until bright orange. Add the pork and stir-fry for 30 seconds. Add the soy sauce and sherry and stir-fry for 30 seconds. Stir the cornstarch mixture again and add it to the boiling sauce.

3   Add the pine nuts and toss 5 times. Turn off the heat. Add the shiitake mushrooms, toss 2 times, and serve.

PORK AND PEPPERS IN BLACK BEAN SAUCE

SERVES 4

The following recipe is the only one in which I like to use black bean sauce for anything other than seafood.

1 pound pork loin, trimmed and sliced into 2½-inch-long by ½-inch-wide by ⅛-inch-thick pieces

1 egg white

3 tablespoons cornstarch

2 cups plus 2 tablespoons vegetable oil

2 green bell peppers, cut into 2½-inch-long thin strips

1 white onion, thinly sliced

SAUCE

3 tablespoons Chinese salted black beans

2 tablespoons chicken broth

2 tablespoons soy sauce

1 tablespoon sherry

1 tablespoon cider vinegar

1 tablespoon finely minced fresh ginger

4 garlic cloves, crushed and minced

2 teaspoons sugar

½ teaspoon freshly ground black pepper

1 teaspoon cornstarch mixed with 1 tablespoon cold water

1   Combine the pork slices with the egg white, cornstarch, and 3 tablespoons cold water. Mix well and reserve.

2   Heat 2 cups of the oil in a wok until 280°F; or place a piece of pork in the oil and when bubbles rise from it like champagne bubbles in a glass, add the rest of the pork. Turn gentle in the poaching oil, and cook until the pork turns tan without any visible signs of pink, approximately 5 minutes. Drain in a colander.

3   Combine the green pepper and onion in a colander. Rinse under cold running water and drain well.

4   Mash the black beans with 2 tablespoons boiling water to make a paste. Stir in the broth, soy sauce, sherry, vinegar, ginger, garlic, sugar, and pepper.

5   Heat the 3 tablespoons oil in a wok until smoking. Add the peppers and onion and stir-fry for 3 minutes, or until the bell pepper is bright green. Add the black bean paste and stir-fry for 1 minute. Add the cornstarch mixture and stir-fry for 1 minute. Serve at once.

PORK AND GREEN BEANS

SERVES 4

When I was in the fifth grade, my family lived in upstate New York in a small town named Fredonia, just west of Buffalo. Our next-door neighbors were Italian. We used to have many joint dinners, and since Chinese produce was not available, my mother would cook recipes like this using Western vegetables. Our Italian neighbors raved about the dish and consumed it heartily, while my mother and I would chow down on their homemade cannelloni and lasagna, which featured a generations-old tomato sauce that used spareribs as the basis of the ragù.

I pound boneless pork loin, trimmed and cut into 2½-inch-long by ½-inch-wide by ⅛-inch-thick slices

I egg white

3 tablespoons cornstarch

2 cups oil plus 3 tablespoons vegetable oil

SAUCE

I cup chicken broth

¼ cup black or mushroom soy sauce

2 tablespoons bean sauce, preferably Koon Chun brand

2 tablespoons dry sherry

4 garlic cloves, crushed and minced

I tablespoon finely minced fresh ginger

I tablespoon sugar

I pound green beans, ends trimmed, sliced on the diagonal into 2-inch pieces

2 tablespoons cornstarch mixed with ¼ cup cold water

1   Combine the pork slices with the egg white, cornstarch, and 3 tablespoons cold water. Mix well.

2   Heat 2 cups of the vegetable oil in a wok to 280°F; or place a piece of pork in the oil and, when bubbles rise from it like champagne bubbles in a glass, add the rest of the pork. Turn slowly in the poaching oil until the pork is cooked, specifically turning tan in color with no pink remaining visible, approximately 5 minutes. Drain in a colander.

3   Combine the chicken broth, soy sauce, bean sauce, sherry, garlic, ginger, and sugar in a small saucepan. Heat to boiling, stirring to dissolve the sugar. Reduce the heat to very low.

4   Heat the remaining 3 tablespoons oil in a wok until smoking. Add the green

beans and stir-fry for 10 minutes, or until they are just tender, not hard, not mushy. Add the pork and stir-fry for 30 seconds.

5   Add the sauce. Stir the cornstarch mixture back into solution and add to the wok. Bring to a boil, stirring until the sauce thickens. Serve at once.

Maple Syrup Spareribs

SERVES 3 TO 4

I believe that the best-tasting pork is not of the tenderloin, but of the spareribs. The following maple syrup marinade makes the very best spareribs.

Everyone loves Chinese spareribs. I like to add this dish to backyard barbecues. I will cook the ribs in the oven as instructed below, and then create cross-hatch marks on the grill. This is the simplest method of barbecuing ribs, but if you are a "barbecue master," cook the ribs according to your own method without baking in the oven first.

1 rack of spareribs (approximately 10 to 15 ribs or 3 lbs), cut into separate ribs	1/4 cup dry sherry
3/4 cup pure maple syrup	2 tablespoons sesame oil
2 tablespoons sugar	8 garlic cloves, crushed and minced
1/2 cup dark or mushroom soy sauce	1 tablespoon freshly ground black pepper
	1 piece fresh ginger, 3 by 1 inch

1   Place the ribs in a baking pan that is at least 2 1/2 inches deep.

2   Combine the maple syrup, sugar, soy sauce, sherry, sesame oil, garlic, and ground pepper. Mix well. Place the ginger on a cutting board. With the flat side of a cleaver, smash the ginger against the board and add it to the marinade.

3   Pour the marinade over the ribs. Turn the ribs in the marinade to coat well. Cover the pan and marinate at least overnight in the refrigerator or for a day or more, turning the ribs every few hours.

4   Preheat the oven to 350°F. Place the pan of ribs in the oven and roast uncovered for 1 hour, turning the ribs every 15 or 20 minutes.

CHA SHA PORK WITH BOK CHOY

SERVES 3 TO 4

Whenever I buy *cha sha* pork, I always buy more than I need. The reason is that, as I cut, for every piece that goes to the side, one goes in my mouth. The slightly bitter bok choy, which is very high in folic acid, provides a nice counterpoint to the sweet roasted pork.

Cha Sha Pork is widely available in Chinese-Asian markets. It is usually in a glass-heated case that has ducks and chickens hanging alongside of it and is reddish in color. When ordering it, you can ask for a whole, uncut piece or have it cut for you. You can also request some sauce in which it was marinated, which you can toss into the stir-fry sauce for extra flavor.

Bok choy is now available in most supermarkets. The larger variety is about the size of celery. It is quite good, but I prefer the baby bok choy that is available in Chinese or Asian markets.

1 pound *cha sha* pork (already prepared and cooked and available in most Asian or Chinese markets)

1 pound bok choy, cut on the diagonal into 3-inch slices

½ pound fresh water chestnuts, peeled, washed, and sliced (optional)

SAUCE

1 cup chicken broth

3 tablespoons black or mushroom soy sauce

3 tablespoons oyster sauce, preferably the Hip Sing Lung brand

2 tablespoons dry sherry

2 tablespoons ketchup

3 tablespoons sugar

4 garlic cloves, crushed and minced

1 tablespoon finely minced fresh ginger

3 tablespoons vegetable oil

2 tablespoons cornstarch mixed with ¼ cup cold water

1   The pork is an elongated piece of cooked meat. Slice this widthwise on a slight diagonal into 3-inch by 1-inch by ¼-inch pieces.

2   Place the bok choy in a colander and rinse thoroughly with cold water. As bok choy is grown in sandy soil, it tends to be sandy. If there is a great deal of sand, soak the bok choy in a large pan of cold water, stirring frequently. Follow this procedure with a thorough rinsing in a colander. To test the bok choy, merely take a piece and eat it.

If it is still gritty, rinse again, if not reserve in the colander. Place water chestnuts on top of the bok choy in the colander.

3   Mix the chicken broth, soy sauce, oyster sauce, sherry, ketchup, sugar, garlic, and ginger in a saucepan. Bring the sauce to a boil and reduce the heat to low or simmer.

4   Heat the vegetable oil in a wok until smoking. Stir-fry the bok choy and water chestnuts until the bok choy is bright green in color.

5   Add the pork and stir-fry for 1 minute. Add the sauce. Stir the cornstarch mixture back into solution and add it a little at a time until the sauce is thickened, which should not be soupy or gummy. Serve at once.

STUFFED CHILIES

SERVES 2

Banana peppers are a good pepper for this dish. Sometimes they are sweet and sometimes they are quite spicy. I remember one time buying them at a roadside stand in New Jersey, and they were some of the hottest peppers I have ever eaten. Other peppers can be used according to taste and tolerance. It is important to try to keep the stuffing from falling out.

6 banana peppers or large chilies of your choice	1 tablespoon dry sherry
½ pound ground pork	3 scallions, finely minced
½ cup minced fresh water chestnuts	1 teaspoon cornstarch
3 garlic cloves, crushed and minced	2 tablespoons vegetable oil
1 teaspoon finely minced fresh ginger	3 tablespoons oyster sauce, preferably the Hip Sing Lung brand
2 tablespoons black or mushroom soy sauce	

1   Cut the stem ends off the banana peppers. Remove the seeds with a small knife. Reserve them if a spicier dish is desired.

2   Sauté the ground pork in a skillet or wok over medium-high heat, stirring often, until no longer pink, 3 to 5 minutes. Add the chili seeds, if desired. Add the water chestnuts, garlic, ginger, soy sauce, and sherry. Sprinkle the cornstarch over the pork filling and blend in. Stir in the scallions and stir-fry for 30 seconds.

3   With a teaspoon, fill each banana pepper with the pork filling, stuffing each pepper tightly.

4   Heat the oil in a skillet until smoking. Add the stuffed peppers and turn gently so that the stuffing will not fall out of the peppers. Pan-fry for approximately 1 minute or until the peppers are bright green in color. Add the oyster sauce. Turn the stuffed peppers in the sauce until well coated, and serve.

LION'S HEAD AND SPRING RAIN

SERVES 3 TO 4

The oversized pork meatballs here represent the lion's head, and the clear noodles the lion's mane.

I pound ground pork

½ cup minced peeled fresh water chestnuts

4 scallions, finely minced

I whole egg

2 tablespoons black or mushroom soy sauce

I tablespoon dry sherry

4 garlic cloves, crushed and minced

I tablespoon minced fresh ginger

½ teaspoon freshly ground black pepper

I cup cooked rice, preferably short-grain

4 cups plus I tablespoon vegetable oil

SAUCE

I cup chicken broth

2 tablespoons black or mushroom soy sauce

I tablespoon regular soy sauce or Kikkoman

2 tablespoons dry sherry

I tablespoon sugar

I tablespoon sesame oil

I packet (I ounce) "spring rain" (clear rice noodles), boiled for 5 minutes and drained

1   Combine the pork with the water chestnuts, scallions, egg, soy sauce, sherry, garlic, ginger, pepper, and cooked rice. Mix well in a mixing bowl with your hands. Form into meatballs the size of golf balls.

2   Heat 4 cups of the oil to 350°F. Deep-fry the meatballs until crusty on the exterior and no longer pink in the center, about 5 minutes. Drain and reserve the meatballs.

3   In a wok, heat the 1 tablespoon vegetable oil until smoking. Add the sauce ingredients and bring to a boil. Add the spring rain, stir, and add the meatballs. Toss gently 4 times and serve.

NOTE There is no cornstarch thickener in this dish. The sauce should be a bit soupy so that it can be absorbed by the spring rain noodles.

Red-Cooked Pigs' Feet

SERVES 4 TO 6

Chinese people are quite fond of eating pigs' feet cooked in this manner. There is something about the chewiness of the skin and the meat of the feet that is particularly appealing. It may not be appealing to all people, however, which is understandable. In that case, it is permissible to substitute fresh ham hocks (not smoked ham hocks), which are more familiar but maintain some of the integrity of the dish.

6 whole pigs' feet or 6 fresh ham hocks

1/3 cup vegetable oil

1/2 cup black or mushroom soy sauce

1/4 cup dry sherry

1 piece fresh ginger, 3 by 1 inch by 1 inch, peeled

6 star anise

1/2 cup rock candy or 1/3 cup granulated sugar

1/2 cup dark brown sugar

1   Rinse the pigs' feet thoroughly in a colander. Fill a large pot with enough water to cover the pigs' feet by at least 2 inches and bring to a boil. Place the pigs' feet in the boiling water and boil for 20 minutes. Drain into a colander and rinse well under cold running water.

2   In a clean heavy pot, such as a Dutch oven, heat the oil over high heat until smoking. Brown the pigs' feet all over, then drain in a colander, reserving 1 tablespoon of residual oil and juices in the pot.

3   Heat the residual oil and juices until smoking. Add the soy sauce, sherry, ginger, star anise, and 1 1/2 cups cold water. Bring to a boil, then add the rock candy and brown sugar. Reduce the heat to low and add the pigs' feet. Stir, then cover, and simmer for approximately 1 hour, frequently turning the meat to expose the braising sauce to all sides.

4   Remove the cover and continue to braise, turning the meat frequently, for an additional 20 minutes. Serve with steamed rice.

Red-Cooked Fresh Picnic Ham with Sesame Biscuits

SERVES 6

1 whole fresh picnic ham, about 4 to 5 pounds

1/4 cup vegetable oil

1/2 cup black or mushroom soy sauce

1/3 cup dry sherry

3/4 cup packed light brown sugar

2 tablespoons sesame oil

8 star anise

4 cinnamon sticks

1 teaspoon freshly grated nutmeg

Peel from 2 tangerines, white pith removed

1 cup raw peanuts

Seasame Biscuits (recipe follows)

1   In a large pot that will hold the ham and has a tight cover, heat the vegetable oil until smoking. Brown the ham on all sides over high heat to the point of bubbling up the skin without burning it. Drain the ham in a large colander, reserving 2 table-spoons of residual oil and juices in the pot.

2   Heat the reserved oil and juices over high heat until smoking. Add the soy sauce, sherry, brown sugar, sesame oil, star anise, cinnamon sticks, nutmeg, and tanger-ine peel. Bring to a boil. Add 4 cups of cold water and place the ham in the pot. Bring the braising liquid to a boil. Add the raw peanuts to the liquid. Reduce the heat to low, cover, and simmer, turning the ham every 15 minutes so it braises evenly, for 2 hours, or until fork-tender.

3   Remove the cover and continue braising, turning the ham, for an addition-al 15 minutes. Test the ham by probing it with a long pronged carving fork in the meati-est part of the ham. If it is soft and easily pliable, the ham is done. If it is still too firm, then continue braising for another 10 to 15 minutes. If it just falls off the bone, the ham has been overcooked.

4   The braising sauce is done when it is thick and bubbly. If the ham is ten-der before the sauce is ready, move the ham to a platter and cover to keep warm while you continue to cook the sauce. If the ham is not done, but the sauce is ready, add 1/4 cup cold water to the pan and braise.

5   Spoon the sauce with the peanuts over the ham. Serve with Sesame Biscuits.

Sesame Biscuits

SERVES 6 TO 8

2 packages (6 biscuits per package) commercial biscuit dough of your choice	½ cup maple syrup or pancake syrup
	I cup untoasted sesame seeds

1   One at a time, unroll each unbaked biscuit and dip the top side in the maple or pancake syrup. Press the syrup side into a plate of raw sesame seeds. Place on a lightly greased baking sheet. Repeat this procedure with each biscuit.

2   Preheat the oven and bake according to the temperature and time indicated on the biscuit package. Serve.

THRICE-COOKED PORK

SERVES 2

The thrice-cooked pork that is offered on most Chinese menus bears no resemblance to the authentic dish. The following recipe is the true recipe and involves literally cooking the pork, or in this case the ham, three times. It is also a lesson in how Chinese people deal with leftovers.

1 pound leftover Red-Cooked Fresh Picnic Ham (page 167), cut into 2½ by ½ by ½-inch chunks

1 cup leftover braising liquid

1 cup cornstarch

2 cups plus 2 tablespoons vegetable oil

3 thin carrots, peeled and sliced on the diagonal into 2-inch slices

3 celery stalks, sliced on the diagonal into 3-inch-long by ⅛-inch-thick slices

3 scallions, sliced diagonally into ½-inch pieces

2 tablespoons cornstarch mixed with ¼ cup cold water

1   Dip the chunks of braised pork in the braising liquid and dredge each piece with cornstarch; shake off any excess.

2   In a deep-fat fryer or large saucepan, heat 3 inches of oil to 350°F. Deep-fry the pork chunks for 2 minutes until crusty but do not overcook, remembering that the pork has already been cooked once. Drain first in the fryer basket and then on absorbent paper. (I prefer brown paper bags from the supermarket.)

3   In a wok, heat the 2 tablespoons vegetable oil until smoking. Stir-fry the carrots, celery, and scallions for 5 minutes or until the carrots are bright orange in color.

4   Add the reserved braising liquid and bring to a boil. Stir the cornstarch mixture into solution. Add it bit by bit to the sauce, thickening it; the sauce should not be gummy or soupy. Add the pork chunks, toss gently 3 times, and serve.

LAMB

No question about it, Chinese people from the far north of China have a love affair with lamb. My maternal grandmother, my Lao-Lao, was from the Beijing region—not far north enough—and, like most Chinese people, was a pork eater. My grandfather, my Lao-Yeh, however, was a Manchu, and he loved lamb. My mother and I inherited this fondness. My favorite lamb dish also happens to be the simplest to make. In Chinese restaurants in the United States, it is called Lamb Mandarin or Mongolian Lamb. It is simply stir-fried lamb with scallions. It is almost sacrilegious, but I like my lamb spicy. So I add 1 tablespoon of finely minced chilies to the scallions before stir-frying.

The only problem with cooking lamb Chinese-style is cutting it. Unlike beef, there is no flank-steaklike cut. In the restaurant, we derive our lamb from boning and filleting the whole leg and then slicing those fillets across the grain. The home cook, however, should use loin lamb chops or cross cuts of the leg. Bone, trim, and slice them, or ask your butcher to do it for you.

LAMB MANDARIN

SERVES 4

1 pound boneless loin of lamb, trimmed and cut into slices 3 inches long, 1/2 inch wide, and 1/8 inch thick	1 bunch of scallions, cut on the diagonal into 1/2-inch pieces
1 egg white	3 garlic cloves, crushed and minced
3 tablespoons cornstarch	2 tablespoons regular soy sauce or Kikkoman
2 cups plus 1 tablespoon vegetable oil	1 tablespoon dry sherry

1   Combine the lamb with the egg white, cornstarch, and 2 tablespoons water; mix well.

2   Heat 2 cups of the vegetable oil in a wok to 280°F; or place a piece of lamb in the oil and, when bubbles rise from it like champagne bubbles in a glass, add the rest of the lamb, approximately 5 minutes. Turn slowly in the poaching oil until the meat turns light brown with just a tinge of pink. Drain in a colander.

3   Heat the remaining 1 tablespoon oil in a wok until smoking. Stir-fry the scallions and garlic for 15 seconds. Add the lamb and stir-fry for 30 seconds. Add the soy sauce and sherry. Stir-fry for 15 seconds and serve.

NOTE THAT THIS DISH DOES NOT use the cornstarch mixture. It is a "dry-cooked" dish. The dish can, however, be finished with a very small amount of cornstarch mixture. Put 1/2 teaspoon of it in a Chinese ladle or kitchen spoon, hold the wok firmly, invert the ladle or spoon, and quickly smack the stem of the ladle or spoon against the side of the wok, spraying it over the ingredients. This will thicken it just a bit and give the dish a nice glaze.

Lamb and Mushrooms

SERVES 4

Please notice that no ginger is used here. I was cooking a lamb dish once and was about to add minced ginger. My mother, who was watching me closely, yelled, "For shame! No ginger with lamb!" But if you like ginger with lamb, go ahead and add 1 tablespoon to the sauce ingredients. I don't think the Mongolian hordes will bolt from the sky on winged horses and lay siege to your home.

1 pound boneless loin of lamb, trimmed and cut into 3-inch-long by $\frac{1}{2}$-inch-wide by $\frac{1}{8}$-inch-thick slices

1 egg white

3 tablespoons cornstarch

2 cups plus 2 tablespoons vegetable oil

2 cups quartered mushrooms

1 medium onion, cut into $\frac{1}{2}$-inch dice

SAUCE

1 cup chicken broth

$\frac{1}{4}$ cup black or mushroom soy sauce

2 tablespoons regular soy sauce or Kikkoman

2 tablespoons dry sherry

6 garlic cloves, crushed and minced

1 tablespoon sugar

1 tablespoon sesame oil

1 tablespoon cornstarch mixed with 3 tablespoons cold water

1   Combine the lamb with the egg white, cornstarch, and 2 tablespoons cold water. Mix well.

2   Heat 2 cups of the vegetable oil in a wok to 280°F; or place a piece of lamb in the oil and, when the bubbles rise from it like champagne bubbles in a glass, add the rest of the lamb. Turn the lamb slowly in the poaching oil and cook until the meat is light brown with just a tinge of pink, approximately 5 minutes. Drain in a colander.

3   Place the mushrooms and onion in a colander and rinse under cold water. Drain well.

4   To make the sauce, mix the chicken broth, both soy sauces, sherry, garlic, sugar, and sesame oil in a small saucepan and bring to a boil. Reduce the heat to low.

5   Heat the remaining 2 tablespoons oil in a wok until smoking. Stir-fry the mushrooms and onion for 30 seconds. Add the lamb and stir-fry for 15 seconds.

6   Add the sauce and bring to a boil. Stir the cornstarch mixture back into solution, add it to the wok, and bring to a boil. Toss 3 times, then serve.

VARIATION LAMB AND SQUASH Substitute 2 cups squash for the mushroom. Cut the ends off either or both yellow squash or zucchini, slice them in half lengthwise, and slice each half into ¼-inch-thick semicircles.

LAMB AND CHINESE EGGPLANT

SERVES 4 TO 6

Lamb and eggplant are a match in any cuisine, such as moussaka in Greek cooking. Chinese egg-plant, however, is special in that it is not acidic like other varieties. It is smaller and narrower, and its skin, which turns a beautiful, iridescent purple when cooked, is edible. Buy the smaller, thinner Chinese eggplant, which are bright purple. They have a rich flavor and hold their texture well.

1 pound Chinese eggplant

2 cups vegetable oil

1 pound loin of lamb, boned, trimmed, and cut into 3-inch-long by 1/2-inch-wide by 1/8-inch-thick slices

1 egg white

3 tablespoons cornstarch

SAUCE

1 cup chicken broth

1/4 cup black or mushroom soy sauce

2 tablespoons regular soy sauce or Kikkoman

2 tablespoons dry sherry

6 garlic cloves, crushed and minced

1 tablespoon sugar

1 tablespoon sesame oil

2 tablespoons cornstarch mixed with 1/4 cup cold water

1   Place the eggplant on a cutting board horizontally in front of you. Looking straight down on the eggplant, place your cleaver or knife straight up and down on the eggplant at a 35 degree angle. Cut the eggplant at this angle. Roll the eggplant toward you 1/4 turn. Cut down again. Repeat this cut for the whole eggplant and others. This is called the roll cut and produces attractive angular cuts of vegetables. Reserve the cut eggplant, but do not rinse in water.

2   In a wok, heat the 2 cups vegetable oil to 350°F on a deep-frying thermometer or place a piece of eggplant in the oil, and when it is floating and sizzling like frying chicken, add the rest of the eggplant. Deep-fry until the Chinese eggplant is bright flu-orescent purple in color, approximately 3 minutes. Remove from the oil with a stainless steel strainer or a brass mesh strainer and drain thoroughly in a colander. Press the egg-plant lightly with a large kitchen spoon to remove more oil, but be careful not to mash it. Leave the oil in the wok.

3   Combine the lamb with the egg white, cornstarch, and 2 tablespoons cold water. Mix well. Reheat the vegetable oil in a wok to 280°F; or place a piece of lamb in the oil and, when bubbles rise from it like champagne bubbles in a glass, add the rest of the lamb. Turn the meat slowly in the poaching oil and cook until the lamb is light brown in color with some tinge of pink. Drain in a colander.

4   To make the sauce, combine the broth, soy sauces, sherry, garlic, sugar, and sesame oil in a small saucepan and bring to a boil. Reduce the heat to low.

5   Place the eggplant in a clean wok and put it on high heat. Stir-fry for 15 seconds. Add the lamb and stir-fry for another 15 seconds. Add the heated sauce and bring it to a boil. Stir the cornstarch mixture back into solution and add it to the wok. Bring to a boil, stirring until thickened. Serve at once.

Red-Cooked Lamb Shank on Bok Choy Lo Mein

SERVES 2 TO 4

This is what Chinese people call hearty country food, which means it tastes good and sticks to your ribs. Believe me, after eating this, you won't be hungry for 15 hours, let alone 15 minutes.

If fresh bamboo shoots are available, as they are in many Asian markets, use them instead of the canned variety. They are so much better. Use the fresh young shoots, which are the shape and size of large asparagus. Slice them on the diagonal into 2-inch pieces.

3 tablespoons vegetable oil

2 lamb shanks, about 1 pound each

1 cup 1-inch chunks bamboo shoots (canned or fresh)

2 cups whole mushrooms

SAUCE

$1/3$ cup black or mushroom soy sauce

$1/4$ cup dry sherry

8 garlic cloves, crushed and minced

1 tablespoon sugar

1 tablespoon sesame oil

1 teaspoon freshly ground black pepper

Bok Choy Lo Mein (recipe follows)

1   Heat the vegetable oil on high heat in a heavy pot, like a Dutch oven, until smoking. Pan-fry the lamb shanks until each side is seared, approximately 2 minutes on each side. Add the bamboo shoots and mushrooms, and pan-fry for 30 seconds.

2   Add the soy sauce, sherry, garlic, sugar, sesame oil, black pepper, and 1 cup cold water. Bring to a boil, then reduce the heat to low, cover, and simmer for 45 minutes, turning the shanks every 10 minutes.

3   Uncover and continue to braise the lamb shanks for 15 minutes, turning them once.

4   To serve individually, place the lo mein on a plate and place one lamb shank on top, ladling some braising sauce on the shank. Surround the shanks with bamboo shoots and mushrooms. If this dish is one of a few or many dishes to be served collectively, place the lo mein on a serving platter and place the shanks on top, the bone of

one facing right and the other facing left. Surround them with bamboo shoots and mushrooms. Ladle braising sauce over the shanks.

Bok Choy Lo Mein

SERVES 4

1 pound fresh lo mein noodles

¼ cup vegetable oil

1 pound bok choy, washed thoroughly and cut on the diagonal into 2-inch slices (see Note)

1 tablespoon sesame oil

1   Cook the noodles in boiling water for 5 minutes. Drain in a colander and rinse immediately in cold water.

2   Heat the vegetable oil on high heat in a wok until smoking. Stir-fry the noodles for 10 minutes, tossing constantly to prevent burning.

3   Add the bok choy and stir-fry for 3 minutes, or until the leafy part of the bok choy is bright green.

4   Add the sesame oil and toss 3 times. Remove from the heat and serve.

NOTE Instead of bok choy, an excellent substitute is Chinese broccoli, known also as rabe. Cut the Chinese broccoli on the diagonal into 3-inch pieces. Stir-fry with the lo mein until bright green in color. Both vegetables complement lamb well because both are just a bit bitter and, thus, have a palate cleansing effect.

Lamb and Pine Nut–Stuffed Squash

SERVES 3 TO 4

Because this is a particularly attractive dish, it is a good choice for banquets or special occasions.

½ pound ground lamb

½ cup pine nuts

4 scallions, finely minced

1 whole egg

2 tablespoons black or mushroom soy sauce

1 tablespoon dry sherry

1 tablespoon cornstarch

2 yellow squash, 8 inches long and 1½ inches wide

2 zucchini, 8 inches long and 1½ inches wide

SAUCE

1 cup chicken broth

3 tablespoons regular soy sauce or Kikkoman

2 tablespoons sweet sherry, such as Dry Sack or Harvey's Bristol Cream

1 tablespoon Worcestershire sauce

¼ teaspoon ground rosemary

6 garlic cloves, crushed and minced

1 tablespoon finely minced fresh ginger

Juice from ½ lime, strained

¼ teaspoon freshly ground black pepper

1 tablespoon sugar

1 tablespoon cornstarch mixed with 3 tablespoons cold water

1   Preheat the oven to 350°F. In a mixing bowl, combine the ground lamb, pine nuts, scallions, egg, soy sauce, sherry, and cornstarch. Mix well, as if making meatloaf.

2   Cut the ends off the yellow squash and zucchini. Use an apple corer to remove the seeds from the center and hollow out the squashes, creating tubes. Fill each squash tube with the lamb filling, packing tightly. Bake in the oven for 20 minutes, or until the yellow and green of the squashes are bright in color.

3   While these are baking, combine the broth, soy sauce, sweet sherry, Worcestershire sauce, rosemary, garlic, ginger, lime juice, black pepper, and sugar in a saucepan. Bring the sauce to a boil, then reduce the heat to low.

4   Stir the cornstarch mixture back into solution. Add it to the sauce in the pan and bring to a boil, stirring until thickened. Ladle the sauce onto serving plates as a base sauce.

5   Place the baked stuffed squashes on a cutting board and cut each into 1-inch slices, being careful to keep the filling intact. With a small spatula, carefully place the disks of stuffed squash on top of the sauce on the plates in a decorative pattern and serve.

GAME

野禽

MY LAO-LAO, MY MATERNAL GRANDMOTHER, had a great love for cooking and eating game, particularly wild birds in China. To her, game included *all* wild birds. I will never forget the time two sparrows flew into the basement of her house. I came downstairs to find her—all 170 pounds and 5 feet, 10 inches of her—chasing the birds with a broom. Thinking of how to get them out, I shooed them back out the basement door.

She yelled at me in Chinese, "Blunt egg ("dummy" in Chinese), I want to eat them!" She then told me the story that sparrows are fair game in China and a delicacy. She described to me a vendor in her Beijing neighborhood who sold sparrows on a stick roasted over an open fire. It was a taste and a memory that she had savored since childhood. As a chef and a hunter, I have inherited her fondness for wild birds and meat, and I try to learn different ways of cooking game from all cultures.

Years later, I went pheasant hunting regularly with friends who had trained bird dogs, a female English setter and a male English pointer, both of which worked beautifully in tandem. The bonus to each hunt was that the other guys didn't like to clean their birds nor did they like to eat pheasant. So, I usually went home with six to eight birds. I told my Lao-Lao this, and she immediately put in her order for a large, old cock pheasant. After all, pheasant was originally a Chinese game bird.

Early one morning, I sleepily walked to the rhythm of the tinkling bells on the two dogs. The sound of the bells accelerated as the dogs found birds. The setter sat on one and one of my friends took it. The pointer was onto a "runner," and I ran after the dog. I huffed through an alfalfa field over a hill. Old cock pheasants run long before setting and flushing, and I knew I had Lao‑Lao's bird. As I crossed the crest of the hill, I didn't hear the pointer's bell. I knew the bird had set and the dog was on point. Proceeding cautiously down the hill, I saw the dog, its nose thrust forward and its tail straight back. As I approached, the pheas‑ant, invisible in the grass, rustled 2 feet farther, followed by the dog that went 2 feet and resumed its point. Walking briefly ahead of the dog, I heard a gobble as the big bird bolted into the air. I took it.

My Lao‑Lao asked that, if I got the bird, to just gut it and bring it whole, head, feet, feathers, and all. I got the bird the day before Thanksgiving. So late that afternoon, I got onto a very crowded Amtrak train to Washington, D.C., car‑rying the pheasant in a brown paper bag, which I folded down so no one would see my strange cargo. But a fresh whole pheasant with feathers has a musty smell to it. Soon, people on the train with a variety of expressions on their faces were looking around for the source of this odor. Wrinkling my brow in a quizzical manner, I joined them in looking around, not wanting to be pegged as the cul‑prit. When the train arrived in Washington, I grabbed my suitcase and the brown paper bag and departed quickly amid scowls and stares that followed me out the door.

But my Lao‑Lao was ecstatic. Holding the pheasant in front of her, she admired its long tail feathers, a testimony to its old age. Why she wanted an old, tough bird was not clear to me until she started cooking it, using a slow braising method of Chinese cooking called "red‑cooking." It's the same reason that an old rooster is used for *coq au vin:* a young tender bird will just disintegrate in the cooking process.

On Thanksgiving Day, she plucked the bird and burned its pinfeathers off over the stove. After washing and drying it thoroughly, she chopped it into pieces. She then took spareribs, which she had also cut into pieces, and browned them in a small amount of oil in a cast‑iron Dutch oven. She then added the pheasant and braised them in a fragrant sauce. This cooked slowly over low heat for about 1 hour. For the final phase of cooking, she added clear noodles, "spring rain," and square pieces of Chinese celery cabbage or napa. It was served in addition to turkey and all the trimmings.

I took a large bowl of rice and served my Lao-Lao a generous portion of the pheasant, and then did the same for myself. As the sensations of this dish traveled through me, I watched my grandmother as she ate. She looked as if she were drifting down a meandering stream to a different time and place.

"How wonderful" I thought, as I looked around, beholding my family in the full glory of a Thanksgiving feast that encompassed thirteen grandchildren, of which I was the eldest. As I savored the pheasant, and the moment, it occurred to me that I was eating a Chinese bird, cooked in a traditional Chinese way, that was many years ago transplanted to America, from whence I plucked it like fruit on a chilly morning in an alfalfa field to the crisp tinkling of bells. And, I thought to myself, "There is, indeed, so much to be thankful for."

Red-Cooked Pheasant and Spareribs

SERVES 4 TO 6

Unless you enjoy whacking away with a heavy cleaver, ask your butcher to cut the spareribs into shorter lengths for you. Likewise, if you order the pheasant from a meat market—rather than harvesting it yourself in the wild—you may as well ask him to hack it into 2-inch pieces for you. In which case, begin with Step 2.

1 large, old pheasant, about 3 pounds, or 2 smaller pheasants

1 pound spareribs, cut into 2-inch lengths

1 pound Chinese celery cabbage (Napa cabbage), cut into 2-inch pieces

3 tablespoons vegetable oil

6 garlic cloves, crushed and minced

2 tablespoons finely minced fresh ginger

$1/3$ cup black or mushroom soy sauce

$1/4$ cup dry sherry

3 tablespoons light brown sugar

1 tablespoon sesame oil

1   Be sure the pheasant is clean and free of pinfeathers. Chop the pheasant into sections approximately 2 inches square. Separate the spareribs.

2   Put the Chinese cabbage in a colander and rinse well under cold water.

3   Heat the vegetable oil in a Dutch oven or heavy pot until smoking. Add the pheasant and spareribs, and stir-fry for 5 minutes, or until the spareribs turn brown. Add the garlic and ginger. Mix in well.

4   Add the soy sauce, sherry, brown sugar, and $1^{1}/_{2}$ cups of water. Stir, cover, and braise for 30 minutes, turning the meat every 10 minutes.

5   Uncover and turn the pheasant and spareribs 3 times. Add the sesame oil. Continue to braise for an additional 15 minutes, uncovered.

6   Add the cabbage and cook for 1 minute, then serve.

MARINATED AND GRILLED WILD BIRDS

SERVES 4 TO 6

This will certainly take the humdrum out of your next backyard barbecue.

6 squab, doves, or wild game birds, such as quail, or 8 woodcock, cleaned and defeathered

¼ cup black or mushroom soy sauce

2 tablespoons dry sherry

2 tablespoons honey

1 tablespoon finely minced fresh ginger

1 tablespoon freshly ground black pepper

1 tablespoon Chinese five-spice powder

3 strips of bacon or aged ham

1   Place the wild birds in a large mixing bowl.

2   In a separate bowl, whisk together the soy sauce, sherry, honey, ginger, black pepper, and five-spice powder until well blended. Pour this marinade over the birds. Mix and cover the bowl of birds with aluminum foil. Marinate in the refrigerator for 24 hours, turning the birds every few hours.

3   Remove the birds from the marinade. Cut the bacon strips in half and stuff ½ piece of bacon into each bird.

4   Place the birds on a hot charcoal or gas grill; I prefer charcoal. Grill, brushing the birds with marinade frequently, until brown on all sides, approximately 3 minutes on each side. (If your grill has a spit attachment, put the birds on the spit attachment and baste frequently.) Elevate the rack, if possible. Close the lid and open the vents to halfway open. Cook for 5 minutes and serve.

Deep-Fried Squab with Roasted Salt

SERVES 4 TO 6

6 squab or doves, or wild game birds,
  such as quail, or 8 woodcock, cleaned

1/4 cup black or mushroom soy sauce

2 tablespoons dry sherry

4 garlic cloves, crushed and minced

1 tablespoon finely minced fresh ginger

6 tablespoons sugar

1 tablespoon freshly ground black pepper

1/2 cup sesame oil

4 cups vegetable oil

Roasted Salt (recipe follows)

1   Place the wild birds in a large mixing bowl.

2   In a separate bowl, whisk together the soy sauce, sherry, garlic, ginger, sugar, black pepper, and sesame oil. Pour the marinade over the birds, cover with aluminum foil and refrigerate for 24 hours. Be sure to turn the birds every few hours.

3   Remove the birds and drain well in a colander.

4   Heat the oil to 350°F. Deep-fry the birds to a mahogany brown color, approximately 4 minutes. Drain the birds in a fryer basket or colander, then on absorbent paper. (I prefer brown paper bags from the supermarket.) Serve with roasted salt.

Roasted Salt

MAKES ABOUT ⅓ CUP

This tasty salt is served with squab, duck, dove, or woodcock.

2 tablespoons kosher salt

1 tablespoon finely minced fresh chilies (jalapeño, serrano, or Asian)

1 tablespoon freshly ground black pepper

1 tablespoon freshly ground white pepper

1 tablespoon Sichuan peppercorns, freshly crushed

1   Mix the kosher salt with the black pepper, white pepper, and Sichuan peppercorns. Heat a heavy skillet, like a cast-iron frying pan, dry without any oil, until hot. Put in the salt and pepper mixture, and stir constantly for 1 minute.

2   Add the minced fresh chilies. Cook for 30 seconds, stirring constantly. Remove and place in a bowl for serving.

Red-Cooked Rabbit

SERVES 2 TO 3

This is the Chinese version of *hasenpfeffer*.

1 small rabbit (about 1 pound), cleaned, disjointed, and chopped into 2-inch pieces

3 tablespoons oil

¼ cup black or mushroom soy sauce

2 tablespoons dry sherry

2 tablespoons brown sugar

1 tablespoon finely minced fresh ginger

1 stick cinnamon

1 teaspoon freshly grated nutmeg

3 star anise

2 tablespoons juniper berries

3 tablespoons sesame oil

1   Place the rabbit in a colander and rinse thoroughly under cold water. Drain well.

2   Heat the oil in a heavy stew pot or Dutch oven over high heat until smoking. Add the rabbit and pan-fry for 5 minutes, or until evenly browned.

3   Add the soy sauce, sherry, brown sugar, ginger, cinnamon, nutmeg, star anise, juniper berries, and 1 cup cold water. Bring the stewing sauce to a boil, then lower the heat to a simmer. Cover and braise for 20 minutes. Turn the meat after 10 minutes.

4   Uncover and turn the meat. Add the sesame oil. Continue to braise for an additional 15 minutes, occasionally stirring the rabbit.

Braised Venison with Quail Eggs and Bamboo Shoots

SERVES 4 TO 6

2 pounds boneless venison, trimmed of
    fat and gristle, cut into 1½-inch cubes

3 to 4 tablespoons vegetable oil

⅓ cup black or mushroom soy sauce

¼ cup dry sherry

6 garlic cloves, crushed and minced

2 tablespoons finely minced fresh ginger

¼ cup dark brown sugar

3 tablespoons sesame oil

2 cups fresh bamboo shoots, sliced on
    the diagonal into 2-inch pieces

1 can (11 ounces) quail eggs, or 1 dozen
    fresh quail eggs, boiled for 20 minutes
    and peeled

1   Put the venison in a colander and rinse thoroughly with cold water. Drain and reserve.

2   Heat the oil in a heavy stew pot or Dutch oven until smoking. Add the venison and sauté until the venison cubes are evenly browned, approximately 3 minutes. Add the soy sauce, sherry, garlic, ginger, brown sugar, sesame oil, and 1½ cups cold water. Bring to a boil.

3   Add the bamboo shoots and quail eggs. Stir in gently. Cover and braise for 45 minutes.

4   Uncover, stir, and simmer for 15 minutes longer, or until the venison is fork-tender.

Peppered Venison Steak

SERVES 4 TO 6

2 pounds venison steak from the haunch, shoulder, or saddle, well trimmed

1/2 cup black or mushroom soy sauce

1/4 cup dry sherry

6 garlic cloves, crushed and minced

2 tablespoons finely minced fresh ginger

1/4 cup sesame oil

2 tablespoons sugar

2 tablespoons freshly ground black pepper

2 tablespoons freshly ground white pepper

1 tablespoon Sichuan peppercorn, freshly crushed

1 tablespoon finely minced fresh chilies (jalapeño, serrano, or Asian)

2 medium onions, thinly sliced

1   Marinate the venison steak in the soy sauce, sherry, garlic, ginger, sesame oil, and sugar. Refrigerate for 24 hours, turning the steak every couple of hours.

2   Remove the steak and season well with the black pepper, white pepper, and Sichuan peppercorns.

3   Place the steak on a large piece of double-thickness aluminum foil. Sprinkle the fresh chili peppers on top. Sprinkle the onions on top. Fold the aluminum foil tightly on all sides, with the seam on the top. Puncture the aluminum foil on the top with a fork 6 times.

5   Preheat the oven to 300°F. Place the venison in a roasting pan and roast for 2 hours, or until the venison steak is fork-tender.

Venison and Onions

SERVES 2 TO 3

1 pound boneless venison saddle, sliced very thinly into silver dollar-size slices

6 tablespoons black or mushroom soy sauce

3 tablespoons cognac or brandy

2 tablespoons dry sherry

1 tablespoon freshly ground black pepper

1 tablespoon cornstarch

2 cups thinly sliced onions

1/4 cup vegetable oil

1   Combine the venison with the soy sauce, cognac or brandy, sherry, black pepper, and cornstarch. Add the onions and mix well. Marinate at room temperature for 1/2 hour or in the refrigerator for 1 hour or longer.

2   Stir the venison and onions. Heat the oil in a wok until smoking. Add the venison and onions, and stir-fry until the venison turns brown and the sauce thickens.

Stuffed Venison Roast

SERVES 6

1 leg of venison, boned and trimmed

⅓ cup black or mushroom soy sauce

¼ cup dry sherry

¼ cup gin

2 tablespoons freshly ground black pepper

3 tablespoons sugar

8 garlic cloves, crushed and minced

3 tablespoons finely minced fresh ginger

FILLING

2 bunches of scallions, finely minced

½ cup pine nuts

1 bunch of cilantro, finely minced

6 garlic cloves, crushed and minced

2 tablespoons finely minced fresh ginger

1 tablespoon freshly ground white pepper

1 tablespoon kosher salt

¼ cup vegetable oil

1   The boned venison roast should lay out flat. Marinate it in the soy sauce, sherry, gin, black pepper, sugar, garlic, and ginger. Refrigerate for 24 hours more, turning the meat every few hours.

2   Combine the scallions, pine nuts, cilantro, garlic, ginger, white pepper, salt, and oil. Refrigerate the filling for 30 minutes.

3   Preheat the oven to 350°F. Take the venison roast from the marinade and drain in a colander for 15 minutes. Lay it out in an oiled baking pan.

4   Stir the filling again. Spread it like peanut butter on bread across the flat top side of the venison roast. Roll the roast into a cylindrical shape. Tie the roast in two places with string.

5   Roast for 1½ hours, basting frequently with the marinade, until tender. To serve, carve into ½-inch-thick slices.

POTSTICKERS, NOODLES, SPRING ROLLS, AND RICE

MY GRANDMOTHER, MY MOTHER'S MOTHER, the infamous shopper and notorious bargainer, is called Lao-Lao in Mandarin Chinese, meaning specifically, "old-old." *Old* in the Asian culture does not mean decrepit and weak. It connotes wisdom and survival, which I label as "smarts with honor."

China in the twentieth century was not an easy place. Invasion by the Japanese and civil war dominated everyday events. Stories abound about the deprivation, starvation, and violence of internal and external political forces. My family was in the midst of that fire. As a teenager, my mother ran messages for the Chinese underground against the Japanese. If she had been caught, she would have been killed, after being tortured. My maternal grandfather, my Lao-Yeh, was the closest friend and aide to John Leighton Stuart, who later became the last American ambassador to China before the Nixon era. My grandfather was beaten by the Japanese for information concerning the Americans. He never talked. The day of Pearl Harbor, he and Dr. Stuart left surreptitiously for Chungking, or, most likely, they would not have survived the day. Dr. Stuart is my namesake.

My grandmother, my Lao-Lao, assumed the helm of the family. There was no food, and the Japanese were relentless. My mother was riding on a bicycle with a friend near the Ming tombs. Shots rang out, my mother fled—an assassination attempt, my grandfather believed later—and but for the grace of God, she emerged unscathed. Lao-Lao held the family together. This was not just the immediate family but also a large extended family consisting as well of aunts, uncles, and cousins. Food was scarce, and the Japanese monitored my family's every move. Lao-Lao was the steel of the family that enabled everyone to stand up to oppression and deprivation without the expectation of better.

Life was so much different in the United States. When I was a child, Lao-Lao came from Washington to New York to help take care of me. She rode the school bus with me and, short and fat, she wasn't a whole lot different in size from my schoolmates. One night, we spent in some sort of place for overnight care. Lao-Lao tucked me in and slept in a chair next to my crib. I didn't sleep well. Lao-Lao snored like a factory.

Although she could not speak English at first, she knew we would be here for quite a while, and she wanted the family to fit in as well as possible. After getting hopelessly lost, she learned the bus routes in Washington, D.C. She then took a cooking course somewhere in the suburbs to learn how to make a tradi-tional Thanksgiving dinner, and from then on, every year we had a traditional American Thanksgiving, from turkey with chestnut stuffing to apple pie, made from apples harvested from the tree in her backyard.

As I knead dough for dumplings, I still feel her warmth. As I fold the dough back and knead it, I hope I convey her love and selfless dedication to fam-ily to my children, and they to their children. As I pinch the dough to test it for readiness, I hear Lao-Lao shouting, "*Wor mein.* Work!" *Wor mein* means to work the dough and tote that barge. Rolling the dough out into a long snake, I cut it into pieces that I roll into balls, flatten, and roll out into disks. Filling those disks, I double them over and crimp them like my grandmother showed me. I place the crescent-shaped dumplings, neatly and evenly spaced, on a floured tray.

I remember how Lao-Lao would set a large plate of the finished steaming potstickers before me. As I bite into one now, the juices capture me with their taste. I grab that thought, hold it, and let it flutter like a butterfly through my memory.

Easy Potstickers— Using Commercial Skins

MAKES 50

Nine out of ten people opt to use commercially made dumpling or potsticker skins. It's easy enough. There are fifty round skins per package. Use the following directions for filling commercial skins.

1   Whisk 1 egg white until foamy in a small bowl.

2   Using 1 commercial skin, which is about a 3½-inch circle, dip half the circle in the egg white.

3   Put about 1 teaspoon filling in the center of the circle. Be sure not to overfill. If filling oozes out after crimping, use less.

4   Fold the bottom to the top to form a semicircle. Pinch firmly with the thumb and forefinger of your dominant hand around the circumference of the semicircle, sealing it.

5   Place this semicircle, which looks like a pirogi, on your nondominant hand on the line where your fingers meet the hand.

6   Using the thumb and forefinger of your dominant hand, crimp the edge of the potsticker to seal it, forming a backward *S*, then pinching it firmly with the thumb and forefinger, repeating these motions every ¼ inch until the whole semicircle is done. Try to give a little twist toward yourself when crimping so that at the end of the crimp you are looking down at your knuckles. Place the potsticker on a lightly floured tray.

7   Repeat this with each potsticker and skin and line up the potstickers in columns on floured trays.

NOTE If the backward *S* crimp is too difficult for you, using the thumb and the forefinger, repinch the circumference of the semicircle, twisting the rounded edge toward you so that you are looking at the top of your knuckles to form a bonnet shape.

HANDMADE POTSTICKER SKINS

MAKES ABOUT 40

Handmade, homemade potsticker skins are so much better. More filling can be added and hand-made skins taste better. For me, it is a matter of tradition and how I was taught by my grand-mother. I am known, however, on occasion to use the commercial skins out of convenience or because I frequently have leftover filling. Forgive me, Lao-Lao.

3 cups all-purpose flour, plus more for kneading	I cup cold water

1   Put the flour in a mixing bowl, and add the cold water a little at time, stir-ring it in with a pair of chopsticks. The flour will get crumbly like piecrust dough.

2   Knead this crumbly dough in the bowl with your hands until it forms a ball. On a lightly floured board, knead the dough ball until smooth. Put it back into the mix-ing bowl and cover it with a damp cloth or paper towel. Be sure it is damp by wringing out the cloth or paper towel. Place the bowl of dough in the refrigerator and let "cure" for ½ hour.

3   Take the dough out and knead it on a lightly floured board for 5 minutes. It should not be too hard or firm like putty, and it should not be too soft like Play-doh®. It should be somewhere in between.

4   Cut the dough in half. Roll each half into a 1-inch-thick snake. Add flour to the board if the dough starts to stick.

5   Cut the dough snake into 1-inch cubes, or a little bit bigger if you like big dumplings like I do. Roll each cube between the palms of both hands to form a ball. Flatten the ball with the floured palm of one hand into a disk. With a floured rolling pin, roll out each disk to be about 4 inches in diameter.

6   Place 2 teaspoons of filling in the center of each disk. The most common mistake in making potstickers is using too much filling. If filling starts to ooze out of the dumpling after you crimp it, use less. With practice, you should be able to use a tablespoon of filling for a 4-inch handmade skin. Fold over the bottom half of the skin

to form a semicircle. Place the potsticker in your nondominant hand on the line where your fingers meet the palm. Using the thumb and forefinger of your dominant hand, pinch the semicircular edge to seal the potsticker. (Note: With handmade skins, no egg white is needed.) Still using your thumb and forefinger, start at the end of the potsticker that is opposite of your dominant hand (i.e., the left side if you are right-handed; the right side if you are left-handed), form a backward *S*, crimp it, move over ¼ inch, make another backward *S*, crimp it, and continue this until the potsticker is done. As you crimp, try to give it a small twist of the hand toward yourself where you are looking down at the top of your knuckles so that the potsticker forms a bonnet shape.

7   Line up the potstickers in columns like "toy soldiers" on a lightly floured board. Don't pile them on top of each other. Otherwise, you will be making one big pot-sticker the size of a volleyball.

Beijing Pork and Chinese Celery Cabbage Potstickers

SERVES 4 TO 6

If the potstickers are busting open when being cooked, it means either you are trying to stuff in too much filling, which is indicated by filling oozing out at the edges, or the filling is too wet, which means you did not drain the filling in a colander.

1 pound Chinese celery cabbage (Napa cabbage)

1 pound ground pork

1 bunch of scallions, finely minced

6 garlic cloves, crushed and minced

1/3 cup black or mushroom soy sauce

2 tablespoons dry sherry

1/3 cup sesame oil

40 to 50 store-bought (8 ounces) or handmade dumpling skins (page 197)

1   I prefer to mince the celery cabbage with a cleaver by slicing across the stalks into thin strips and then cutting across these strips into a mince. Continue to chop the minced celery cabbage into a fine mince. This can be done with a food proces-sor, but this tends to "mush" the vegetable.

2   Using a clean cloth, such as a clean dishtowel, place the minced celery cab-bage in the center of the cloth. Gather up the ends and edges of the cloth to form a ball. Twist the ball in one direction while twisting the ends and edges in the other direc-tion. Squeeze out most of the water from the celery cabbage, retaining some water which will add juices to the potstickers when they are cooked.

3   Put the cabbage into a mixing bowl. Add the ground pork, scallions, garlic, soy sauce, sherry, and sesame oil. Mix well with a pair of chopsticks, as if making a meat-loaf. Place the filling in a colander to drain.

4   If using the store-bought commercial skins, dip half of each skin in egg white and place 1 teaspoon of filling in the center of the skin. Fold and crimp. If using the handmade skins, place 2 teaspoons of filling in the center of each skin. Fold and crimp. For both, line up the potstickers on a floured tray like soldiers.

5   Bring a large pot of water to a full boil. Put in enough potstickers to form one solid layer of potstickers on the bottom of the pot. Immediately, with a wooden spoon, slowly and gently stir the potstickers in a circular motion to prevent them from sticking to the bottom of the pot (hence, the name "potstickers"). The potstickers should start to float in the water. Bring the water to a full boil (do not cover the pot), and immediately add 1 cup of cold water. When the water comes to a boil again, add another cup of cold water. Repeat this procedure one more time, a total of three times, and remove the potstickers with a small brass mesh strainer or slotted spoon. Serve with dipping sauce.

PAN-FRIED POTSTICKERS Pan-fried potstickers are generally made with left-over potstickers. Using a heavy skillet, like a cast-iron frying pan, dip a paper towel in some vegetable oil and brush a thin veneer of oil on the bottom of the skillet. Heat the pan to hot over medium-high heat. Line the skillet with potstickers facing in the same direction. Cover for 1 minute, then uncover and use a small spatula to check the potstickers. When they are crusty brown on one side, they are done. If they need more time, sprinkle a little water on the potstickers, cover, and cook for another minute. Then check them again. They are cooked only on one side.

IT SEEMS THAT EVERY TIME I mix the dipping sauce for dumplings, I remember my good friend Joe Rossi, one of the first friends I made when I was a freshman at Rutgers. Potstickers were his favorite Chinese food, but they are labor intensive. Also, like most Chinese people, I don't make a few. I make a lot. I tried to teach Joe once how to wrap dumplings, but his end products looked liked ugly little gnomes that inevitably burst open when cooked. So he would just watch me make them. It must have been torture for him because the filling was redolent of sesame oil, garlic, and soy sauce. Oh, anticipation, anticipation.

I never seem to make the dipping sauce until the potstickers are done and on the table, their steam rising to the ceiling, beckoning all to snatch them up. It doesn't take long to make the dipping sauce. But as I did it at the table, Joe would sit forward with his elbows on the table, chopsticks in his hand, cocked back like a heron ready to pluck a fish from water. When the sauce was done, the heron would strike and consume its prey. No matter how many times he tasted them, Joe always said the same thing after eating his first potsticker, "Yeah, these are great."

Dipping Sauce

SERVES 4 TO 6

½ cup regular soy sauce or Kikkoman

½ cup wine vinegar, cider vinegar, or balsamic vinegar

1 teaspoon finely minced fresh chili peppers (jalapeño, serrano, or Asian; optional)

Mix these ingredients in a small bowl. Let your guests serve themselves.

LAMB AND SQUASH POTSTICKERS

SERVES 4 TO 6

One year, my garden did fantastically well. The squash and zucchini were huge and plentiful. After tiring of the squash cooked in traditional ways and of zucchini bread, I made about one thousand lamb and squash potstickers to the delight of family and friends.

1 pound zucchini and/or yellow squash, finely minced	2 tablespoons dry sherry
1 pound ground lamb	$^1/_4$ cup sesame oil
1 bunch of scallions, finely minced	$^1/_2$ teaspoon freshly ground black pepper
5 garlic cloves, crushed and minced	40 to 50 store-bought or handmade dumpling skins (page 197)
2 tablespoons regular soy sauce or Kikkoman	1 egg white, lightly beaten (optional)
1 tablespoon black or mushroom soy sauce	Dipping Sauce (page 202)

1   Place the squash in the center of a cloth. Bundle it up by gathering the sides and corners of the cloth and up and over the squash to form a ball. With one hand grabbing the bottom of the ball and the other hand holding the bundle of sides and corners, twist each in opposite directions to squeeze the water out of the squash.

2   Place the squeezed squash in a mixing bowl. Add the lamb, scallions, garlic, regular soy sauce, black soy sauce, sherry, sesame oil, and black pepper to the squash and mix well with a pair of chopsticks.

3   If using store-bought commercial skins, dip half of each skin in egg white and place 1 teaspoon of the lamb filling in the center of the skin. Fold and crimp and place each potsticker on a floured tray. If using handmade skins, place 2 teaspoons of lamb filling in the center of each skin. Fold and crimp, placing each one on a floured tray.

4   Bring a large pot of water to a full boil. Add enough potstickers to make one solid layer on the bottom of the pot. Immediately, stir the potstickers with a wooden spoon in a slow, circular motion to suspend them in water and to prevent them from sticking to the bottom of the pot. When the potstickers are all floating, stop stirring and bring the water to a boil, at which time add a cup of cold water. Repeat this procedure once more, a total of 2 times. Remove the potstickers and serve with dipping sauce.

SHRIMP AND CRAB POTSTICKERS

SERVES 4 TO 6

1/2 pound shrimp, peeled, deveined, and minced

1/2 pound fresh crab meat, picked over to remove any cartilage or shell fragments

10 chives or 4 scallions, finely minced

1 tablespoon finely minced fresh ginger

1 tablespoon sesame oil

1 tablespoon dry sherry

1 teaspoon salt

1/2 teaspoon freshly ground white pepper

1 egg white

40 to 50 store-bought or handmade dumpling skins (page 197)

1 egg white, lightly beaten (optional)

Dipping Sauce (page 202; optional)

1   Combine the shrimp, crab meat, chives or scallions, ginger, sesame oil, sherry, salt, white pepper, and egg white. With a pair of chopsticks, mix well.

2   If using store-bought skins, dip half of each skin in egg white and place 1 teaspoon of shrimp and crab filling in the center of each skin. Roll and crimp, then place on a floured tray. If using handmade skins, place 2 teaspoons of shrimp and crab filling in the center of each skin. Fold and crimp. Place each one on a floured tray.

3   Bring a large pot of water to a full boil and add enough potstickers to form a solid layer on the bottom of the pot. Immediately stir the potstickers with a wooden spoon in a circular motion so that they won't stick to the bottom of the pot. When they are floating, stop stirring and bring the water to a boil. Remove the potstickers with a brass net strainer or slotted spoon. Serve with dipping sauce, if you wish. (I prefer to eat these plain.)

LOBSTER AND SCALLOP POTSTICKERS

SERVES 4 TO 6

This is a delicate, delicious potsticker. The objective is to keep the filling moist but not dry. If it is too wet, the potstickers will burst in the water. If it is too dry, the filling will be hard and gummy. My advice is to fill a few, cook them, and eat them to get the hang of it. It is an enjoyable test.

½ pound fresh uncooked lobster meat	I egg white
½ pound scallops	I teaspoon cornstarch
2 teaspoons minced fresh ginger	40 to 50 store-bought or handmade dumpling skins (page 197)
I tablespoon dry sherry	
3 scallions, minced	I egg white, lightly beaten (optional)
I teaspoon salt	Dipping Sauce (page 202; optional)
I teaspoon freshly ground white pepper	

1   With a cleaver or knife, mince the lobster meat and scallops. Place in a bowl and add the ginger, sherry, scallions, salt, white pepper, egg white, and cornstarch. Mix well with a pair of chopsticks. Place the mixture in a colander, which should be on a plate or in a bowl to catch the juices.

2   Before filling the potstickers, pour any juices back into the colander and mix well. Using a teaspoon, take filling from the top layer first, working toward the bottom, and place 1 teaspoon of filling on a store-bought skin (remember to dip half the store-bought skin in egg white) or 2 teaspoons of filling on a handmade skin. Fold, crimp, and place like soldiers on a lightly floured tray.

3   Bring a large pot of water to a full boil. Put enough potstickers in the pot to form one solid layer. As quickly as possible, stir the potstickers in a slow, circular motion with a wooden spoon, suspending them in the water. When they begin to float, stop stirring. Bring the water to a boil again and remove the potstickers with a brass mesh strainer or slotted spoon. This may be served with the dipping sauce, but I recommend you eat them plain.

BEEF AND TOMATO POTSTICKERS

SERVES 4 TO 6

1 pound ground chuck

3 medium tomatoes (preferably vine-ripened), finely minced and drained well in a colander

1 bunch of scallions, finely minced

6 garlic cloves, crushed and minced

1 whole egg

3 tablespoons black or mushroom soy sauce

2 tablespoons dry sherry

5 tablespoons sesame oil

1 tablespoon freshly ground black pepper

1 tablespoon finely minced fresh chilies (jalapeño, serrano, or Asian)

40 to 50 store-bought or handmade dumpling skins (page 197)

1 egg white, lightly beaten (optional)

Dipping Sauce (page 202)

1   Combine all the ingredients in a mixing bowl except the dumpling skins, egg white, and sauce and mix well with a pair of chopsticks. Put the filling in a colander to drain.

2   If using store-bought skins, dip half the skin in egg white and place 1 teaspoon of filling in the center of each skin. Fold, crimp, and place on a lightly floured tray. If using handmade skins, place 2 teaspoons of filling in the center of each skin. Fold, crimp, and place on a floured tray.

3   Bring a large pot of water to a full boil. Put enough potstickers in the pot to form a solid layer on the bottom of the pot. Immediately stir the potstickers in a slow, circular motion with a wooden spoon to suspend them in the water, so that they will not stick to the bottom. When they begin to float, stop stirring.

4   Bring the water to a boil, then add 1 cup of cold water. Bring to a boil again and again add 1 cup of cold water. Return to a boil. Remove the potstickers with a brass mesh strainer or a slotted spoon. Serve with the dipping sauce.

Vegetarian Potstickers

SERVES 4 TO 6

2 pieces of soft tofu, 3 inches square and
   1 1/2 inches thick

2 pieces of pressed tofu, 3 1/2 inches
   square and 1/2 inch thick, finely minced

1/2 cup grated carrot

1/2 cup minced broccoli

1/2 cup fresh or frozen green peas

1/2 cup minced white button mushrooms

1/2 cup minced shiitake mushrooms

1/4 cup minced green bell pepper

1/4 cup minced red bell pepper

1/4 cup minced peeled fresh water
   chestnuts

4 scallions, minced

2 tablespoons black or mushroom soy
   sauce

2 tablespoons dry sherry

3 tablespoons sesame oil

1 tablespoon freshly ground white pepper

40 to 50 store-bought or handmade
   dumpling skins (page 197)

1 egg white, lightly beaten (optional)

Dipping Sauce (page 202)

1   Mash the soft tofu with a fork. Put it in a clean cloth and wring the water out of the tofu. It should look a bit like cottage cheese. Put it in a mixing bowl.

2   Add all the rest of the ingredients except the dumpling skins, egg white, and sauce, and mix well with a pair of chopsticks. Put the filling in a colander. Place a plate that fits within the circumference of the colander on top of the filling. Put a weight, such as a large can, on top of the plate. (I use a small weight from my weight-lifting set.) Let the filling sit this way for a half-hour so that the water from the vegetables will drain.

3   Remove the weight and the plate. Remix the filling with chopsticks. If using store-bought commercial skins, dip half the skin in egg white and place 1 teaspoon of filling in the center of each skin. Fold, crimp, and place on a lightly floured board. If using hand-made skins, place 2 teaspoons of filling on each skin. Fold, crimp, and place on a floured tray.

4   Bring a large pot of water to a full boil. Add enough potstickers to form a solid layer on the bottom of the pot. Immediately, slowly stir the potstickers with a wooden spoon in a circular motion, placing them in suspension and preventing them from sticking to the bottom of the pot. When the potstickers are floating, stop stirring. Bring to a boil and remove them with a brass mesh strainer or a slotted spoon. Serve with the dipping sauce.

Mandarin Pancakes

MAKES 20 TO 30 PANCAKES

These light, thin pancakes with their tempting sesame flavor are used to wrap *moo shu* dishes and for Peking duck. For an attractive presentation, after steaming the pancakes, fold each one in half to a semicircle and then fold it again into a quarter circle. Place these quarter circles on a round plate, overlapping each other and fanned out in a circle.

3 1/2 cups all-purpose flour	6 tablespoons sesame oil
1 1/2 cups boiling water	3 tablespoons vegetable oil

1   Put 3 cups of the flour in a mixing bowl. Slowly add the 1 1/2 cups boiling water, stirring and mixing constantly with a pair of chopsticks. When finished, it should look crumbly, like piecrust dough. Let the crumbly mixture cool.

2   Knead the cooled mixture in the bowl. Then, on a lightly floured board, knead the dough ball until smooth. Kneading should consist of alternately folding the dough over itself and pressing it into the board. Lean into the dough for effective kneading. Place the kneaded dough ball back in the bowl and cover with a moist (not wet) cloth or paper towel. Put the bowl in the refrigerator and let the dough rest for 1/2 hour.

3   Take the dough out of the refrigerator and knead it again on a lightly floured board. Use small amounts of flour, as needed to keep the board and your hand floured. Cut the dough ball in half and roll each half into a 1-inch cylinder. Cut the cylinder into 1-inch cubes. Line up the cubes on the board in a column of twos. Putting each cube between the palms of your hands, roll them into balls. Continue to place the balls in a column of twos on the floured board.

4   Put the sesame oil into a bowl or small saucer. With floured hands on a lightly floured board, flatten each ball into a 2- to 3-inch disk. Put them back into the column of twos when finished. Dip one side of the disk liberally in the sesame oil and place its corresponding disk in the column on top of it—think of it as a sesame oil sandwich. Twist the disks one quarter turn to spread the sesame oil evenly. Then, use a rolling pin

to roll the disk sandwiches into pancakes. Be sure to turn the disks as you roll to get as circular a pancake as possible. Each pancake should be between 5 and 7 inches in diameter.

5   Dip a paper towel into some vegetable oil. Brush a thin veneer of oil onto the bottom of a heavy skillet, like a cast-iron frying pan. Heat the skillet on medium heat for 3 minutes. Reduce the heat to low and put a rolled-out disk in the pan. When it begins to bubble up, turn it with a spatula. If it has a few small, light brown spots, it is fine. Cook the same way on the second side. Remove it with the spatula and place it on a plate. Put another disk in the skillet. Meanwhile, use a small knife to make a small separation of the two pancakes in the cooked disk. If you look carefully, a thin line is evident on one of the sides of the cooked disk. From that point of separation, carefully pull the pancakes apart. Pile them like pancakes on a plate.

6   Before serving, set up a steamer in a pot that will fit the plate by placing a footed rack in the pot and filling the pot with water to the surface of that rack. Bring the water to a full boil, place the plate of separated pancakes on the rack, cover, and steam for 5 minutes. Remove the plate carefully with mitts or gloves and serve.

PORK AND CABBAGE SPRING ROLLS

MAKES ABOUT 50 SPRING ROLLS

These spring rolls, which most people erroneously think of as egg rolls, are much tastier than the ones in Chinese restaurants. It is not necessary to use mustard and plum sauce, but if you want these condiments, buy the real plum sauce, made from Chinese plums—Koon Chun makes a good one. For mustard, mix $1/4$ cup powdered mustard with $1/4$ cup of cold water.

1 green cabbage, approximately $1 \frac{1}{2}$ pounds	3 tablespoons black or mushroom soy sauce
1 bunch of scallions, finely minced	2 tablespoons regular soy sauce or Kikkoman
2 carrots, finely minced	2 tablespoons dry sherry
1 cup minced peeled fresh water chestnuts	1 teaspoon freshly ground white pepper
6 garlic cloves, crushed and minced	2 packages store-bought spring roll skins (not eggroll skins), 50 skins per package
1 tablespoon finely minced fresh ginger	
3 tablespoons vegetable oil	2 egg whites, lightly whisked
1 pound ground pork, sautéed until brown, drained	Oil for deep-frying

1   Core the cabbage by cutting the heart out. Slice the cabbage thin, as if making coleslaw. Cut across the cabbage into 3-inch strands. Put the cabbage in a colander. Add the scallions, carrots, water chestnuts, garlic, and ginger. Rinse under cold water.

2   Heat the oil in a wok until smoking. Stir-fry the vegetables for 10 minutes or until the cabbage is wilted. Add the cooked pork, soy sauces, sherry, and white pepper.

3   Drain the stir-fried filling in a colander. Place a plate that will fit within the circumference of the colander on top of the filling. Put a weight like a large can on top of the plate. (I use a small weight from my weight-lifting set.) Let this sit for a half-hour to drain.

4   Take the skins out of the plastic packages. They are like phyllo dough sheets stuck together. Pull the skins apart, first into halves, then into quarters, eighths, etc., until each skin is single and separated. Place the skins back in the plastic package and cover with a damp cloth. This will prevent the skins from drying out.

5   Place one skin in front of you on a flat surface, a cutting board, or counter or table. Position it diagonally in front of you. Imagine it to be a baseball diamond with you behind home plate. Place 2 tablespoons of drained filling side by side on the diamond a bit off center toward the bottom, just below the pitcher's mound. Fold the bottom corner (home plate) over the filling. The tip of the bottom corner should touch midway between the pitcher's mound and second base. Fold the first-base corner over the right end of the spring roll and hold it in place. Fold the third-base corner over the left end of the spring roll. Roll the spring roll toward second base and stop midway between the pitcher mound, the center, and second base. Dip your forefinger and middle finger into the egg white and brush the egg white on the second-base corner. Continue rolling until the spring roll is a complete cylinder. Slide the second-base side 2 or 3 inches on the flat surface to complete the sealing of the spring roll. Line up the spring roll on a tray. Do not put one spring roll on top of another or they will stick to each other.

6   Heat the oil to 350°F or put a small piece of spring roll skin in the oil. If it pops up immediately and turns light brown, the oil is ready. Deep-fry the spring rolls in batches until golden brown. Do not crowd them in the oil. Drain first in the fryer basket or colander, then on absorbent paper. (I use brown paper shopping bags from the supermarket.) Serve hot.

COMBINATION LO MEIN

SERVES 3 TO 4

Buy fresh noodles labeled as "lo mein noodles." Other fresh noodles are better suited to soup and are very yellow in color. Dried spaghetti can also be used. Boil them until al dente.

I pound fresh lo mein noodles

$\frac{1}{2}$ pound flank steak, sliced against the grain into pieces 3 inches long by $\frac{1}{2}$ inch wide by $\frac{1}{8}$ inch thick

$\frac{1}{2}$ pound skinless, boneless chicken breast, cut into pieces 2 inches long by $\frac{1}{2}$ inch wide by $\frac{1}{8}$ inch thick

$\frac{1}{2}$ pound small shrimp, peeled and deveined

2 egg whites

$\frac{1}{4}$ cup cornstarch

$2\frac{1}{4}$ cups vegetable oil

I cup broccoli florets, in 3-inch-long by I-inch-wide pieces

I cup 2-inch diagonally sliced celery

I cup snow peas or snap peas, tips and strings removed

I cup quartered mushrooms

$\frac{1}{2}$ cup thinly sliced carrots, cut on the diagonal

$\frac{1}{2}$ cup fresh water chestnuts, peeled, washed, and sliced

SAUCE

$\frac{1}{2}$ cup chicken broth

2 tablespoons black or mushroom sauce

2 tablespoons regular soy sauce or Kikkoman

2 tablespoons dry sherry

4 garlic cloves, crushed and minced

I tablespoon finely minced fresh ginger

$\frac{1}{2}$ teaspoon freshly ground white pepper

2 tablespoons cornstarch mixed with $\frac{1}{4}$ cup cold water

1   Boil the lo mein noodles for 5 minutes. Drain in a colander and rinse thoroughly in cold water. Drain well.

2   Mix the beef, chicken, and shrimp with the egg whites, $\frac{1}{4}$ cup cornstarch, and $\frac{1}{4}$ cup cold water. Heat 2 cups of the vegetable oil to 280°F; or put a piece of "meat" in the oil and, when bubbles rise from it like champagne in a glass, add the rest of the beef, chicken, and shrimp. Turn the meat slowly in the poaching oil until the beef is tan, the chicken white, and the shrimp curled. Drain in a colander.

3   Combine the broccoli, celery, snow peas or snap peas, mushrooms, carrots, and water chestnuts in a colander and rinse under cold water.

4   Mix the chicken broth, two soy sauces, sherry, garlic, ginger, and white pepper in a small saucepan. Bring the sauce to a boil; reduce the heat to very low.

5   Heat the remaining ¼ cup oil in a wok until smoking. Stir-fry the noodles for 8 to 10 minutes, tossing frequently, until they become firm. Add the vegetables and stir-fry until bright in color, approximately 5 minutes. Add the meat and stir-fry for 30 seconds.

6   Add the sauce and bring to a boil. Stir the cornstarch mixture back into solution, add it to the wok, and bring to a boil. Toss 5 times and serve.

Happy Birthday Noodle Cake

SERVES 4 TO 6

Instead of a piece of cake with that ridiculous sparkler, I would send this, with my compliments, to good customers who were celebrating a birthday. No candles are necessary.

1 pound fresh lo mein noodles

1 cup plus 2 tablespoons vegetable oil

SAUCE

1 cup chicken broth

1 tablespoon black or mushroom soy sauce

3 tablespoons oyster sauce, preferably the Hip Sing Lung brand

2 tablespoons dry sherry

2 tablespoons ketchup

1 tablespoon sugar

4 garlic cloves, crushed and minced

1 tablespoon finely minced fresh ginger

1 pound bok choy, rinsed thoroughly under cold water and sliced on the diagonal into 2-inch pieces

2 tablespoons cornstarch mixed with $1/4$ cup cold water

1 pound Chinese roast pork (*cha sha pork*), thinly sliced on the diagonal

1   Boil the lo mein noodles for 5 minutes. Drain in a colander and rinse under cold water.

2   Heat the 1 cup oil in a deep skillet (at least $2^{1/2}$ inches deep) to 350°F; or place a piece of noodle in the oil and, when it pops up to the surface quickly and starts to turn brown, add the rest of the noodles carefully without splashing. Move the noodles around so that the "cake" forms to the shape of the pan. Check the noodles from time to time by lifting the cake a bit with a spatula to see how brown the bottom is. When it is crisp and golden to light brown, using two spatulas (I prefer a large and a small one), carefully turn the noodle cake to cook on the other side. When it is golden to light brown, carefully remove it and drain the cake on absorbent paper. (A large brown paper bag works great.) Place the noodle cake on a large circular serving platter.

3   Combine the chicken broth, soy sauce, oyster sauce, sherry, ketchup, sugar, garlic, and ginger in a small saucepan. Bring to a boil, then reduce the heat to low.

4   Heat the remaining 2 tablespoons vegetable oil in a wok until smoking. Stir-fry the bok choy until bright green in color, approximately 3 minutes. Add the sauce and bring to a boil. Stir the cornstarch mixture back into solution, add it to the wok, and bring to a boil. Add the roast pork, toss 3 times, and pour the roast pork and bok choy with sauce over the noodle cake. To serve, cut the noodle cake as you would cut a cake.

URING THE HOT SUMMER MONTHS, CHINESE people are fond of eating cold noodle dishes. The next two recipes are favorites of my family that can be made on cool nights and eaten during the hot days to follow. The peanut sauce made here refrigerates well. It does, however, have to be stirred again with chopsticks before serving.

DAN-DAN COLD PEANUT NOODLES

SERVES 4 TO 6

1 pound fresh lo mein noodles

2 tablespoons vegetable oil

SAUCE

1 cup smooth peanut butter

4 garlic cloves, crushed and minced

2 scallions, finely minced

3 tablespoons black or mushroom soy sauce

1 teaspoon dry sherry

1 teaspoon chili paste

1 tablespoon sesame oil

1   Boil the lo mein noodles for 5 minutes. Drain in a colander and rinse well under cold water. Add the vegetable oil and mix into the noodles. Refrigerate until cold.

2   Put the peanut butter in a 1-pint measuring cup. Little by little, add 1 cup cold water, stirring the peanut butter with a pair of chopsticks, each time water is added. When the water is finished, the sauce should be thick but smooth.

3   Add the garlic, scallions, soy sauce, sherry, chili paste, and sesame oil. Blend in well with chopsticks. The peanut sauce should be brown.

4   For each serving, put 1 cup of the chilled, lightly oiled noodles in a bowl and spoon 1 to 3 tablespoons of the sauce on top. Mix well and eat.

CHA CHA MEIN

SERVES 4 TO 6

1 pound fresh lo mein noodles

2 tablespoons vegetable oil

1 pound ground pork

$\frac{1}{2}$ cup coarsely minced bamboo shoots, preferably fresh

$\frac{1}{2}$ cup finely minced onion

3 tablespoons bean sauce

1 tablespoon hoisin sauce

2 tablespoons dry sherry

$\frac{1}{2}$ cup chicken broth

1 teaspoon sugar

5 garlic cloves, crushed and minced into $\frac{1}{2}$ cup of ice water

1 tablespoon finely minced fresh chilies in $\frac{1}{2}$ cup balsamic vinegar

2 crisp apples, cored and sliced into wedges

1 cucumber, peeled and cut into spears

1   Boil the lo mein noodles for 5 minutes. Drain in a colander and rinse under cold water. Mix the oil into the noodles. Refrigerate until cold.

2   Sauté the ground pork in a skillet or wok, stirring to break up any lumps, until no longer pink. Add the bamboo shoots, onion, bean sauce, hoisin sauce, sherry, chicken broth, and sugar. Mix well. Simmer for 10 minutes, or until the liquid is reduced by half.

3   For each serving, put one 1 cup or so portion of chilled noodles in a bowl. Spoon 1 or 2 tablespoons of the cha cha sauce on the noodles and mix well with chopsticks. Top each portion of noodles with about 1 tablespoon each garlic and water and chiles and vinegar, 2 or 3 apple slices, and few cucumber spears.

My FAMILY USUALLY EATS FRIED RICE for lunch, since leftover rice is always on hand. Any kind of rice can be used, but long-grain rice is the best. Short-grain tends to be sticky and will clump a bit when stir-fried. I use it anyway if I feel like fried rice and leftover short-grain rice is all I have. The cooked rice should be spread out on a baking sheet and permitted to dry for an hour or two. If I am to buy rice specifically for fried rice, I will buy converted rice (not instant rice), since the grains cook up dry and separate. Note: Each of these recipes feeds four people as a main course but will stretch to six if offered as a side dish.

SHRIMP FRIED RICE

SERVES 4 TO 6

½ pound converted rice	3 eggs, beaten
7 tablespoons vegetable oil	3 tablespoons black or mushroom soy sauce
½ pound small shrimp, peeled and deveined	1 teaspoon freshly ground white pepper
1 bunch of scallions, cut on the diagonal into ½-inch pieces	

1   Put the rice in a pot that has a tight cover. Fill the pot with water to 1 inch above the surface of the rice. Cover and bring the water to a full boil. Uncover and stir with a spoon. Boil the water over high heat until the level is just above the surface of the rice. Cover and reduce the heat to low or simmer. Cook for 13 minutes. The rice should be pretty dry, but not burnt. (Or use a rice cooker with the same measurement of water. Whatever you do, never follow the directions on the box for cooking rice.) Spread the rice out on a cookie sheet and let dry for an hour or more.

2   Heat 1 tablespoon of the oil in a nonstick skillet and sauté the shrimp. Just as they start to curl, take the skillet off the heat and drain in a colander. The shrimp should be a little undercooked, but remember they will be cooked a second time.

3   In a hot wok, heat 4 tablespoons of the oil to smoking. Add the rice and stir-fry vigorously. If the rice starts to stick to the pan, scrape it loose with a spoon, Chinese ladle, or spatula. Toss frequently and stir-fry for 5 minutes. Add the shrimp and scallions. Stir-fry for 30 seconds.

4   Tilt the wok so that it is at an angle facing you. Push the rice and other ingredients upward on this angle. Heat the remaining 2 tablespoons of oil in the space created on the bottom of the wok. Scramble the beaten eggs in the hot oil, trying as best as possible not to mix the scrambling eggs with the rice. When the eggs are solid, mix them in with the rest of the fried rice.

5   Add the soy sauce and white pepper. Toss 5 times, or until the soy sauce is well mixed into the rice, then serve.

LAO-LAO'S FRIED RICE

SERVES 4 TO 6

This is my Lao-Lao's recipe for fried rice, and it is the best. It also bears little resemblance to the fried rice served in restaurants.

5 tablespoons vegetable oil

1/4 cup minced aged Smithfield ham

4 cups leftover cooked rice, preferably long-grain

I cup boiled or baked ham, cut into 1/4-inch cubes

1/2 cup chopped onion

3 eggs, beaten

1/2 cup green peas

I teaspoon salt

I   Heat 3 tablespoons of the oil in a wok over medium-low heat. Add the Smithfield ham and cook for 3 minutes to release its flavor into the oil. Remove the ham with a slotted spoon and reserve.

2   Turn the heat to high and heat the flavored oil until smoking. Add the rice and stir-fry vigorously for 5 minutes, scraping up any rice that may stick. Add the cubed ham, reserved Smithfield ham, and the onion. Stir-fry for 3 minutes.

3   Tilt the wok so it is on an angle facing you. Push the fried rice up on this angle. Heat the remaining 2 tablespoons of oil in the cleared space in the wok. Scramble the eggs in the oil, and when they are solid, mix the scrambled eggs into the rice.

4   Add the peas and salt. Toss 3 times and serve.

Star Anise Beef with Bok Choy Shantung Noodles

S E R V E S   6   T O   8

I have loved licorice since I was a boy and, thus, am quite partial to food cooked with star anise. Beef and anise bond particularly well. The bok choy's slight bitterness cuts the sweetness, while Shantung noodles tie it all together.

4 tablespoons vegetable oil	1/2 teaspoon freshly ground black pepper
2 pounds boneless chuck steak, cut into 1 1/2-inch cubes	5 star anise
1/4 cup black or mushroom soy sauce	1/3 cup dark brown sugar
2 tablespoons dry sherry	1 pound bok choy, sliced on the diagonal into 1 1/2-inch pieces
1/2 teaspoon cinnamon	1 pound fresh Shantung white noodles, boiled, drained in a colander, and rinsed in cold water
1/2 teaspoon nutmeg	

1   Heat 2 tablespoons of the vegetable oil in a heavy stew pot, like a Dutch oven, to the smoking point. Sauté the beef on high heat until well seared on all sides, approximately 4 minutes. Drain the beef in a colander and reserve.

2   Reserve 1 tablespoon of oil and fat in the heavy pot. Heat until smoking, then return the seared beef to the pot. Add the soy sauce, sherry, and 1 1/2 cups cold water. Bring to a boil.

3   Add the cinnamon, nutmeg, black pepper, star anise, and brown sugar. Stir in well. Reduce the heat to low, cover, and simmer for 30 minutes, or until the beef is fork-tender. The beef should not be tough, nor should it fall apart when forked. Uncover the beef and cook for 15 minutes, to reduce the sauce, stirring occasionally.

4   Meanwhile, rinse the bok choy thoroughly in cold water, since bok choy can be somewhat sandy.

5   In a separate pan, preferably a wok, heat the remaining 2 tablespoons oil and stir-fry the bok choy until a bright garden green in color. Add to the anise beef, stir, and serve on the Shantung noodles.

VEGETABLES AND TOFU

蔬菜和豆腐

"YOU CANNOT EAT THAT AND EXPECT to live a long time," Ah Gung said to me when I was a little boy, pointing to the Hershey bar I was eating and the Pepsi Cola I was drinking. *Ah Gung* means "uncle" in Chinese, and although he was not a blood relative, he was a good friend of my paternal family dating back to its Shanghai days. (All good family friends were addressed by children as uncle or aunt in respect and with affection.) I pushed the Pepsi and candy bar aside, although I did go back later and finish them. Ah Gung patted me on both my shoulders and smiled. He was a devout, practicing Buddhist. He stayed in the basement of my grandparents' house, where he kept a gilded Buddha sitting in a lotus position on a front-loading washing machine in his room.

One time I came into his basement room and found him in a meditative trance in front of the Buddha. I thought he was watching the circling suds in the window of the washing machine. He needs to get out more, I thought. Actually, the only enjoyment he had was once a month, when he would go to Radio City, sit in the front row, and watch the Rockettes.

It was through Ah Gung that I first became familiar with Chinese vegetarian cuisine, because devout Buddhists are pure vegetarians. He did not eat any animal products or by-products. For protein, he relied heavily on beans, especially soybeans. When I was a teenager, I went to the refrigerator to look for something to eat. Ah Gung pulled out a large jar of pickled soybeans. These were soybeans still in their husks, and when Au Gung pulled one out with a pair of chopsticks, it looked like a hairy bug. But I ate it anyway and enjoyed it. Before I could sit down, he placed a whole plate of these hairy bugs before me.

Ah Gung was a true ascetic—with the exception of the Rockettes. Chinese vegetarian cuisine is not so austere. In fact, as I found out when I was in China, it is quite fancy. It is common to shape the food to look like meat. A favorite dish of mine was stuffed "fish," which was delicate minced vegetables stuffed into bean curd skin and shaped like a whole fish in a delightful sauce. But I could not really understand why, if a person does not want to eat animals or fish so as not to kill them, would he want to fantasize that he is eating an animal or fish?

SPICED SOYBEANS

SERVES 3 TO 4

Fresh soybeans are wildly popular these days. This treatment serves them up as a tasty snack, easy on the cook, because guests shell their own beans as they eat them.

3 cups fresh green soybeans, unshelled	I teaspoon kosher salt
I teaspoon finely minced fresh green chilies	I teaspoon freshly ground black pepper

1   Clip off the ends of the soybean pods and remove any visible strings.

2   Bring a large pot of water to a boil. Add the soybeans, chilies, salt, and black pepper. Boil for 15 minutes; drain.

3   Refrigerate the spiced beans until cold. Serve chilled.

HOMESTYLE TOFU

SERVES 4

5 soft tofu squares, 3½ inches by 3½ inches by 1½ inches

1 cup cornstarch

4 cups plus 2 tablespoons vegetable oil

1 cup diagonally sliced fresh bamboo shoots, in 1-inch pieces

SAUCE

1 cup vegetable broth

2 tablespoons black or mushroom soy sauce

1 tablespoon regular soy sauce or Kikkoman

2 tablespoons dry sherry

6 garlic cloves, crushed and minced

1 tablespoon finely minced fresh ginger

1 tablespoon sugar

1 tablespoon sesame oil

2 tablespoons cornstarch mixed with ¼ cup cold water

1   With a cleaver or knife positioned parallel to the cutting surface, cut horizontally across the width of each tofu. Then cut straight down from one corner to the opposite corner, creating four triangles. Dip each triangle of tofu in the cornstarch and coat well on all sides. Do not pile the tofu pieces on top of each other.

2   In a large saucepan or deep-fryer, heat the 4 cups oil to 350°F; or place a piece of tofu in the oil and, when it pops up to the surface and begins to start frying like chicken, the oil is ready. Deep-fry the tofu pieces until crisp and golden yellow in color, approximately 3 minutes. Drain well on absorbent paper.

3   Put the bamboo shoots in a colander, rinse, and reserve.

4   Combine the vegetable broth, soy sauces, sherry, garlic, ginger, sugar, and sesame oil in a small saucepan and bring the sauce to a boil. Turn the heat to low.

5   Heat the remaining 2 tablespoons oil in a wok until smoking. Add the bamboo shoots and stir-fry for 30 seconds. Add the sauce and the tofu triangles and braise for 5 minutes, turning the tofu about halfway through.

6   Stir the cornstarch mixture back into solution, add to the wok, and bring to a boil, stirring gently until thickened.

Mapo Tofu

I don't care what anybody says, my Mapo Tofu is the best. My daughter and sister will attest to this claim. But I must admit that I learned this authentic recipe from chefs in Sichuan Province.

Crushed Sichuan peppercorns are a key ingredient here. If not available crushed, put a tablespoon of the Sichuan peppercorns between two pieces of aluminum foil or wax paper and crush with a rolling pin. Since this is a spice I use frequently, I take a small quantity, like $1/4$ cup of Sichuan peppercorns, and grind them in a coffee grinder or blender. Then I put the powder in a jar.

For a spicier version, add 1 tablespoon or more of crushed chili peppers (jalapeño, serrano, or Asian) with the ginger and garlic.

3 tablespoons vegetable oil	$1^{1}/_{2}$ cups vegetable broth
$^{1}/_{2}$ teaspoon crushed Sichuan peppercorns	5 soft tofu squares, $3^{1}/_{2}$ inches by $3^{1}/_{2}$ inches by $1^{1}/_{2}$ inches, cut into $^{3}/_{4}$-inch cubes
$^{1}/_{2}$ teaspoon freshly ground black pepper	
$^{1}/_{2}$ teaspoon freshly ground white pepper	2 cups diced portobello mushrooms, in $^{3}/_{4}$-inch pieces
1 teaspoon chili paste, or to taste and tolerance	2 tablespoons sesame oil
6 garlic cloves, crushed and minced	4 tablespoons cornstarch mixed with $^{1}/_{2}$ cup cold water
1 tablespoon finely minced fresh ginger	
3 tablespoons black or mushroom soy sauce	4 scallions, cut on the diagonal into $^{1}/_{2}$-inch pieces
2 tablespoons dry sherry	

1   Heat the vegetable oil in a deep heavy skillet, such as a cast-iron frying pan, which has a tight lid, until smoking. Add the Sichuan peppercorns and black and white pepper. Immediately add the chili paste, garlic, and ginger. Stir once. Quickly add both soy sauces and the sherry. Add the vegetable broth and stir.

2   Add the tofu cubes and portobello mushrooms. Fold them in gently with a wooden spoon. Add the sesame oil. Cover the pan with a lid and braise for 15 minutes on medium heat. Uncover. Stir gently and slowly with the wooden spoon. Continue to braise uncovered for 10 more minutes.

3   Stir the cornstarch mixture back into solution, add it to the skillet, and bring to a boil, stirring gently until thickened. Add the scallions. Stir and serve.

IF A NONVEGETARIAN VERSION IS DESIRED, substitute ½ pound sautéed ground pork for the portobello mushrooms.

STEAMED TOFU IN OYSTER SAUCE

SERVES 3 TO 4

3 soft tofu cubes, 3½ inches by 3½ inches by 1½ inches

2 scallions, finely minced

½ cup oyster sauce with "oyster flavoring," meaning no seafood is used

1   Set up a steamer using a large pot that will fit the steaming plate. Place a footed rack on the bottom of the pot and fill with water to the level of the top of the rack. Heat the water to a full boil.

2   Place the tofu cubes on a round plate. Place the plate of tofu carefully in the steamer. Sprinkle the tofu with the scallions. Cover and steam for 15 minutes.

3   Meanwhile, heat the oyster sauce either in a saucepan on the stove or in a glass receptacle in the microwave.

4   When 15 minutes have elapsed, uncover the pot. Remove the plate of tofu carefully with gloves or mitts. Pour the heated oyster sauce on top of the tofu and serve.

Sichuan Green Beans

SERVES 4

This is by far the most popular vegetable dish for vegetarians and nonvegetarians alike.

1 pound Chinese long beans or regular green beans, cut on the diagonal into 2-inch pieces

1 tablespoon bean sauce, preferably Koon Chun brand

2 tablespoons black or mushroom soy sauce

2 tablespoons vegetable or chicken broth

1 tablespoon dry sherry

1 tablespoon sugar

2 teaspoons cornstarch

1 teaspoon chili paste, or to taste and tolerance

1 tablespoon sesame oil

3 tablespoons vegetable oil

1   If using regular green beans, parboil them for 5 minutes. (Regular green beans are thicker than Chinese long beans.) Put the cut beans in a colander and rinse thoroughly.

2   Combine the bean sauce, soy sauce, sherry, sugar, cornstarch, chili paste, and sesame oil in a bowl. Add 2 tablespoons cold water.

3   Heat the oil in a wok until smoking. Add the green beans and stir-fry for 10 minutes, or until the beans are bright green in color and slightly wrinkled.

4   Add the sauce ingredients and stir-fry until the sauce thickens.

Chinese Broccoli in Oyster Sauce

SERVES 4

1 pound Chinese broccoli or rabe, sliced on the diagonal into 1-inch pieces

3 tablespoons vegetable oil

4 garlic cloves, crushed and minced

1 tablespoon dry sherry

$\frac{1}{4}$ cup oyster sauce with "oyster flavoring," meaning no seafood is used

1   Place the broccoli in a colander and rinse thoroughly under cold water.

2   Heat the vegetable oil in a wok until smoking. Add the broccoli and garlic, and stir-fry until the broccoli is bright green in color, approximately 5 minutes.

3   Add the sherry and stir-fry for 30 seconds. Remove from the heat and add the oyster sauce. Toss 5 times and serve.

Bok Choy in Oyster Sauce

SERVES 4

1 pound bok choy, cut on the diagonal into 2-inch pieces

3 tablespoons vegetable oil

3 garlic cloves, crushed and minced

2 tablespoons dry sherry

$\frac{1}{2}$ cup oyster sauce with "oyster flavoring," meaning no seafood is used

1   Wash the bok choy thoroughly, since it can be quite sandy. If after washing two or three times the bok choy remains sandy, soak it in a large pot of cold water and stir it with your hand 3 times. Remove the bok choy with a strainer and place in a colander to wash again. The best way to test to see if the bok choy is still sandy is to take a piece and eat it. If there is a lot of crunch to it, wash it some more.

2   Heat the vegetable oil in a wok until smoking. Add the bok choy and garlic, and stir-fry until the bok choy is bright green in color, approximately 3 minutes. Add the sherry and toss 3 times.

3   Turn the heat off. Add the oyster sauce. Toss 5 times and serve.

Stir-Fried Collard Greens

SERVES 4

One summer, I picked a mislabeled flat of vegetables to plant in my garden, which later turned out to be collard greens. I am not a great fan of the traditional American way of cooking collard greens, so I chopped my collard greens and sautéed them. They were delightful and reminded me of the fresh mustard greens I had eaten in China.

1 pound collard greens, chopped

3 tablespoons vegetable oil

4 garlic cloves, crushed and minced

1 tablespoon finely minced fresh ginger

1 teaspoon sugar

2 tablespoons regular soy sauce or Kikkoman

1 tablespoon dry sherry

1 tablespoon sesame oil

1   Rinse the collard greens in a colander.

2   Heat the vegetable oil in a wok until smoking. Add the collard greens, garlic, ginger, and sugar. Stir-fry until the collard greens are bright green in color, approximately 3 minutes.

3   Add the soy sauce, sherry, and sesame oil and stir-fry for 1 minute. Serve at once.

DEEP FOREST MUSHROOMS

SERVES 2

Shiitake mushrooms are very delicate in flavor. For this reason, I add them at the end of cooking a dish to avoid overcooking.

¼ pound portobello mushrooms, thinly sliced

¼ pound white button mushrooms, thinly sliced

¼ pound fresh shiitake mushrooms, thinly sliced

3 tablespoons vegetable oil

SAUCE

2 tablespoons black or mushroom soy sauce

2 tablespoons dry sherry

2 tablespoons vegetable broth

1 teaspoon cornstarch mixed with 1 tablespoon cold water

1   Combine the portobello and white mushrooms in a colander. Rinse under cold water and reserve. In a separate colander or strainer, rinse the shiitake mushrooms.

2   Heat the vegetable oil in a wok until smoking. Add the portobello and white mushrooms and stir-fry for 2 minutes. Add the soy sauce, sherry, and broth.

3   Stir the cornstarch mixture back into solution, add to the wok, and bring to a boil, stirring until thickened.

4   Toss 3 times. Turn off the heat. Add the shiitake mushrooms, toss twice, and serve.

POTATO STICKS WITH SICHUAN PEPPERCORNS

SERVES 4

Yes, potatoes are a part of Chinese cuisine. Potatoes along with tomatoes, long-grain rice, and peanuts were introduced to China in the 1700s. This new plentiful food source was largely responsible for a population explosion that, in a relatively short historical period, ballooned China's population to 1 billion people.

3 cups potato strips, in thin julienne pieces 3 inches long	1 cup plus 1 tablespoon vegetable oil
¼ cup cornstarch	1 teaspoon Sichuan peppercorns, crushed
	2 scallions, finely minced

1   Place the potato sticks in a colander and rinse under cold water for 5 minutes. This will remove the potato starch, which would become gummy in the cooking process. Drain thoroughly, then mix with the cornstarch.

2   Heat the 1 cup oil in a wok to 350°F; or put a potato stick in the oil and, when it pops up to the surface and fries like french fries, add the rest of the potato sticks and deep-fry until the potato sticks are just cooked, approximately 4 minutes. Drain in a colander, then on absorbent paper.

3   Heat the 1 tablespoons of oil in a wok until smoking. Add the Sichuan peppercorns and stir once. Add the scallions and stir once. Add the potato sticks. Toss 5 times, then serve.

STIR-FRIED WATERCRESS AND GARLIC

SERVES 3 TO 4

2 bunches of watercress

6 garlic cloves, crushed and minced

3 tablespoons vegetable oil

1 tablespoon dry sherry

$\frac{1}{2}$ teaspoon salt

1   Cut the stem ends off the watercress. Chop the rest of the watercress into 1-inch segments. Wash thoroughly in a colander. Place the garlic on top of the watercress.

2   Heat the oil in a wok until smoking. Add the watercress and garlic, and stir-fry for 30 seconds.

3   Add the sherry and salt. Toss 5 times and serve.

VARIATION SPINACH WITH GARLIC Prepare the dish as described above, substituting 8 ounces fresh spinach for the watercress. I prefer the baby spinach now available in most supermarkets.

WATERCRESS AND FERMENTED BEAN CURD SAUCE

SERVES 3 TO 4

This is an old family recipe, a dish I like to eat in the morning with rice porridge (rice congee). My mother called the sauce "Martini bean curd sauce."

2 bunches of watercress

4 cubes fermented bean curd measuring 1 inch by 1 inch by ½ inch

2 tablespoons dry sherry

1 teaspoon gin

2 tablespoons vegetable oil

1   Cut the stem ends off the watercress. Chop the watercress into 1-inch segments, place in a colander, and wash thoroughly under cold water.

2   With a fork, mash the fermented bean curd. Add the sherry and gin. Mix in and mash to a paste.

3   Heat the oil in a wok until smoking. Stir-fry the watercress for 30 seconds. Add the bean curd and stir-fry, mixing thoroughly, for 30 seconds. Serve hot.

BUDDHIST VEGETABLES

SERVES 4 TO 6

These are the vegetables commonly used in Chinese restaurants for Buddhist Vegetables. I, however, use whatever vegetables are available. When my vegetable garden is in full bloom, I use squash, different kinds of peas, tomatoes—whatever vegetable is ripe and ready. There is nothing like vegetables picked 5 minutes before you cook them.

2 cups broccoli florets

1 cup snow peas or snap peas, tips and strings removed

1 cup carrots, sliced on the diagonal into 1-inch pieces

1 cup quartered white mushrooms

2 celery stalks, sliced on the diagonal into 1-inch pieces

1 cup vegetable broth

2 tablespoons dry sherry

4 garlic cloves, crushed and minced

1 tablespoon finely minced fresh ginger

1/4 teaspoon salt

1 tablespoon sesame oil

1/2 teaspoon freshly ground white pepper

3 tablespoons vegetable oil

2 tablespoons cornstarch mixed with 1/4 cup cold water

1   Place the vegetables in a colander and rinse thoroughly under cold water.

2   Combine the broth, sherry, garlic, ginger, salt, sesame oil, and white pepper in a small saucepan and bring the sauce to a boil. Reduce the heat to low.

3   Heat the vegetable oil in a wok until smoking. Add all the vegetables and stir-fry until the vegetables are bright in color, approximately 5 minutes.

4   Add the sauce to the wok and bring to a boil. Stir the cornstarch mixture back into solution and add it to the sauce. Bring to a boil, stirring until thickened. Serve at once.

VARIATION SICHUAN BUDDHIST VEGETABLES Merely add 1 teaspoon of chili paste, or to taste and tolerance, to the sauce when it is simmering.

VEGETARIAN ROLLS

SERVES 4 TO 6

8 bean curd skins

1 tofu square, 3$\frac{1}{2}$ by 3$\frac{1}{2}$ by 1$\frac{1}{2}$ inches

1 pressed tofu, 3$\frac{1}{2}$ inches by 3$\frac{1}{2}$ inches by $\frac{1}{2}$ inch, finely minced

1 cup chopped spinach, boiled, drained, squeezed dry

1 cup minced shiitake mushrooms

$\frac{1}{2}$ cup chopped cilantro

4 scallions, finely minced

1 tablespoon finely minced fresh ginger

4 garlic cloves, minced and crushed

2 tablespoons sesame oil

1 egg white

3 tablespoons vegetable oil

SAUCE

$\frac{1}{4}$ cup vegetable broth

2 tablespoons mushroom soy sauce

1 tablespoon dry sherry

1 teaspoon sugar

1 tablespoon cornstarch mixed with 3 tablespoons cold water

1　Soak the bean curd skins in cold water to cover for 20 to 30 minutes, or until soft.

2　Mash the fresh tofu and place it in a cloth to wring the water out of it. Place in a colander. Add the pressed tofu, spinach, shiitake mushrooms, cilantro, scallions, ginger, garlic, and 1 tablespoon of the sesame oil. Mix well.

3　Pat bean curd skins dry with a paper towel. Place 2 tablespoons of the filling on the middle of a bean curd skin. Fold it into a blintz shape by first folding the bottom flap over the filling and then by folding the side flaps inward. Brush the top edge of the top flap with some egg white. Make the final fold and seal. Place the vegetable roll with the seam side down on a plate. Repeat with remaining skins and filling.

4　Heat the vegetable oil in a skillet until smoking. Fry the vegetable rolls seam side down until light brown. Turn them so that they fry on the opposite side. Place the rolls on a serving platter.

5　Add the broth, soy sauce, sherry, and remaining 1 tablespoon sesame oil to the skillet. Stir the cornstarch mixture back into solution and add it 1 teaspoon at a time to thicken the sauce. The sauce should not be soupy or gummy. Pour the sauce over the rolls and serve.

DESSERTS

饍後甜食

THERE IS REALLY NO CONCEPT OF dessert in Chinese cuisine, as there is in Western cooking. A meal may end with tea, or in certain regions of China, it ends with soup. But there is no concept of something sweet and special to end a meal. There are sweet dishes, such as sweet-and-sour foods or General Tso's Chicken, served as an entree. Sweet pastries and cakes are generally eaten as snacks. One "dessert" that is usually served ceremoniously in a multi-course wedding or birthday banquet is Eight-Jeweled Precious Pudding. Consisting of glutinous, or "sweet," rice molded with an inner filling of sweet red bean paste, the "cake" is adorned with brightly colored citron, other fruits, and nuts. So when it is presented before being cut and served, it looks like a crown with glistening jewels. It is beautiful, but most Americans don't particularly care for it. To soften its impact, I prefer to serve it with an almond cream sauce, which greatly enhances its acceptability.

I served Eight-Jeweled Precious Pudding as the dessert for a banquet held in my mother's restaurant, The Court of the Mandarins in Washington, D.C., for my son's one-month birthday, a tradition for Chinese families. I asked the American guests how they liked the pudding and they responded, "It tastes like glue."

Funny that they should say that. When I was in China, while touring the Great Wall, I was told that the Great Wall was constructed 2,000 years ago from large stone blocks joined together with cement derived from glutinous rice. But Chinese people absolutely love Eight-Jeweled Precious Pudding. And so, because it is something "sweet and special" for Chinese families, I provide its recipe for you to make up your own mind.

If you don't like the pudding and find that Spun Sugar Apples are too difficult, you can always bake your favorite cake or pie. Many Chinese families living in the United States do just that. In fact, my favorite dessert to serve as a poetic ending to a Chinese dinner is strawberry cream meringue torte, a type of schaumtorte, which my sister, Adriane Fugh Berman, perfected.

I remember when my sister first started baking. She was eight years old when I bought her one of those light-bulb ovens and baking sets for her birthday. She spent many hours mixing and baking cookie powders enclosed in little envelopes, stirring them in little metal bowls with little plastic utensils, and pouring the batter into little cake and cookie pans, which she inserted into her little light-bulb oven. Then, she would anxiously wait for the final product, clapping her hands and jumping up and down. She learned not to open the little oven door prematurely so that her baked goods would be thoroughly cooked. Her pigtails bobbing and with a smile that filled our house, she served me her little cookies and cakes. They resembled an assortment of droppings of various small creatures. Some of them were still powdery, some slimy, some hard as pebbles. But I ate them with great gusto, always finishing with an "Umm, good."

Adriane has become a master baker of great renown in the family and among her friends. The week or so before Christmas, her kitchen literally whirls, spinning out Bundt cakes, fruit tortes, chocolate truffles, and Norwegian almond cookies. A great gift from her is a plate of these cookies, which are called "Jan Hagels." I like serving them with ice cream or sorbet as a light dessert, a good finish to a good meal.

It seems like so many years have passed since those days when Adriane baked her light-bulb oven cakes and cookies. Our father died suddenly in India at the age of 39, where he, my mother, and sister were residing on his sabbatical year off. I was in my junior year at Rutgers. I waited with other family members at Dulles Airport for my mother and sister to arrive from India, but we were informed that their flight was delayed and would not arrive until early the next morning. That night I slept in a spare bedroom in my grandmother's house. Early the next morning, my uncle left by himself to go to the airport as I slept. I was awakened by the trample of little feet on the stairs. My sister burst into the room, tears streaking her face and welling up in the bottom of her blue-framed glasses. Tears gushed from me as I hugged her, not wanting ever to let go. And, for the entire funeral, I never let go of her.

EIGHT-JEWELED PRECIOUS PUDDING

SERVES 6 TO 8

2 cups sweet rice (glutinous rice)

1/4 cup sugar

1/2 cup candied citron in various colors, including green and red

1/2 cup mandarin orange slices (canned are fine)

1/2 cup pitted maraschino cherries, sliced in half

1 cup canned lichees, sliced in half

8 whole blanched almonds

5 fresh dates, pitted and sliced in half

3 tablespoons vegetable oil

1 can (18 ounces) sweetened red bean paste

Almond Cream Sauce (recipe follows)

1   Put the rice in a saucepan and add enough cold water to measure 1 inch above the surface. Cover with a tight lid and bring to a full boil. Uncover and stir well. Boil uncovered until the water is reduced to just above the surface of the rice. Cover tightly, reduce the heat to low, and simmer for 13 to 15 minutes. Remove the pot from the heat. Let sit for about 10 minutes.

2   Put the cooked rice, which should still be warm, in a mixing bowl. Add the sugar and mix well. Set aside.

3   Grease a sturdy bowl, such as a mixing or Pyrex bowl (either 7-inch diameter by 4 inches high, or 9-inch diameter by 3 inches high) well with vegetable shortening, oil, or cooking spray. Line the bowl with plastic wrap by placing a strip of it across with an 8-inch overhang on both sides. Repeat, crossing the first strip with the same length of plastic wrap to form a cross.

4   Working in a concentric pattern and starting in the center of the greased bowl, adorn the bowl with alternate patterns of colors. I like making the center a large flat red piece of citron or a maraschino cherry. Next, make a circle of mandarin oranges. Place half a maraschino cherry in the pit cavity of each lichee half and make a concentric circle of lichees with the cherry side facing outward. Finally, place an almond in the middle of each split date and build the final circle with the almond side facing outward.

5   By this time, the rice should have cooled enough to be handled. With wet or greased hands, pack the sweet rice to the contours of the bowl up to 1 inch below

the rim, leaving a 1½-cup depression or bowl in the middle of the rice. Be sure to reserve enough rice to seal the mold with a lid of rice.

6   In a wok or frying pan, heat the oil to the smoking point. Scoop out the red bean paste into the hot oil and sauté, turning and stirring frequently, for 3 minutes or until the paste is cooked through. It should be much more pliable after sautéing.

7   Place the pan-fried bean paste in the depression in the rice. Mold the lid from the remaining sweet rice and place it on top of the paste, leveling the lid with the bowl rim. Seal as best as possible with wet or oiled hands. Fold the crisscross flaps in, tucking the excess plastic wrap between the rim and the pudding.

8   Put a round footed steamer rack in a large pot big enough to hold the bowl. This pot should have a tight-fitting lid. Add enough cold water to reach just below the rack. Cover and bring the water to a full boil. Put the bowl in the steamer, cover, and steam for 1 hour.

9   Remove the pudding carefully with gloves or mitts. Open the plastic wrap-flaps. Place a serving plate or platter over the top of the bowl, and invert the pudding to unmold. Remove the plastic wrap carefully to reveal the "jewels" in their full glory. Serve hot, with the almond cream sauce on the side.

Almond Cream Sauce

MAKES ABOUT 2 ½ CUPS

This sauce can be ladled over an entire pudding for added effect in presentation, and then it can be ladled again over individual portions.

⅓ cup cornstarch	1 tablespoon almond extract
2½ cups cold water	¼ cup heavy cream
½ cup sugar	

1   Dissolve the cornstarch in 1 cup cold water. Set aside.

2   Bring the remaining 1½ cups water to a boil in a saucepan. Add the sugar and stir to dissolve. Add the almond extract.

3   Stir the cornstarch mixture well and thicken the sauce by adding the mixture a little at a time. The sauce should be thick, but not soupy or gummy. Add the cream and stir for 10 seconds. Serve warm.

Peking Snow

The following dessert is a simple dessert that my mother used to make for me since I always loved whipped cream. It was a dessert popularized around the beginning of the 1900's when cream products made their appearance in the culinary landscape of China.

Although not traditional, I like to roast the crisscrossed chestnuts for about 30 minutes, let them cool, and shuck them of their meat. The roasted chestnut meat imparts a rustic taste to the dessert.

1 pound fresh chestnuts (see Note)

1 cup whipping cream

1/4 cup sugar

1 pint fresh strawberries, preferably small

2 kiwis, sliced

1   Cut a crisscross in each chestnut. Boil in a large saucepan of water for 1 hour; drain. Peel each chestnut with a paring knife. Coarsely chop and reserve the meat.

2   Using a chilled bowl and chilled beaters, beat the heavy cream until stiff.

3   Fold in the chestnuts and turn into a shallow bowl or a glass pie plate. Decorate the top with whole strawberries and sliced kiwis. Chill for at least 1 hour before serving.

NOTE For convenience, you can use a can of vacuum-packed peeled cooked chestnuts or 1 cup unsweetened chestnut puree.

Spun Sugar Apples

SERVES 6 TO 8

This dessert is difficult to accomplish, and you must be careful with the hot sugar syrup. After the candy syrup is made and the apple chunks are deep-fried, everything must be done as quickly as possible. Bananas can be used instead of apples. I prefer bananas on the greener side.

1 cup sugar	1 egg
3 cups cold water	4 cups vegetable oil
5 apples (crisp and tart, like Granny Smith or Winesap), peeled and cored	½ teaspoon baking powder
2 cups cornstarch	1 tablespoon sesame seeds
2 cups all-purpose flour	Large bowl of ice water

1   In a heavy saucepan, heat the sugar and 2 cups cold water. Boil until the syrup reaches the hard-crack stage, 400°F on a candy thermometer. Put a drop of sugar syrup in cold water and it should turn immediately into hard candy. Keep the syrup hot.

2   Cut the apples into 1-inch chunks. Using 1 cup of cornstarch, coat the apple chunks well.

3   Using a whisk, mix the remaining 1 cup cornstarch with the flour, egg, 1 cup of the vegetable oil, and remaining 1 cup water in a bowl. When well blended, add the baking powder and stir in. Let the batter sit for 15 minutes, at which point small bubbles should be percolating in the batter. Add a handful of apple chunks to the batter and turn to coat.

4   Heat 3 inches of oil in a deep-fryer or a deep saucepan to 350°F. Add the coated apple chunks, one chunk at a time with tongs, into the oil and fry until the chunks are yellowish white, approximately 4 minutes. Drain well. Wait 5 minutes and refry a second time for 1 minute, or until golden in color. Drain again.

5   As quickly as possible, add the deep-fried apple chunks to the candy syrup and turn the chunks until well coated. Quickly remove the chunks with 2 large spoons pulling upward, like pulling taffy, elongating the bundle of candied apple chunks. Place the candied apples on a large platter and sprinkle with the sesame seeds.

6   Using a portion of 4 to 5 apple chunks, quickly dip them, using the spoons, into a bowl of ice water. Turn them once or twice, and lift them out immediately and shake once to get the excess water off. When the apples are removed from the candy syrup, the sugar coating is still hot and pliable, and the sections can be separated with two forks and pulled in the individual 4- to 5-chunk servings. Place on a serving plate and serve immediately. Do each portion in this way as quickly as possible. When done properly, the end result is wonderful. The spun sugar apple chunks should be cold and crisp on the outside and hot on the inside.

FRUITS MARINATED IN PLUM WINE

SERVES 6 TO 8

Although good alone and a nice finish to any meal, marinated fruits are also great served with a fine vanilla ice cream and thin cookies or wafers. Quite a bit of liquid is rendered from macerating the fruit and from the plum wine. This liquid, mixed with $1/2$ ounce of vodka or light rum and topped with a splash of club soda on ice, makes a refreshing cocktail. Garnish with a little of the leftover fruit.

$1/2$ ripe cantaloupe	I pint raspberries
$1/2$ ripe honeydew	I can lichees, drained
$1/2$ cup fresh or unsweetened canned pineapple chunks	$1 1/2$ cups plum wine
I pint strawberries, halved if large	$1/2$ cup sugar

1   Slice the honeydew and cantaloupe crosswise into 1-inch slices and remove the seeds. Cut the rind off and cut into 1-inch chunks.

2   Combine the fruit, including the lichees, in a serving bowl. A glass serving bowl is the best for a pretty presentation.

3   Add the plum wine and sugar. Mix well and refrigerate from 30 to 60 minutes.

I PREFER GEKKEKAN PLUM WINE, WHICH is made from real plums. Other cheaper versions are sweetened grape wine with plum flavoring.

Adriane's Jan Hagels

SERVES 8

2 sticks (8 ounces) butter, softened

1 cup plus 2 tablespoons sugar

2 cups all-purpose flour

$\frac{1}{2}$ teaspoon vanilla extract

$\frac{1}{2}$ teaspoon almond extract

2 eggs, separated

1 cup sliced almonds

$\frac{1}{2}$ teaspoon cinnamon

1   Preheat the oven to 350°F. In a mixing bowl, combine the butter, 1 cup of the sugar, flour, vanilla, almond extract, and egg yolks. Blend well. Press the dough into a 9 by 13-inch baking pan.

2   Beat the egg whites with a fork until foamy. Spread the beaten egg whites over the dough. Scatter the sliced almonds evenly on top. Mix the remaining 2 tablespoons sugar and the cinnamon and sprinkle evenly over the dough.

3   Bake for 20 to 25 minutes, or until a pale golden brown. Cool and cut into squares. Serve warm or cold.

MENUS

COMPOSING THE MENU IS AN IMPORTANT part of any meal, and if you haven't grown up eating Chinese food, you may not know how to combine different dishes and flavors. There is a menu for every occasion. I have crafted seven menus for seven occasions, serving two to twelve people.

MENUS FOR TWO

A Romantic Dinner—An Intimate Interlude

In the beginning of a relationship, traditionally when one pursues another, it is so romantic to cook for the intended and to present a great dinner that excites the palate and pleases the eye. It is much more expressive of a lover's intentions and adulation than merely giving flowers or going out to a restaurant. The dinner should also be on the light side so as not to bear down heavily on either party.

The Sesame Vegetables, Fruits Marinated in Plum Wine, and garnishing for the shrimp can be done hours ahead and held in the refrigerator. After it has been thickened, keep the soup on low heat. Add the asparagus to it 5 minutes before serving and the crabmeat just before serving. Reserve the jade-green base sauce over low heat. Velvetize the shrimp and coat in the peppers, then set aside. Serve the Sesame Vegetables, the champagne, and then the soup. Stir-fry the coated shrimp, set on top of the sauce, and garnish. Serve immediately.

Sesame Vegetables

Crab and Asparagus Soup

Sichuan Blackened Shrimp

Steamed Rice

Fruits Marinated in Plum Wine

Champagne

A Get to the Movies on Time Dinner

Lamb and Zucchini Potstickers

Kosher Salt Shrimp with Fresh Chilies

Use potstickers previously made and frozen.

MENUS FOR FOUR

A Casual Get-Together for Good Friends

When friends get together, they should devote some time to cooking a meal, each one contributing what he or she can do best. Bonded friendship is best realized when everyone sits down to a good meal collectively prepared.

Hot-and-Sour Soup

Pork and Cabbage Potstickers

Shrimp and Scallops in Garlic Sauce

Stir-Fried Watercress and Garlic

Tsingtao beer

A Special Dinner for Four

Eggroll Soup

Shrimp Croquettes

Steamed Chilean Sea Bass

Sichuan Green Beans

St. Emilion or Pouilly Fuissé wine

MENUS FOR MORE

A Family Dinner for Six

A family dinner including children is tough to do. If the food is too "adult," the kids won't eat it, and if the food is too "kid-like," the adults won't eat or will eat only reluctantly. The following is a menu that will make both little and big people happy.

Wonton Soup

Spring Rolls

Sweet-and-Sour Pork

Shrimp Lo Mein

Yon Hagels and ice cream

A Sensational Dinner for Eight

Hot-and-Sour Soup

Deep-Fried Marinated Fish with Dipping Sauce

General Tso's Chicken or Chicken in Orange Sauce

Mussels in Black Bean Sauce

Mapo Tofu

Peking Snow

Chardonnay wine

A Banquet for Twelve

Crab and Asparagus Soup

A cold platter of sliced Drunken Chicken (using boneless breast), sliced Cha Sha Pork, Hot-and-Sour Cucumbers, Tea Eggs, chilled White and Red Radishes, Marinated Mushrooms

Steamed Clam Soufflé with Sausage Rice

Sichuan Blackened Shrimp

Shanghai Steamed Whole Fish

Pine Forest Pork

Chicken and Walnuts

Eight-Jeweled Precious Pudding

CONCLUSION

MY MOTHER AND I TRAVELED TO China together before Americans were permitted to enter the country. The Chinese people were just recuperating from the excesses and oppression of the Cultural Revolution. We stayed most of the time in Beijing, where many of our family members still resided. They had so little in those days: a cramped place to live in, a bed to sleep on, a small table to eat at, and some small, hard chairs to sit on. Heat for cold Peking nights came from a coal-fed potbelly stove. Night light was provided by a solitary electric bulb hanging from a cord pinned to the ceiling.

Our Beijing family treated us with great generosity. Although meat was stringently rationed at that time, they gathered up all their ration coupons and bought pork for making potstickers. It was an all-family affair. Some made the filling, redolent of scallions, garlic, and sesame oil, while others mixed the dough. Cousins rolled out the skins into small dough disks and filled them, crimping the pastries into crescent shapes and lining them up like toy soldiers on a large floured board. A cauldron of boiling water was outside, attended diligently by two uncles who were responsible for the final transformation of those floured soldiers into steamy morsels that burst in my mouth with the first bite, fireworks of tastes that conveyed the celebration and the joy of family lost and then found.

Many of us spend our lives trying to find out who we are, and so much of that depends on discovering and knowing where we came from. My trip to China was full of insights and revelations, some of which had immediate impact on me, and much of which unfolded slowly over the following years.

My mother and I received many visitors at our hotel. Family members related to my Lao-Lao, peasants from the countryside north of Beijing, visited us for a few days. A grandmother, my Lao-Lao's cousin, her granddaughter and her husband, and their baby daughter slept on the floor of our hotel room since they were not allowed to occupy a room of their own in this "vistors only" hotel. It was a treat for them to eat with us in the hotel dining room.

The daughter of my great-grandfather's concubine came to see my mother. She expressed her appreciation and gratitude to my Lao-Lao, who, in a visit to Beijing some years earlier, declared to the entire family that she accepted her as a true relative, despite her being the descendant of my great-grandfather's concubine, thus sealing a family schism that had endured for four generations. It was from this woman that I learned that my Lao-Lao, early in her life, broke from the traditional mode of the compliant, submissive wife and became a progressive advocate of women's rights—this at a time when young girls in many parts of China were still having their feet bound.

The one visitor I remember most was my grandfather's cousin, who appeared at our hotel room door one day and, in impeccable, accentless English, inquired, "Does Aline Fugh [my mother's maiden name] reside here? If so, would it be possible for me to speak with her?"

I called him San Yeh-Yeh, or third grandfather. He and my Lao-Lao attended English classes together at the Peking YMCA in the 1920s. San Yeh-Yeh kept up his English by reading English books for two hours every morning, reciting much of what he read out loud, but in a low voice, since, during the Cultural Revolution, it was a crime to speak English. He lived with my Lao-Yeh's extended family during the war years and used to walk my mother, her sisters, and her cousins to school everyday. He was an accomplished artist and master calligrapher. His artwork hangs in my house today.

I had more of a rapport with San Yeh-Yeh than with any other Peking family member. He was quite a character, one I found to be quite likeable. He was also an accomplished martial artist in a type of wrestling particular to northern China. As a young man, he was known for feats of strength.

Often San Yeh-Yeh would say to me in English, "When you go back to the United States, please convey my warmest regards to your grandparents and tell them I am still strong!" He would always follow this with a he-man pose and a wide, toothless smile. San Yeh-Yeh told me that when he was young, on a bet, he lifted a large cast-iron woodbin with only his teeth.

"This was quite foolish," he explained. "All my teeth fell out one by one."

Because we had such a good rapport, I asked San Yeh-Yeh if he would be willing to be interviewed on tape and film. He consented. Sitting stoically in our hotel room, he sipped tea and answered my questions, initially in slow, perfect English. He told me he was a city policeman for the Nationalist government in the precommunist years. When the communists came to power, he was imprisoned and later sent to a "re-education camp." After being released, he supported himself with his calligraphy, painting signs for stores and businesses.

It was when I started asking him about his family and his childhood that he unconsciously switched from speaking English to speaking Chinese. Emotionally, he spoke of his father, who was a revolutionary with Sun Yat-Sen in the revolution of 1911, the upheaval that founded the modern Republic of China. His father believed fervently in the Three Principles, written by Sun, which are essentially a reiteration of the U. S. Bill of Rights. After Sun's death, San Yeh-Yeh's father was imprisoned and tortured by Sun's successor, the warlord dictator Yuan Shih-Kai. San Yeh-Yeh, his mother, and his siblings would go daily to the wall outside the part of the Forbidden City where prisoners were tortured, and wail, begging for his father's life. His father was eventually released, but he emerged a broken man, incapable of supporting or leading his family.

San Yeh-Yeh also spoke affectionately of his aunt, his father's sister, his Goo-Goo. She was poor without any means of support. As his lips quivered and tears rolled down the wrinkled terrain of his cheeks, he said his Goo-Goo would always bring him and his siblings something good to eat, like a Chinese pear, even though she had nothing to eat herself. She later died of starvation, he told me.

Wiping his tears away, San Yeh-Yeh said he also had good memories. He told me when he was a small boy, his grandfather, an opium smoker, would take him to a pavilion, an inn, in the mountains where other old opium smokers went.

The pavilion was enchanted, he thought. There were all kinds of songbirds in ornate bamboo cages hanging throughout the pavilion. The birds sang incessantly because they were fed chili peppers. The cacophony of bird song lifted the old men in their opium daze. Thus encouraged, the old men would also sing songs. San Yeh-Yeh remembered one song in particular, which he sang for me. It was about a fisherman whose family was starving. He fished for days in the hot sun in his boat on a lake without even a bite. But one day, a torrential storm pelted him with rain. The turbulent lake threatened to overturn his boat and drown him. The storm lifted and departed quickly, leaving the lake as placid as glass. The sun emerged. Burning off the mist of the storm, it beamed a glorious rainbow that encompassed the mountains. The fisherman caught one fish after another, all the colors of the rainbow, quivering in his boat like the glistening jewels they were.

After the interview, there was a knock on the door. I opened the door and I thought I beheld an apparition. Standing before me was an old man with a flowing white beard and piercing blue eyes, dressed in traditional Mandarin garb: a blue silk tunic, a black skull cap, and cloth shoes. He greeted me in *ke-chi hua*, a cultured and polite manner of speaking typical of the classic Mandarin of Peking many years ago. Stating he was an old friend of my grandfather, he asked for my mother. I invited him in.

When he spotted San Yeh-Yeh, the old man beamed. Extending his arms, he looked upward and said in Chinese, "Glory be to God." Although they had both lived in Peking, they had not seen each other for thirty years. Because the old man was a scholar, an intellectual, and a devout Christian, he also suffered greatly in the years following the revolution.

San Yeh-Yeh bolted up to face the old man. They grasped each other's elbows, facing each other for the first time in years—years in which neither knew whether the other was alive or dead. And, together, they said in unison, "Glory be to God."

For years, after being divorced, I prepared dinner for my son. Dinner was an important daily ritual for us. "Are you cooking yet, Dad?" my son would ask, as I gathered up ingredients in the kitchen.

He anticipated the meal as well as the intimacy of sitting down with me, which made it an event we both looked forward to. Every day, I would come home after work, and he would greet me in the driveway to help unload the groceries. I prepared the evening meal, and my son and I would sit down, eat, and talk about our day.

I still cook for my family. Now, after cubing chicken fillet, I combine it with egg white, cornstarch, and a little water. As I stir with a pair of chopsticks, I think about the difficulties we have endured over the years. Seeding green peppers, I cut them with a cleaver into diamonds and place them in a colander. As I slice scallions on an angle, I remember fondly how my children used to "help" me cook dinner by cutting vegetables with dull, little knives. The rice pot is boiling over. I remove the lid, stir the rice, replace the lid, and lower the heat.

From a fresh hand of ginger I shave off paper-thin slices, stack them, and cut them into thin strips. I cut across the strips to produce a fine mince, adding it to the contents of the colander. Quickly I rinse vegetables under cold water, put them aside, assemble the sauce in a bowl, and reserve it by the stove.

Smashing cloves of garlic with the broad side of my cleaver, I give the garlic a quick mince and add it to the sauce. My son can do this as well; he is quite a good cook, which impresses and delights his classmates. Poaching the coated chicken cubes in oil, I drain them in a colander and put them by the stove. Lastly, I open a can of cocktail peanuts. Tossing a few in my mouth, I know I have to do this last because, otherwise, none will be left for the dish. I'm ready to cook, I say to myself.

In a hot wok, that predates my birth, given to me by my mother, I heat a little oil until it smokes. I hear a key in the door and know my son has arrived. I dump the vegetables in the wok; the flash and crackle tell me the meal will be ready in minutes. Walking into the kitchen, my son pops a few peanuts in his mouth, and he asks, "Are you cooking, Dad?"

D

Deep Forest Mushrooms, 231
Deep frying
   in electric deep-fryer, 67
   poaching-in-oil technique, 12, 21
   safety precautions in, 21-22
Desserts, 239-249
   Almond Cream Sauce, 244
   Apples, Spun Sugar, 246-247
   Eight-Jeweled Precious Pudding, 239-240, 242-243
   Jan Hagels, Adriane's, 240, 249
   Peking Snow, 245
Dim sum, in China, 71
Dipping Sauce
   with Fish, Deep-Fried Marinated, 42
   for Potstickers, 202
Drunken Chicken, 41
Dumplings. *See* Potstickers

E

Edamame (Soybeans), Spiced, 224
Egg(s)
   in Chicken, Red Cooked, 126
   in Fried Rice, Lao-Lao's, 220
   in Moo Shu Dishes
      Beef, 144-145
      Chicken, 108-109
      Pork, 150-151
   Pancakes for Egg Roll Soup, 38
   Quail, Braised Venison

with Bamboo Shoots and, 189
   in Shrimp Fried Rice, 218-219
   Soufflé, Steamed Clam, with Sausage Rice, 96
   Tea Eggs, 48
Eggplant, Chinese, Lamb and, 174-175
Egg Roll Soup, 38
Eight-Jeweled Precious Pudding, 239-240, 242-243
Enoki Mushrooms, in Flounder, Whole Steamed with Vegetables and Three Mushrooms, 56-57
Equipment, selecting, 7-12

F

Firepot, Mongolian, 129-131
Fish, 51-69
   Bluefish, Deep-Fried Marinated, 42
   Braised Fillet in Garlic Sauce, 53
   Braised Whole, "Suyu", 58-61
   Chilean Sea Bass Fillet, Shanghai Steamed, 62-63
   Crispy Fillet with Roasted Seasoned Salt, 68
   Deep-Fried Marinated, 42, 43
   Flounder, Whole Steamed, with Vegetables and Three Mushrooms, 56-57
   Hot-and-Sour Slices, Beijing (variation), 66-67

   selecting, 51-52
   Soup, Hunan Honey, 37
   Squirrel Fish, Crispy, in Garlic Sauce, 64-65
   Steamed Chilean Sea Bass Fillet, Shanghai, 62-63
   Steamed Whole Flounder with Vegetables and Three Mushrooms, 56-57
   Steamed Whole, Shanghai, 54-55
   steamers for, 12
   Sweet-and-Sour Slices, Beijing, 66-67
   Swordfish, Sichuan Cubed, 69
   Trout, Pan-Fried, 10
   See also Shellfish
Flounder, Whole Steamed with Vegetables and Three Mushrooms, 56-57
Fried Rice. *See* Rice, Fried
Fruits Marinated in Plum Wine, 248

G

Game, 181-192
   Birds, Marinated and Grilled, 185
   Pheasant and Spareribs, Red-Cooked, 182-184
   Rabbit, Red-Cooked, 188
   Squab, Deep-Fried, with Roasted Salt, 186
   Venison
      Braised, with Quail Eggs and Bamboo Shoots, 189
      and Onions, 191